Rahu and Spirituality
A Triveni of Parashari, Nakshatra, and Nadi Astrology

Rahu and Spirituality
A Triveni of Parashari, Nakshatra, and Nadi Astrology

Richa Shukla; MA, PhD
Jyotish Alankar, Jyotish Acharya
Faculty and Founding Director *Dev Jyotish*, Gurgaon, India

Ranjan Pal; MS, PhD
Research Scientist, Faculty Member
Massachusetts Institute of Technology, USA
Jyotish Research Scholar, *Dev Jyotish*

Ekta Jain; BTech, MBA
CEO, Alliance Consultants, Atlanta, USA
Jyotish Research Student, *Dev Jyotish*

Ranjan Pal is rigorously and personally trained in *jyotish* (research) by Dr. Richa Shukla, equivalent to the requirement of titles *Jyotish Alankar* and *Jyotish Acharya*.

MOTILAL BANARSIDASS INTERNATIONAL
DELHI

First Edition : Delhi, 2025

© MOTILAL BANARSIDASS INTERNATIONAL
All Rights Reserved

ISBN : 978-93-48911-98-8

Also available at
MOTILAL BANARSIDASS INTERNATIONAL
H.O. : 41 U.A. Bungalow Road, (Back Lane)Jawahar Nagar, Delhi - 110 007
4261 (basement) Lane #3,Ansari Road, Darya Ganj, New Delhi - 110 002
203 Royapettah High Road, Mylapore, Chennai - 600 004
12/1A, 2nd Floor, Bankim Chatterjee Street, Kolkata - 700 073
Stockist : Motilal Books, Ashok Rajpath, Near Kali Mandir, Patna - 800 004

No part of this book may be reproduced in any form or by any electronic or mechanical means including information storage and retrieval systems without permission in writing from the publishers, excepts by a reviewer who may quote brief passages in a review.

Printed in India
MOTILAL BANARSIDASS INTERNATIONAL

ॐ श्री गणेशाय नमः॥

Dedication

Richa Shukla dedicates this work to her late father and jyotish scholar Dr. J. P. Agnihotri, her mother Shrimati Nandini Agnihotri, and the Almighty.

Ranjan Pal dedicates this work to his late father and jyotish scholar Dr. M. N. Pal, his mother Shrimati Mohua Pal, his undying spirit, and the Almighty.

Ekta Jain dedicates this work to her family, her large thirst for jyotish knowledge, and Lord Ganesha.

Ranjan Pal and Ekta Jain dedicate this work to their revered, inspiring jyotish Guru Dr. Richa Shukla.

The book is written without salutations to conform with global writing norms. The authors use salutations uniformly in the 'Acknowledgements' section to honor their Gurus, astrology masters, and colleagues helping the authors in their journey.

Preface

Rahu is a planet that is often associated (astrologically signifies) with materialism, ambition, greed, mischief, fear, dissatisfaction, obsession, confusion, mystery, science, and occultism. All these factors are often (if not always) the opposite of achieving spiritual bliss and/or *moksha*.

In the *puranas*, Rahu is represented by the *Varaha* (boar) avatar (incarnation) of Lord Vishnu, with each of the nine planets associated with one of the nine avatars of Lord Vishnu. Rahu, when operating on its higher principle, can protect and save the universe (as was the main purpose of all the avatars of Lord Vishnu). Rahu is also related to the energy of Goddess Durga and likewise worshiping the Goddess helps us elevate our Rahu energy to please the Goddess by putting such energies to the right use.

More specifically, Rahu, the cosmic shadow, personifies *moha* — illusion, desire, and distortion of truth. *Devi* Durga is both the source and the conqueror of that *moha*, the *Sakti* who tests and liberates simultaneously. When Rahu clouds the mind with insatiable ambition or confusion, it is Durga who grants the courage (*durg* = *fortress*) to withstand and transcend. Philosophically, Rahu is the exam, Durga, the teacher and redeemer. Together, they represent the dialectic of bondage and liberation: Rahu exposes the shadow, while Durga transforms it into wisdom. In invoking her, the aspirant gains the strength to master

Rahu's turbulence. We rightly have the following *shloka* from the scripture ***Devi Mahatmyam*, 5.16:**

या देवी सर्वभूतेषु मोह रूपेण संस्थिता।
नमस्तस्यै नमस्तस्यै नमस्तस्यै नमो नमः॥

To that Goddess who abides in all beings as delusion (moha), we bow again and again.

It is then hard to believe that Rahu energies will not enable spiritual development for a native when Lord Vishnu and Goddess Durga represent this planet.

The Main Essence of the Book

This argumentative essay wants to answer the all-important question: *what is the truth behind the spiritual ethos of Rahu?* Alternatively, does Rahu seed and/or give spirituality or not? (note that seeding is not equivalent to giving) The novelty of this question in the broader literature of Vedic astrology is that there has been no documented finding (backed up with logical and rigorous analysis) on Rahu not having the capacity to give spirituality to a native.

The popular consensus is that Rahu is a malefic that mostly drives the materialistic, anti-spiritual aspect of human behavior, and is incapable of seeding spirituality. While this consensus may still hold true, we were motivated to conduct a systematic astrological study backed by a rigorous analysis to put more statistical weight for/against this statement. After all, the major pain point of Vedic astrology in the last 100 years has been a mountain pile of diverse opinions on the subject without much thought and logic, and most importantly not backed by appropriate analysis on horoscopes. Such analyses provide unshakeable statistical confidence in any opinion. In the context of this essay, the consensus opinion that demands to be statistically tested (for or against) by astrological data analysis is *Rahu is incapable of giving spirituality to a native.*

The book extends a *Parashari-Nakshatra* based prequel titled *Does Rahu Give Spiritual Ethos? An Argumentative Analysis in Jyotish* by Ranjan Pal by conducting a rigorous argumentative amalgamation of *Parashari, Nakshatra,* and *Nadi* astrology analysis to statistically establish using numerous horoscopes the fact that Rahu does not give spirituality as per popular consensus; however, it has a significant role in seeding, sustaining/supporting, and externally (outwardly) manifesting already inherent spirituality (that is seeded by other elements other than Rahu) in a native. This 'secondary' role of Rahu is not a necessity for every native on the path of spirituality. However, for natives where Rahu plays a prominent secondary role in their spiritual development and sustenance, the astrological logic that establishes this secondary role is quite involved and deserves a systematic description for students and aficionados. We have done exactly that via the effort in this book as part of *Dev Jyotish* research.

Now one may ask: *why amalgamate Parashari, Nakshatra, and Nadi astrology in order to establish a hypothesis?* Astrological analysis gains depth and precision when approached through multiple systems. When combined, these perspectives create a layered, holistic picture. Cross-verification between systems increases predictive confidence: if *Parashari* system's *dasha* analysis integrated with a *nakshatra* analysis and *Krishnamurti Paddhatai's* (KP's) *nakshatra* sub-lord analysis converge, accuracy is reinforced. Moreover, the interplay between systems highlights the philosophical tension between *dridh* (fixed) and *adridh* (modifiable) *karma*, offering a nuanced view of destiny and free will. Using multiple approaches also reduces interpretive bias and helps triangulate the truth. As is the wise saying from the ***Atharva Veda* (12.5.47):**

अनेकानि हि दृष्टय:, एकं सत्यं न विद्यते ।
सर्वे पन्था: समायान्ति, एकं सत्यं सनातनम् ॥

There are many perspectives; truth is not captured by one alone. All paths converge toward the one eternal truth.

How Have We Written this Book?

The author list comprises engineers and philosophers by graduate education and with elite higher education and research credentials. While these points might be perceived as being "pompous", there is no denying the fact that there are three things that most engineers and philosophers (if not all) love and live by: (i) infallible logic to construct arguments, (ii) validation of arguments using a well-founded data and/or statistical analysis, and (iii) extending theory to practice by repeated application and validation. In this book, we examine a significant connection of Rahu with spiritual ethos in a native using the work ethic and philosophy that an academic practices. However, the need for the hour is the stepwise scientific application and integration of these principles resulting in a "spiritual ethos" analysis framework that is replicable across charts to check how Rahu influences spirituality in a native. We satisfy this need in the book via a novel analysis integrating *Parashari*, *Nakshatra*, and *Nadi jyotish*.

We have organized this book in the form of a collection of **seven case studies** studying our hypothesis related to Rahu's influence on a native's spiritual ethos. Each case study comprises of **five sections** (i) a brief narrative of the spiritual philosophy of the native, (ii) an analysis using an integration of *Parashari* and *Nakshatra jyotish*, (iii) a *Bhrigu-Nandi Nadi* (BNN) analysis, (iv) a BNN analysis using *nakshatras* and *KP* principles on *nakshatras*, and (v) an analysis based on the *karmic* philosophy of BNN astrology.

We note that a brief narrative of the native's spiritual philosophy in relation to our hypothesis on Rahu provides the essential context for astrological analysis. It frames the horoscope not as a mechanical chart of fate but as a reflection of the native's journey and silencing the arguments (for a reader not knowing astrology) on how Rahu contributes to the journey. This also reveals how the native approaches *karma* and *dharma*, distinguishing fixed tendencies from areas open to growth. The spiritual narrative thus humanizes destiny and frames reflecting our analysis of the hypothesis as a dialogue between *karma* and consciousness.

A Critique on Existing Books on Rahu

There are multiple books available in the market that have discussed Rahu, and nearly all of them (barring a very selective few) can be classified as "run of the mill" efforts with absolutely no substance in terms of astrological predictions and analysis. As part of this "run of the mill" efforts, all of these books mention the mythology of Rahu, its significance in the materialistic world, and then broadly go on to provide "sermons" of what happens when Rahu is placed in a certain house, *rashi*, *nakshatra* etc. In other words, these efforts are redundant and more importantly incorrect when it comes to referring them to match events/character in a native. The great astrologer K. N. Rao has spoken enough about the drawbacks of these "run of the mill" efforts (not particular to Rahu only) in many of his classic books, and we need not elaborate.

The keen student of astrology knows quite well that just like a machine is built using integral parts connected with nuts and bolts, astrological analysis and predictions are only meaningful when many of these "sermons" as mentioned above can be connected with a rigorous and logical analysis framework. The irony is that this logical framework is missing in nearly all the books studying Rahu. Either the authors of these books are only keen to provide a grossly incomplete astrological picture to the public, or do not want to release their trade secrets of analysis. The first category of authors is misleading the readers with their very incomplete knowledge of Rahu on human affairs. The latter category of authors is duping their readers (many budding Vedic astrologers) into buying their works that eventually have very little use when using them for predictions and assessments related to Rahu.

There have been four exceptions to authorship mediocrity (in the sense mentioned above) on the topic of Rahu: *The Mystery of Rahu in a Horoscope* by Shiv Raj Sharma (edited by K. N. Rao); *Karmic Control Planets* by Manik Chand Jain; *Rahu and Ketu in Predictive Astrology* by Manik Chand Jain; and *Kaal Sarpa Dosha: Why Such Fright?* by K. N. Rao. The common positive of all these four books is the fact that apart from the necessary "run of the mill" material that should necessary be provided in any general book on Rahu (and/or Ketu), there is a presence of a logical analysis framework that allows one to see beyond the simple independent *sutras* (i.e., the "sermons") on Rahu and get a hold of how these *sutras* can be tied up together in an integrated and logical analysis framework to make correct predictions and assessments on native matters influenced by Rahu.

One book in the "exceptions" category mentioned above that faintly touches upon the topic of Rahu and spirituality is *The Mystery of Rahu in a Horoscope* by Shiv Raj Sharma (edited by K. N. Rao). However, the book lacks the substantial *Parashari* rigor and statistical significance in the analysis (as spirituality was not the focus) — only giving the topic a handful of pages with astrological arguments made in a hand waving fashion. In this book, we extend their efforts in a major overhauling fashion to ensure statistical significance of the underlying unified conclusion drawn from numerous analyzed case studies.

The only other book in the "exceptions" category, and that surpasses all other books on the topic of Rahu and spirituality in rigor and depth is *Does Rahu Give Spiritual Ethos? An Argumentative Analysis in Jyotish* by Ranjan Pal. This study challenges the assumption that Rahu is inherently unspiritual. By situating Rahu within Vedic cosmology as one of the *navagrahas* — avatars of Vishnu — it reframes him not as a mere demon, but as a cosmic agent whose role deserves inquiry. Through a *Parashari-Nakshatra* approach, the analysis grounds itself in empirical case studies and statistical rigor. The benefit of this synthesis is clarity: Rahu does not originate spirituality but functions as a catalyst, amplifying or revealing what is already latent in the chart. This conclusion corrects simplistic demonization, situates Rahu within cosmic harmony, and extends previous research with deeper philosophical and methodological precision. Our effort in this book extends the analysis to integrate *Bhrigu-Nandi Nadi* astrology and *KP* astrology.

Richa Shukla, September 2025, India

Ranjan Pal, September 2025, USA

Ekta Jain, September 2025, USA

Acknowledgements

This research treatise is derived in part from an effort of astrological research conducted by Ranjan Pal and Ekta Jain under the guidance of their revered teacher and Vedic astrologer Richa Shukla; MA, PhD, *Jyotish Acharya*, *Jyotish Alankara*. Ranjan Pal acknowledges that without the fiery inspiration, guidance, and love of Richa Shukla, the essay would not have materialized. In this regard, Ranjan Pal acknowledges the countless chats of both encouragement and banter, between himself and Richa Shukla, that pushed the author to relentlessly pursue excellence in astrological analysis. The outcome of this beautiful relationship led to a series of research efforts - this being one of them. As the popular belief goes: the ardent seeker only needs a seed flame; the author acknowledges Richa to be the primary source of this flame. Richa mutually acknowledges Ranjan to be the exceptional (but 'naughty and frisky') mind and talent who is the deserved candidate among her many students to take *Jyotish* research forward like no other student.

Ranjan Pal acknowledges Ekta Jain, a very diligent research student of Vedic astrology who is a true friend in need, and someone with a great heart who was always there for her co-authors whenever they wanted to discuss their research. This is despite her multiple family commitments. Ekta was instrumental many times to help the co-authors get case study charts and related data in shape, and proofreading arguments put forward by her co-authors. It is big-hearted and sacrificing friends like the lovely Ekta Jain who always wish well for their near and dear-ones, and such mindsets make such research efforts truly meaningful and successful.

Ranjan Pal acknowledges Bodhibrata Nag, a Vedic astrology student of Dr. Richa Shukla, to always be there for him in terms of clearing obstacles related to publishing innovative and insightful ideas, be it in astrology or otherwise. Bodhibrata Nag is himself a research scholar of repute and recognizes the fact, along with the co-authors, that doing quality work is only half the battle won, the rest of the battle is won using negotiations with top publication agencies to announce the work to the world.

Finally, Ranjan Pal acknowledges Shri K. N. Rao, being their astro-academic grandfather (the *jyotish* Guru of Dr. Richa Shukla) for his superb and brilliant insights through his many books on analysis. Ranjan Pal also especially acknowledges Dr. B. V. Raman, Shrimati Gayatri Devi Vasudev, Shri S. C. Mishra, Shri J. N. Bhasin, and Shri A. K. Gaur for the lucid, conceptual, and detailed *Parashari* wisdom they impart through their books. He is indeed an *Eklavya* to these modern masters.

Ekta Jain considers herself incredibly blessed and fortunate to have crossed path with phenomenal mentors and guides and be able to learn from them starting from her first Guru, her mother, Shrimati Trilesh Jain and her grandmother, Shrimati Bimla Devi Jain. She humbly and with heart filled with gratitude, acknowledge all her mentors and guides in life for shaping parts of her.

Acknowledgements (xvii)

Ekta Jain acknowledges her revered Vedic astrology teacher, Dr. Richa Shukla who introduced her to the fundamental concepts of *Parashari jyotish* and *Nakshatra* and Mrs. Anuradha Sharda for sharing knowledge on *Nakshatra jyotish*. Ekta Jain acknowledges Dr. Ranjan Pal who is not just a colleague and friend, but also a mentor, guide and source of inspiration to the author. Even though the fundamental concepts of astrology were introduced to the author by Dr. Richa Shukla, it was Ranjan who spent a huge amount of his time personally mentoring and coaching Ekta Jain like a Guru, using a systematic, methodical and logical approach. Ekta feels blessed to have had the opportunity to interact with brilliant (and 'mischievously playful') minds like Ranjan and be able to have extensive and exhaustive discussions on varied topics and concepts in Vedic astrology. Ekta Jain also acknowledges Dr. Richa Shukla and Ranjan's benevolence for providing her the opportunity to co-author this book, despite they being far senior, knowledgeable, and experienced in this subject in comparison to her.

Ekta Jain acknowledges her parents, Shrimati Trilesh Jain, Shri Pavan Kumar Jain, and family who have always been a source of strength and encouragement to her. She acknowledges her daughter, Aarushi Jain and husband, Mr. Sandeep Jain, who have been her rock and colossal pillars of strength by providing unconditional support in all her endeavours. Aarushi has been Ekta's most emphatic and vocal cheer leader, providing unfaltering backing in all situations and circumstances. Ekta acknowledges Mr. Sandeep Jain for his stoic love, wisdom, and fortitude.

The authors would like to thank Mr. Abhishek Jain and Mrs. Poonam Taneja from the Motilal Banarsidass (MLBD) International for providing them with the opportunity to publish this book in their prestigious and historic publishing house. They also thank the anonymous editing staff of this esteemed publishing agency.

Contents

Preface .... *(vii)*

Acknowledgements .... *(xv)*

Introduction 1

Proem

Part 1: Can Rahu Give Highest Spiritual Ethos? 8

Part 2: Can Rahu Drive Spiritual Ethos? 13

* Each of the following case studies can be read independently.

Case Studies

Case Study 1

   A Political Diplomat and Freedom Fighter 19

   1.1 A Narrative of Spiritual Philosophy 19

   1.2 *Parashari-Nakshatra* Analysis 22

   1.3 A *Nadi* Commentary 27

        1.3.1 Method 1 (*Bhrigu-Nandi Nadi*) 27

        1.3.2 Method 2 (BNN with *Nakshatra*) 33

        1.3.3 Method 3 (BNN with *Karmic* Angles) 40

Case Study 2

   A Religiously Confused and Agnostic Politician 50

   2.1 A Narrative of Spiritual Philosophy 50

   2.2 *A Parashari-Nakshatra* Analysis 53

   2.3 A *Nadi* Commentary 59

        2.3.1 Method 1 (*Bhrigu-Nandi Nadi*) 59

      2.3.2 Method 2 (BNN with *Nakshatra*) 66
      2.3.3 Method 3 (BNN with *Karmic* Angles) 72

Case Study 3

A Controversial Spiritual Leader 82
  3.1 A Narrative of Spiritual Philosophy 82
  3.2 A *Parashari-Nakshatra* Analysis 85
  3.3 A *Nadi* Commentary 91
      3.3.1 Method 1 (*Bhrigu-Nandi Nadi*) 92
      3.3.2 Method 2 (BNN with *Nakshatra*) 98
      3.3.3 Method 3 (BNN with *Karmic* Angles) 107

Case Study 4

A Renowned Holy Saint 117
  4.1 A Narrative of Spiritual Philosophy 117
  4.2 A *Parashari-Nakshatra* Analysis 120
  4.3 A *Nadi* Commentary 125
      4.3.1 Method 1 (*Bhrigu-Nandi Nadi*) 126
      4.3.2 Method 2 (BNN with *Nakshatra*) 133
      4.3.3 Method 3 (BNN with *Karmic* Angles) 141

Case Study 5

A Renowned Corporate Executive 154
  5.1 A Narrative of Spiritual Philosophy 154
  5.2 A *Parashari-Nakshatra* Analysis 157
  5.3 A *Nadi* Commentary 164
      5.3.1 Method 1 (*Bhrigu Nandi Nadi*) 165
      5.3.2 Method 2 (BNN with *Nakshatra*) 170
      5.3.3 Method 3 (BNN with *Karmic* Angles) 175

Case Study 6

A Renowned Yogi 184
  6.1 A Narrative of Spiritual Philosophy 184

    6.2   A *Parashari-Nakshatra* Analysis 187
    6.3   A *Nadi* Commentary 193
          6.3.1 Method 1 (*Bhrigu-Nandi Nadi*) 194
          6.3.2 Method 2 (BNN with *Nakshatra*) 198
          6.3.3 Method 3 (BNN with *Karmic* Angles) 202

Case Study 7

A Spiritual Communication Businesswoman 212
    7.1   A Narrative of Spiritual Philosophy 212
    7.2   A *Parashari-Nakshatra* Analysis 215
    7.3   A *Nadi* Commentary 222
          7.3.1 Method 1 (*Bhrigu Nandi Nadi*) 223
          7.3.2 Method 2 (BNN with *Nakshatra*) 228
          7.3.3 Method 3 (BNN with *Karmic* Angles) 233

Conclusion 241
Bibliography 243
Biographies 246

ॐ अर्धकायं महावीर्यं चन्द्रादित्यविमर्दनम्।
सिंहिकागर्भसंभूतं तं राहुं प्रणम्यहम्॥

Salutations to Rahu, half-bodied, of great valor, who seizes the Sun and Moon, born of Simhika. To him I bow.

(Atharva Veda, Rahu Stotra mantra)

राहुं शिरसि धृत्वा तु नित्यं पश्येद्य एव हि।
सर्वपापविनिर्मुक्तो ब्रह्मलोकं स गच्छति॥

He who contemplates Rahu daily with reverence is freed from all sins and attains the realm of Brahman.

(Brihat Parashar Hora Shastra, Rahu Stuti)

Introduction

Rahu, also called the North Node of the Moon, is a shadowy planet in Vedic astrology. In the context of astronomy and physics, these nodes are strategic vortexes that are formed via the interaction between powerful magnetic and other cosmic fields of the Earth, the Sun, and the Moon. Hence, despite being shadowy in nature and having no physical presence, these planets can exert a significant influence on life sustained on Earth. Philosophically, Rahu represents the paradox of *asat* (the unreal) exerting a real impact. Just as shadows reveal the existence of light by contrast, Rahu discloses the hidden patterns of desire, illusion, and disruption that shape human destiny. Vedic seers treated Rahu not as a void but as a *Karmic* force — an archetype of *avidya* (ignorance) that tests the soul. Thus, Rahu's significance lies not in physicality but in its capacity to bend perception, drive evolution, and ultimately point toward truth by making us confront illusion.

On one hand, Rahu is a planet often associated (astrologically signified) with materialism, ambition, greed, mischief, fear, darkness, dissatisfaction, obsession, confusion, mystery, science, and occultism. Such a perception of Rahu is primarily derived from the mythological lore associated with the *samudra manthan* (ocean churning) event mentioned in the *puranas*. All these factors are often (if not always) the opposite of achieving spiritual bliss and/or *moksha* (the ultimate spiritual bliss). The myth also reveals Rahu's deeper symbolism: as the *asura* who partook of *amṛita* (nectar of immortality) before being exposed, he embodies the soul's thirst for eternity but in distorted form. Rahu's ceaseless craving represents *avidya* (ignorance) binding beings to *sansara*. However, Vedic philosophy teaches that even illusion (*maya*) is part of the divine play (*lila*). Thus, Rahu becomes paradoxically both obstacle and teacher — forcing seekers to confront desire and illusion as the very thresholds to liberation.

On the other hand, in the *puranas* Rahu is represented by the *Varaha* (boar) avatar (incarnation) of Lord Vishnu. Consequently Rahu, when operating on its higher principle, can protect and save the universe (as was the main purpose of all the avatars of Lord Vishnu). It is often related to the *kundalini* — a metaphysical serpent (mentioned first in the *Upanishads*) which sits coiled inside the human body along an axis that runs between the *ajna chakra* and the base of the spine. A sleeping *kundalini* drives a native towards baser material attachments. In this sense, Rahu symbolizes the raw evolutionary drive — disruptive when unconscious, liberating when directed. Philosophically, Rahu's darkness is not mere negation but an alchemical ground where ignorance can be transmuted into wisdom. This also explains Rahu's association with Goddess Durga: she embodies the capacity to master illusion (*moha*) and channel shadow into *sakti*. Worship of the Goddess, therefore, elevates Rahu energy, aligning it with *dharma*. When seen through this lens, Rahu is not an enemy of *mokṣha* but a paradoxical ally: its trials compel the soul to awaken. Indeed, the very turbulence Rahu generates and can become a form of *tapas*, a crucible of inner discipline. Just as eclipses obscure light only to restore it, Rahu conceals truth in order to deepen longing for it. Thus, Rahu serves as both veil and revealer — the shadow that ultimately gestures toward illumination. In view of this argument, the following shloka from the *Brhadaranyaka Upanishad (1.3.28)* becomes relevant for Rahu.

तमसो मा ज्योतिर्गमय ।
From darkness, lead me to light.

In view of the above arguments, it is hard to be convinced that Rahu energies will not enable spiritual ethos of varying degrees for a native when it is related to the *kundalini* significance, and more so when Lord Vishnu, and Goddess Durga represent this planet as both its guardians and higher transformative archetypes within Vedic cosmology.

This book wants to answer the all-important question: *what is the truth behind the spiritual ethos of Rahu?* Alternatively, does Rahu give or seed spirituality or not? The novelty of this question in the broader literature of Vedic astrology is that there has been no documented finding (backed up with logical and rigorous astrological analysis) on Rahu not having the capacity to give spirituality to a native. The popular consensus is that Rahu is a malefic that mostly drives the materialistic, anti-spiritual aspect of human behavior, and incapable of giving spirituality. While this consensus may still hold true, we were motivated to conduct a systematic astrological study backed by a rigorous analysis to put more statistical weight for/against this statement. Here, the term 'statistical' implies verifying the statement (in favor or against) through an analysis of several horoscopes to promote as much generality for/against the statement.

In this research, we infer jointly via arguments based on (a) scriptural annotations and (b) analysis of astrological case studies, i.e., horoscopes, whether (including to what degree) and how Rahu influences a native's spiritual side. One boundary of spirituality (as mentioned in the *Bhagavad Gita*) is achieving oneness with God (also termed as *moksha* in Hinduism) through (as example) intense adherence to either *Bhakti Yoga, Karma Yoga, Jnana Yoga,* or *Sankhya Yoga*. The other boundary is the extreme opposite or the non-spiritual space where a native is mostly interested in experiencing and enjoying the baser desires. In between these two boundaries is the space where most natives live. A good way to imagine this boundary space is a spiritual pyramid wherein the top/peak (one of the boundaries) of the pyramid represents the rare and small class of individuals who are highly evolved and spiritual achieving oneness with the Divine. The bottom broad base (the other boundary) of the spiritual pyramid consists of natives whose main goal and actions in life are solely to satisfy their baser desires. In between these two boundaries lie the zone where the spiritual ethos of an individual grows rapidly as we approach the peak of the pyramid. The main question here to examine astrologically is: *can Rahu place an individual to be nearer to the peak of the pyramid in terms of their spiritual ethos?* After all, Lord Krishna instills curiosity via his following *shloka* in the **Bhagavad Gita (10.30)** where he identifies himself with Rahu and showcases that

Introduction

Rahu's disruptive trials are not outside *dharma* but instruments of it. Thus, Rahu **can** paradoxically pull a native upward on the pyramid, by eclipsing false lights and compelling the soul to seek the true Light.

प्रह्लादश्चास्मि दैत्यानां काल: कलयतामहम्।
मृगाणां च मृगेन्द्रोऽहं वैनतेयश्च पक्षिणाम्।।

Among the Daityas, I am Prahlada... among the reckoners of time, I am Time itself... among the planets, I am Rahu who swallows the Sun and Moon.

As a pathway to answering the question above via statistical and astrological logic given divine wisdom of Lord Krishna's words from the Gita as a steering compass, we first extensively survey classics to screen out *shloka* outcomes that are related to a native achieving *moksha*. This concept of *moksha* is synonymous with the native being at the peak of the spiritual pyramid or very much nearer to the peak. We figure out this connection of Rahu in the *shlokas* (aphorisms) to screen the *shlokas* where (or whether) Rahu acts as a necessary condition for attaining *moksha* in native. In the event that we find Rahu not giving (as is the popular opinionated consensus) natives the high spiritual bliss states, we examine whether Rahu plays a significant role to seed spiritual ethos in natives who are higher up in the spiritual pyramid. Specifically, we examine using an amalgamation of *Parashari, Nakshatra,* and *Nadi jyotish* more than 50 diverse horoscopes (to ensure statistical significance) of such natives to check for the role of Rahu to influence their spiritual ethos. We get two very interesting findings (discovery) as an outcome of our analysis on these horoscopes.

First, **Rahu does not appear in any of the *shlokas* in the classics that mention the necessary conditions for a native to directly attain/get *moksha*.** However, we cannot rule out the possibility of Rahu playing a strong seeding and/or 'supporting' role to the spiritual ethos of a native who is at the peak of the spiritual pyramid or inside the space closer to the peak when compared to the base. This calls for a more rigorous horoscope analysis than simply and hurriedly making a snapshot inference in the negative based on these *moksha*-related *shlokas*.

Second, from the astrological case studies, we statistically establish as a conjecture (simply because statistical analysis cannot prove any statement to work in each and every chart - it can only provide an increased confidence) the following: **Rahu can support a spiritual lifestyle in a native, can seed a native towards *moksha*/high spiritual state, can sustain high spiritual ethos/*moksha* attained in other periods (i.e., the planetary *dashas*), but cannot be the giver of *moksha*/high spiritual states.** Simply put, Rahu can support/seed/ spiritual ethos but cannot be the giver of such an ethos. We establish this result using *Parashari*, *Nakshatra*, and *Nadi jyotish* analysis.

This conjecture makes very good sense from the view of both, keeping the consensus significance of Rahu intact (that Rahu is in general anti-*moksha* in nature), but also establishing that positive energies of divine Rahu can be leveraged to seed, contribute and/or sustain the flame of *moksha* (under suitable astrological conditions) or high spiritual ethos that has already been given by other planets (e.g., via astrological combinations that grant *moksha* or high spiritual states to a native) in their periods. In essence, our research infers that though each planet is an avatar of Lord Vishnu who is a giver of *moksha*, the primary functions of each avatar are compartmentalized in Vedic astrology. Each planet has its own unique contribution, but together they all serve the larger purpose of spiritual evolution. So, while Rahu doesn't originate spirituality, it can push a person (explained via appropriate astrological combinations) closer to *moksha* or high spiritual ethos by (for example) breaking attachments and intensifying the search for truth. Rahu can accelerate the soul's detachment, compelling deeper yearning for truth. The native is forced to see through false attachments, and this confrontation becomes a stepping-stone toward higher realization.

Proem
Part 1

Can Rahu Give Highest Spiritual Ethos?

We extensively survey and exhaustively state from definitive classic sources (*Brihat Parashara Hora Sastra* popularly abbreviated as BPHS, *Brihat Jataka, Skanda Hora, Jaimini Sutras, Chandra Kala Nadi*) necessary conditions for a native to gain *moksha* in the current birth.

Note here that we have extended the related work: *Does Rahu Give Spiritual Ethos? An Argumentative Analysis in Jyotish* by incorporating *nakshatra jyotish* in depth in addition to *Nadi jyotish*. However, the crux of *nakshatra jyotish* lies in lords, pada lords, sub-lords that are the *navagrahas* forming combinations among them in the *rashi* and divisional charts (e.g., in the *navamsa* charts) in *Parashari* and *Jaimini jyotish*. It is through such *graha* combinations; we eventually decode the spiritual ethos of a native. Connecting this with the above paragraph rationalizes why it is sufficient to survey conditions from the sources mentioned. *(Bhrigu-Nandi) Nadi jyotish* is based on orthogonal principles of analysis and does not corroborate with the principles from the classics mentioned in the first paragraph above, and we do not historically have a collection of *sutras* laid down by sages that state the *Nadi* combinations for achieving spiritual ethos.

Proem (Part 1)

We revisit the definition of *moksha* in our research to be equivalent to any of the following: (a) achieving oneness with the Almighty, (b) experiencing the state of ultimate spiritual bliss, and (c) being blessed with the highest spiritual ethos.

We now list the relevant *sutras* from classics on the necessary conditions for a native to gain *moksha*. After each sutra, we briefly comment on whether and how Rahu plays a role in the necessary conditions. In the rest of *Part One* of this essay, when we mention benefic(s) or malefic(s), it implies natural benefic(s) and malefic(s).

BPHS

If the Lord of Lagna is in the 9th, the 9th Lord is in the 2nd, Jupiter is in the 10th, and the Moon is endowed with strength gives *moksha*; **there is no mention of Rahu.**

If Jupiter joins the 9th lord while the 7th and 2nd are in order in the 9th and the 2nd, gives *moksha*; **there is no mention of Rahu.**

The Moon, Jupiter, the Lagna lord and that of the 9th being together in the 10th house while the 10th lord is in the 9th gives *moksha*; **no mention of Rahu.**

Should the Lagna lord be in the 2nd while the 5th is occupied by Jupiter, as the 10th lord is with strength, giving *moksha*; **there is no mention of Rahu.**

Should the lords of the 9th and 10th houses be in the Lagna unaspected by malefics while the Lagna lord is in the 2nd unafflicted by Saturn, gives *moksha*; **there is no mention of Rahu.**

If the 9th house is tenanted by the lords of the Lagna and 10th house in aspect to a benefic, gives *moksha*; **there is no mention of Rahu.**

If there is a benefic in 12th house (of a *punya* chart – a chart casted at the time of death of the native), while its lord is exalted, or is in *yuti* with or receives a *drishti* from a benefic, one will attain the final emancipation (a stronger version of *moksha*); **there is no mention of Rahu.**

Brihat Jataka

If Jupiter in exaltation occupies 6th, 8th or any *kendra* gives *moksha*; **there is no mention of Rahu.**

If Pisces is Lagna occupying beneficial *navamsas*, (*e.g., trines of a D9 chart*) and planets other than Jupiter are powerless, the native attains *moksha*; **there is no mention of Rahu.**

Skanda Hora

If Saturn in 9th house is in his own sign or exalted, then the native has come from *Vaikuntha* (the abode of Sri Vishnu). After living in accordance with *Dharma*, he shall again attain *Vaikuntha"*. There **is no mention of Rahu.**

Jaimini Sutras

If Ketu is in the 12th from *Karakamsa* and conjunct or aspected by *subha grahas* then the person gets *moksha*; **there is no mention of Rahu.**

Ketu in the 12th [from *Swamsa* = *Navamsa* Lagna] and aspected by benefics gives final emancipation of the soul (stronger version of *moksha*); **there is no mention of Rahu.**

If Ketu is in the 4th or 12th (and having no malefics) from *karakamsa* final emancipation will be granted; **there is no mention of Rahu.**

If benefics in friendly sign are in trines from *Varnada Lagna*, *Arudha Lagna* or Venus, the native is on the path of liberation; **there is no mention of Rahu.**

Chandra Kala Nadi

If the 12th lord is with a benefic planet and both aspects the 12th house, *moksha* is granted; **there is no mention of Rahu.**

If Jupiter with Ketu or Ketu is next to Jupiter, *moksha* is granted; **there is no mention of Rahu.**

If Jupiter or Venus are in a *kendra* in Rasi and in 12th from *Navamsa* Lagna, *moksha* is granted; **There is no mention of Rahu.**

Moksha Yoga (Saturn, Mars and Ketu *yuti* or in 3rd, 5th, 7th or 9th of each other): *Japa siddhi*, *moksha*, visit to *tirthas*, attainment of Divine grace in old age; **There is no mention of Rahu.**

Jagad Guru (a type of *Shakti Avesha Yoga*) *Yoga* (according to this *yoga*, Saturn, Jupiter, Ketu *yuti* or should be in 3rd, 5th, 7th or 9th from each other): the native with this *yoga* will be the guide of society as a whole, he has been entrusted with the sacred task of propagating the means and ways of getting *moksha* to the man and entire humanity; he will offer food to the needy; knowledge and experience in the science of chemistry; he will travel extensively; goes to Vaikuntha (*moksha*) after death; **there is no mention of Rahu.**

It is obvious from the above-mentioned sutras from astrological classics that no *moksha sutras* comment on the direct role of Rahu in a native attaining *moksha*. We want to be statistically conservative in our comment here by stating that we do not rule out the theoretical possibility of a *sutra* tying a direct role of Rahu to a native attaining *moksha*. After all there are hundreds of thousands of *sutras* in Vedic astrology, and finding one *sutra* is akin to finding a needle in a haystack. However, given our focused study of the classics, and commentaries by modern masters on Rahu, there is a very low likelihood of the event that Rahu directly gives *moksha*.

Hence, we can infer with statistical confidence based on *sutra* churning that Rahu does not directly make a native attain *moksha* or the highest spiritual ethos. However, we cannot rule out the possibility of Rahu providing a strong indirect seeding effect or inculcating and supporting spirituality characteristics leading towards *moksha* or significant spiritual development and ethos of a native. This skepticism (or lack of) is subject to a rigorous study we conduct in the subsequent parts of this detailed research effort.

Proem
Part 2

Can Rahu Drive Spiritual Ethos?

In this part of the book, we borrow the inference from *Part One* and move towards examining as to whether and to what degree there is a seeding and/or supporting influence of Rahu in driving a native towards attaining spiritual states (including *moksha*) or inculcating a spiritual ethos - even if Rahu cannot give *moksha* to a native. There are two steps to this examination. The *first step* is laying down a structured/methodical list of primary (but not exhaustive) elements that should be analyzed in order to establish whether and to what degree Rahu can drive a native towards inculcating a spiritual ethos. The second step is to perform a rigorous analysis of these elements on multiple horoscopes to arrive at a conjecture with statistical confidence on whether Rahu can inculcate/drive spiritual ethos in a native. We list elements of the *first step* as follows:

(1) An examination of the basic potential (promise) of a native to achieve varying degrees of spiritual ethos based on a mind-body-soul synchronization (with respect to astrological reasoning) analysis. A good synchronization increases the potential (but does not guarantee) of the native achieving spiritual ethos.

(2) An examination of the basic potential of Rahu to provide spiritual ethos to a native.

(3) The *Vimshottari dasha* period always (among many other things) talks about the psychological evolution of a native during that period. Since we are talking about spirituality (a type of psychological evolution in any native) and Rahu, we need to importantly investigate the effect of the Rahu *mahadasha* (MD) of a person on his/her spiritual mindset and consequently find astrological connections of Rahu with necessary conditions for spiritual development of a native. In relevant settings, we also need to see the effect of Rahu *antardasha* (AD) on the spiritual evolution of a native.

(4) The Rahu MD is 18 years, and quite a long time. Since we are looking into the effect of Rahu on spirituality of a native and already given that Rahu has no direct effect on a native attaining *moksha* (from *Part One* of this essay), it is sufficient to study the role of Rahu on a native's ability to attain *moksha* ONLY in the Rahu MD of 18 years (maximum). In other words, if Rahu influences a person's spirituality, then it must show significant effects in that person's Rahu MD. One could argue here that if Rahu is conjunct with a planet(s) then the MD of that planet(s) should also be studied for spiritual achievements. While this is true, it cannot be denied at all that the conjunct planet(s) are giving the result here due to the amplifier effect of Rahu, and not Rahu itself. We are

interested in the very conservative scenario of what Rahu itself can give, and hence we only look at the Rahu MD in our analysis to make conservative assessments.

(5) Rahu acts as the lord of the house where he is placed, and the planet it represents. As an example, if Rahu is placed in the 4th house of a Leo ascendant, then Rahu will act like Mars and give effects of the 4th lord.

(6) There are basic static conditions (extending step (2) above) that need to be satisfied in a chart of any native for that native to be *helped by Rahu* (either in a materialistically positive or negative way) on the path of spirituality, even if Rahu does not directly promote *moksha/* spirituality. **Without these conditions in a chart (especially D1/D9) being satisfied, it is fair to say that Rahu will not contribute to spirituality in a native in its MD or surrounding periods.** Prominent among them (but not limited to) are (i) Rahu being associated with Jupiter; (ii) Rahu's association with the fifth or ninth lord (with or without Jupiter); (iii) Rahu's association with the fifth or ninth lord (Saturn playing a role) especially if Sun and Moon are involved; (iv) Rahu and Jupiter are in the same sign as Jupiter (Pisces or Sagittarius), this combination can lead to spiritual development in any of the *moksha sthana* (the 4th, 8th, or 12th houses); (v) Rahu is placed in Mercury's *gandanta nakshatra* (especially in the fourth *pada*); and (vi) the basic spiritual propensity of a horoscope as

evident from a D1 chart. Such combinations usually bring some big changes in a native's life either during the Rahu MD or otherwise that propels the latter towards a spiritual lifestyle later in the Rahu MD or otherwise.

(7) We are interested in judging the overall effect Rahu has on a native's spiritual journey, and not necessarily on the exact timing and the essence of spirituality. Hence, it is sufficient to work with the D1 (and relevant divisional charts such as the D9) chart (without transits) of a native. If there is no Rahu power to promote spirituality in D1, it is safe to say that for that native, looking into divisional charts will be of less use (if at all).

(8) Finally, but not the least important is the fact that while conducting horoscope analysis, a viewpoint (whether it be in relation to Rahu or otherwise in general) should be established by summing up sub-analysis on multiple dimensions of the horoscope. The outcome of an analysis on each dimension adds or subtracts strength to the final viewpoint on a question that is being examined.

(9) *Parashari* astrology with *nakshatras* excels in structural rigor: *yogas*, planetary strength, and *dasha* systems map the broad *karmic* framework of a native's life. Bhrigu–Nandi Nadi (BNN) astrology, by contrast, works narratively by reading planetary exchanges, *karaka* linkages, and directional flows to describe how Rahu impacts spiritual ethos with striking specificity. When combined, the two methods balance

each other: *Parashari* offers the architecture of destiny, while BNN astrology provides the storyline of *karma*. Cross-checking events through both systems enhances predictive accuracy, reveals subtler nuances (e.g., spiritual versus material outcomes), and reduces interpretive bias in deciphering the role of Rahu in a native's spiritual ethos. We do this inter-systems analysis in our book and also add in the *Krishnamurti Paddhati* system of astrology in the integration that sharpens precision of analysis through the concept of cuspal sub-lords and stellar subdivisions, and their use.

The *second step* consists of selecting numerous horoscopes (as **case studies**) for analyzing the influence of Rahu on a native's spiritual ethos. We re-emphasize that public opinion on Rahu and spirituality is mostly without any proof - in a way of hearsay. Opinions may still hold true, but it is imperative that one proves them first through analysis. To this end, we selected 50 horoscopes of individuals who are either spiritual, and/or publicly perceived to be spiritual in order to examine whether and how Rahu played a role in shaping their (perceived) spirituality. We present the analysis of 7 such horoscopes (created using the *Parashara Lite 9.0* software) without loss of generality.

The list of the 7 horoscopes for our case studies are as follows:

1. A Political Diplomat and Freedom Fighter
2. A Confused and Agnostic Politician

3. A Controversial Spiritual Leader
4. A Renowned Holy Saint
5. A Renowned Corporate Executive
6. A Renowned *Yogi*
7. A Spiritual Communication Businesswoman

Disclaimer: Note here that Rahu is not necessary for spiritual evolution, and we are not testing this fact. What we are testing is whether Rahu, like any other planet, has the potential to drive the spiritual ethos of a native. Hence, we select charts where we show, based on hypotheses collected from historical life events of a native, how the placement of Rahu (using a logical combination of *Parashara, Nakshatra,* and *Nadi* analysis) and its major periods (in the case of a logical combination of *Parashara* and *Nakshatra* analysis) contributed to seeding or giving or sustaining the spiritual ethos of the native.

Case Study 1
A Political Diplomat and Freedom Fighter

Section 1.1:
A Narrative of Spiritual Philosophy

During the years spent in South Africa (1893–1914), the native entered a crucible of personal transformation. Exposed to systemic injustice and racial humiliation, the native began to search for a deeper response that would not merely oppose oppression but transcend it. It was here that the ideals of *satya* (truth) and *ahimsa* (non-violence) were not abstract principles but lived realities, resonating with the Vedic vision of $ṛta$ — the cosmic order upheld by truth, justice, and self-restraint. Practices such as fasting, celibacy, and simplicity were cultivated, echoing the yogic vows (*yamas* and *niyamas*) set out in the *Upanishads*, transforming the native's lifestyle into a field of spiritual discipline.

Upon returning to India in 1915, these seeds matured into a mission that transcended the personal and entered the collective. The doctrine of *satyagraha* became both a moral vow and a social instrument, embodying the Rigvedic dictum *"Satyameva jayate"* — truth alone triumphs. Political resistance was framed not as a contest of force but as a sacred *yajna*, a sacrifice of ego and comfort offered for the liberation of the people. This was not merely a political technique, but a spiritual movement aimed at aligning the nation with *dharma*.

By integrating personal austerity, truth, and non-violence with collective struggle, the native demonstrated the Vedic principle that the purity of the individual soul sustains and uplifts the destiny of the community. Thus, the freedom movement became more than politics; it was a spiritual renaissance of India, reclaiming its ancient ethos through modern action.

The native's spirituality was profound, yet not absolutely pure, for it unfolded within the contradictions of human life. He pursued *satya* (truth) and *ahimsa* (non-violence) with relentless devotion, but often imposed his experiments on family and colleagues, reflecting ego as much as renunciation. His vows of celibacy and austerity were sincere, yet some practices — such as testing self-control in controversial ways — blurred the line between discipline and lapse. Rabindranath Tagore described him as a *"great soul struggling with human clay,"* capturing the tension between saintly aspiration and embodied flaws. Politically too, his compromises with authority diluted his principles, showing the difficulty of keeping spiritual ideals intact within practical leadership. The native himself admitted, *"I am painfully conscious of my imperfections. I claim to be a seeker of truth. I admit that I have not yet found it"* His spirituality was luminous but unfinished — not perfection, but a striving, restless search for truth that shone brightly yet carried inevitable human shadows.

Case Study 1: A Political Diplomat and Freedom Fighter

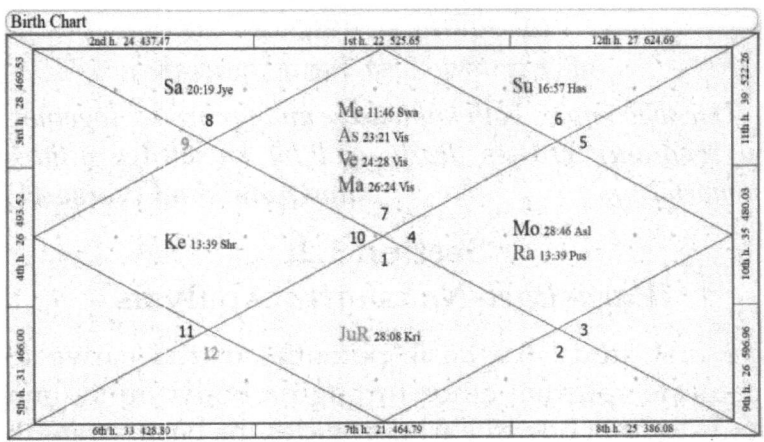

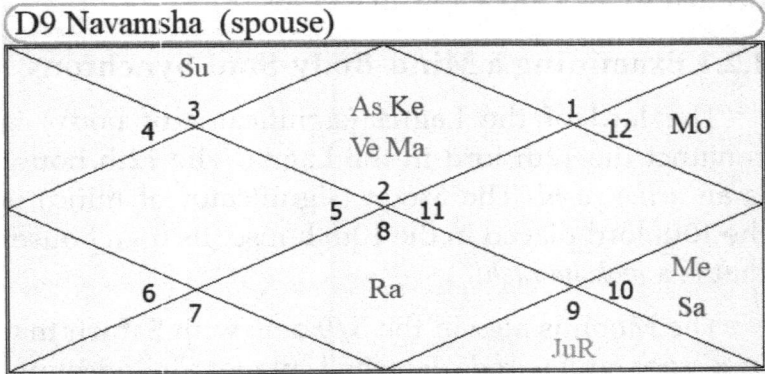

Birth Chart				
As	23:21:51	Vishakha	Too	2,Ju/Sa/Ra
Su	16:57:01	Hasta	Nuh	3,Mo/Sa/Mo
Mo	28:46:17	Ashlesha	Doh	4,Me/Sa/Ve
Ma	26:24:22	Vishakha	Too	2,Ju/Ke/Sa
Me	11:46:16	Swati	Ray	2,Ra/Sa/Mo
Ju	28:08:04 R	Krittika	Ah	1,Su/Mo/Me
Ve	24:28:07	Vishakha	Too	2,Ju/Me/Ve
Sa	20:19:56	Jyeshtha	Yah	2,Me/Ve/Ra
Ra	13:39:27	Pushya	Dah	4,Sa/Ra/Sa
Ke	13:39:27	Shravana	Khu	2,Mo/Ra/Mo

DOB - 2nd October 1869, Time - 8:35 AM, Porbandar, India

विद्यां चाविद्यां च यस्तद्वेदोभयं सह ।
अविद्यया मृत्युं तीर्त्वा विद्ययाऽमृतमश्नुते ॥

He who knows both knowledge and ignorance together, by ignorance crosses death, and by knowledge attains immortality. **Isha Upanishad (verse 11)**

Section 1.2:
Parashari-Nakshatra Analysis

We first study the basic potential of the native to inculcate spiritual ethos through a body, mind, and soul study of how the trio provides the basic strength needed to develop a spiritual ethos.

1.2.1 Examining a Mind-Body-Soul Synchrony

The lord of the Lagna (significator of body) is conjunct the 12th lord in the Lagna. The 12th house is an *artha rashi*. The Moon (significator of mind) is the 10th lord placed in the 10th house (its own house) that is a *moksha rashi*.

The Moon is also in the 5/9 axis with Saturn that is a separative and detached planet. In addition, the *Manasa nakshatra* (24th *nakshatra* from the *Janma nakshatra* in the 27 *nakshatra* scheme) that signifies the nature of thoughts in the mind, is *Mrigashira* and lorded by Mars. Mars is conjunct Mercury who is the 12th lord and 9th lord, and Venus who is the Lagna lord and the 8th lord. Hence, the Moon placement of the native drives the natives towards a spiritual bent of mind who is detached from titles and status that characterize the 10th house.

In addition, the *Manasa nakshatra* (*Mrigashira*) is a *manda nakshatra* (a *nakshatra* type in the *andhadi*

Case Study 1: A Political Diplomat and Freedom Fighter

nakshatra set) gives this native a hard working mental attitude to achieving one's goals. The *Nakshatra Lord* is aspected by Jupiter who is lord of *upachaya* (gain) houses, and orthogonal to dharmic purity - in this case the gain mindset is amplified by Jupiter aspecting its own house. The *Janma nakshatra* is also a *manda nakshatra* and denotes that the native will have to work hard to obtain his goals of "detachment". Alternatively, the native will not be spiritually gifted. Hence, the nature of the *Janma* and *Manasa nakshatras* together contribute to the "gain"-driven, slow, and hardworking progress towards imbibing a spiritual ethos in life.

Sun (the significator of the soul) is placed in the 12th house in an *artha rashi*. In the D9, Lagna is with Ketu in *artha rashi* and so is Lagna lord and is conjunct 12th lord. Moon is in the 11th house (9th from its own house) but in a *moksha rashi* and aspected by Saturn from 9th house as 9th lord (causing a *sannyas yoga* signifying detachment) who is conjunct 5th lord. Sun is aspected by Jupiter who is 8th lord and who is placed in the 8th house in a *dharma rashi*.

Hence, the above astrological arguments show sufficient potential in the native to experience spiritual ethos of a certain degree given the mind-body-soul connection.

1.2.2 Influence of Rahu on Spiritual Potential

The native has Rahu in the 10th house in Cancer — a *moksha rashi*. Hence it acts like the 10th lord and exhibits properties of the Moon that is itself in the *Ashlesha nakshatra* of transformation in *gandanta* position. The *nakshatra* is a *manda nakshatra* - hence the native would have to work hard for transformations. Rahu is also in the *nakshatra* of the 5th lord and *yogakaraka* Saturn. Here, *Pushya* is an *andha nakshatra*, where the native does not care about the surroundings, i.e., blind or *andha* to the surroundings, but only about focusing and achieving a greater goal. The *nakshatra* lord being the 4th lord, and the 5th lord supports this goal more. The Moon, being the 10th lord, is also in the 10th house with Rahu. Rahu is also on the 1/7 axis in the D9 chart and sitting in a *moksha rashi*. Hence, *Rahu as a planet here will promote spiritual ethos in the native* via a focused and hardworking goal. The placement of Rahu in the 10th house in D1 likely indicates a revolutionary at the workplace with non-conventional thinking. The native is also blessed with a *Gajakesari Yoga* between Jupiter and Moon with Jupiter in a *dharma rashi* gives immense fame and popularity to the native (influencing the 7th and 10th houses) in public spheres.

1.2.3 *Dasha* Analysis

Take note that the dispositors of the birth ascendant and Sun - Venus and Mercury, respectively are mutual friends; and the dispositor of Moon, i.e., Moon is not mutually friendly Venus and Mercury. The majority of the three dispositors are friends of the ascendant lord. Hence, while analyzing *dasha* periods, and in accordance with the *Sudarshan Paddhati* (SP) principles from the *Parashari* code of *dasha* analysis, we need not perform a logical analysis from all the three reference points (Lagna, Sun, Moon) to arrive at conclusions/inferences. We, however, do it for completeness for this case study.

Case Study 1: A Political Diplomat and Freedom Fighter

This native in the Moon MD advent suddenly started to exhibit and lead a never-seen-before attitude (a representation of outlier-ish behavior) of non-violence (an important factor in spirituality) at the workplace (as Moon is in house 10) despite facing sufficient injustice. This sudden change in attitude had its seed placed in the Sun MD where Sun (the significator of the soul) is in the 12th house (a house of spirituality) of the native. Note that making Sun as the ascendant lord by SP principles places Sun in the 2/12 axis from its own house and contributes to 12th house significances. The native in the Moon MD also turned to celibacy (another important factor in spirituality) in the Moon-Rahu period (Moon on the Rahu-Ketu axis and Ketu is in 7th from the Moon as the 7th house represents marital non-celibacy). Note that in D9, Moon and Rahu are in the 5/9 axis of each other, and both are in *moksha rashis*. In the Mars MD, the native sustained (maintained) both, the nonviolent behavior at the workplace (Moon with Rahu in 10th from MD lord Mars) and the spiritual personality (LL with 12th lord conjunct MD lord) that he developed in the prior Moon MD and seeded in the Sun MD. Note that in D9, Sun is aspected by Jupiter, the 8th lord, from the 8th house - adding weight to the seeding argument. Returning to the D1 chart, taking Moon ascendant here, makes Mars conjunct with the 12th lord Mercury, and consensus is there of 12th house influence among the three reference points.

In the entire Rahu MD, the native became obsessed (Rahu is associated with obsession) with motherland (represented by Moon) and went to extreme lengths of materialistic sacrifices (an important factor in spirituality) to protect his motherland through an amplified (Rahu is an amplifier) set of sacrificial events. The sequence of these events spread the fame of the native (especially for outlier-ish non-violence traits in workplace) far and wide due to the *Gajakesari Yoga* formed between Moon and Jupiter by the effect amplified by Rahu in the 10th house (that indicates social image and fame/popularity). In addition, in D9, Rahu is in the 7th house (the *bhavat bhavam* of the 10th house); 5th from its position in D1, signifying the increase in fame/popularity. Taking the Moon, as the ascendant, Jupiter is in the 10th house and amplifies the positive social image and following of the native in relation to non-conventional attitudes. Hence, we have consensus on workplace fame in the Rahu MD according to SP principles. The *Gajakesari Yoga* also gave results in the Moon MD, but the duration/amplification of such results are in the Rahu MD due to the 18-year period of Rahu and the amplifier effect controlled by the MD lord.

1.2.4 Summarizing Inference

The seed of a significant degree of spirituality in the native was planted and inculcated in the MDs of the Sun/Moon/Mars (that also sustained the spiritual behavior over time) because of the soul/mind significances and connections with the 12th house (with respect to the *Sudarshan paddhati*). The Sun/Moon/Mars MDs had a significant role in inculcating spiritual ethos in the native. Rahu MD had the role in amplifying the public impact of the positive role of spirituality on the good of the motherland **but** cannot be taken as the primary direct contributor to the genesis of spirituality within the native. It is also possible that the Rahu MD showcased an exaggerated spiritual development of the native in public than the case actually in reality. We establish for this native that **Rahu did not give him spiritual ethos,** but sustained the spiritual ethos given by other periods.

Section 1.3:
A *Nadi* Commentary

We provide THREE alternative, concise, and precise methods of analysis – based on *Bhrigu-Nandi Nadi* (BNN) astrology complementing the *Parashari* analysis of Case Study 1. **The goal is to establish the *Parashari* inference from Case Study 1 independently for each of the alternative methods of analysis.**

The essence of a good astrological analysis is the necessity for it to be validated from multiple schools of Vedic astrological thought. We choose the BNN approach as the alternative school of thought in this book — however, we smoothly integrate and blend an in-depth *nakshatra jyotish* analysis with the BNN framework, as we did with the *Parashari* analysis. While a strong *Parashari* education and a unique predictive *nakshatra jyotish* course are the pillars of the *Dev Jyotish* school of astrology, the BNN analysis was self-learned by Ranjan Pal under the personal guidance of Richa Shukla, and then the learning imparted to Ekta Jain by Ranjan Pal and Richa Shukla.

1.3.1 Method 1 (*Bhrigu-Nandi Nadi*)

The significator of spirituality is Ketu. In BNN

astrology, only this planet can grant spiritual realization to a native. Hence, unlike in the *Parashari* analysis we need not check whether Rahu provides a spiritual ethos. It cannot. Simply put, BNN saves us effort to test this that takes a significant effort to test via *Parashari jyotish*. It is sufficient to see **(a) whether the placement of Ketu is of sufficient strength to provide a spiritual outlook to the native and (b) whether and to what extent Rahu influences Ketu to support the native realizing spiritual ethos.** Unlike in *Parashari jyotish*, there is no need to do a dynamic analysis in BNN astrology (e.g., via progressions and transits) of Rahu to establish its quantum of influence on native spiritual ethos. This is because the static *Nadi* analysis is sufficiently causal to judge the quantum of Rahu's effects.

Decision Making Factor #1

For the native in Case Study 1, we have **Ketu + Sun** (trines with each other in ascending order of degree). As part of the 7th house from Ketu analysis, we have **Rahu + Saturn + Moon** (in trine from the 7th house from Ketu in ascending order of degree).

The Ketu + Sun combination makes the native famous (Ketu is the flag that stands out) via the government and on lines of his spiritual ethos as both Ketu and Sun are friends at the soul level. One indicates the purity of soul and the other of detachment of the soul from materialism. This combination is a *karmic* call to shed ego and worldly pride, pushing the native toward inner realization. It is both disruptive and liberating — **a classic *moksha-***

Case Study 1: A Political Diplomat and Freedom Fighter

oriented combination, but one that often unfolds through painful detachment.

Rahu + Saturn + Moon indicates work (signified by Saturn) in a foreign land (signified by Rahu) and that work (or the workplace) is changing (signified by the Moon) in nature. Ketu + Sun that normally leans toward ego-dissolution and spirituality. But under Rahu + Saturn + Moon's impact, the path becomes heavy and chaotic — marked by illusions, emotional suffering, and *karmic* obstacles. Yet, precisely through this turbulence, profound detachment and spiritual depth can emerge, provided grace (e.g., Jupiter's influence) stabilizes the mind. In the native's case, the Rahu + Saturn + Moon combination happens in the *artha* houses (2nd, 6th, 10th) that indicate material struggles with spirituality emerging late in life.

However, all three planets (Rahu, Saturn, Moon) are in *moksha rashis*, and together with Rahu gives high spiritual impetus to the native though late in life. However, Ketu and Sun are in *artha rashis*. **The realization isn't ultimate — no blissful *moksha*.**

The elements in the same trine from the 7th house from Ketu have a strong modifying/influencing effect to the significance impact of Ketu of making a native realizing (or not) spiritual ethos. Rahu is always part of this trine to no surprise, the interesting thing to see is how the other planets together with Rahu shape the quantum of impact, as we have done above. It might be tempting to also check for the trines from the 2nd to the placement of Ketu – however, since we are interested in the role of Rahu, we skip this step for now and will return to the analysis of such trines when we integrate *nakshatra* astrology with BNN astrology.

Decision Making Factor #2

For the native in Case Study 1, we have Jupiter as the lord of the 12th house from **Ketu**. Since Ketu is the significator of spirituality in BNN astrology one must check for the 12th from Ketu (12th house is the house of *moksha/dissolution* from any signification). We have a retrograde **Jupiter** standing alone on the trines from the 12th house from Ketu in a *dharma rashi* — hence, the philosophical Jupiter also provides influence on Ketu here from the *moksha rashi* of Pisces via Rahu that is in trine with Jupiter considered from Pisces. With Jupiter in trine from the 12th from Ketu, spiritual fruition is delayed and comes through loss, sacrifice, or detachment via relationships and passions. In other words, Jupiter's 12th-from-Ketu status shows an indirect *mokṣha karma*: liberation not given outright, but through trials of loss, emotional detachment, and exhaustion of desires. However, retrogression also makes Jupiter more philosophically intense: the native questions relationships deeply, seeks higher meaning, and eventually integrates detachment into relational life.

The trine from the 7th from Jupiter (and also from the 7th from the 12th house from Ketu) form the combination **Mercury + Venus + Mars** (in ascending order of degree). The Mercury–Venus–Mars cluster becomes the *karmic* stage where desires are lived out, drained, and finally sublimated. Alternatively, this combination becomes both temptation and teacher— relationships may begin in passion but end in disillusionment, pushing the soul toward Ketu's higher calling.

Rahu and its trine combination have no direct influence role to play here on Ketu significance based on sign placement (if we do not include a *nakshatra* analysis here that is left for subsequent Methods 2 and 3).

Decision Making Factor #3

For the native in Case Study 1, we have Mars as the lord of the 11th house from **Ketu**. We also have Saturn placed in the 11th from Ketu. Since Ketu is the significator of spirituality in BNN astrology one must check for the 11th from Ketu (11th house analysis checks for catalytic factors contributing to a significator – in our case Ketu of spirituality). We have **Rahu + Saturn + Moon** (in ascending order of degree) in *moksha rashis*. **Relate this combination to Decision Making Factor #1 earlier, and it is evident why Rahu is a big catalytic factor in the spiritual journey of the native.** This configuration suggests that the native's spiritual awakening is delayed, *karmically* heavy, and emotionally turbulent. Rahu + Moon agitate the mind, while Saturn enforces discipline and *karmic* repayment. Since Saturn is 11th from Ketu, the endurance of these struggles fulfills old *karmas* (social and/or material) and prepares the native for liberation. If we take the trines from the 7th from the 11th house from Ketu, we get Ketu and Sun that being in *artha rashis*, spoils the non-materialistic essence towards ultimate spiritual realization. There is no blissful *moksha*.

If we now consider Mars as the lord of the 11th house from Ketu, we have the combination **Mercury + Venus + Mars** (in ascending order of degree). The Mercury–Venus–Mars cluster becomes the *karmic* stage where desires are lived out, drained, and finally sublimated. Alternatively, this combination becomes both temptation and teacher — relationships may begin in passion but end in disillusionment, pushing the soul toward Ketu's higher calling. If we consider a retrograde Jupiter placed in the 7th from this combination in a *kaam rashi*, we can see the influence of Rahu on the trine from the Jupiter presence in Pisces due to its retrograde nature. **Rahu gives considerable spiritual impetus to the native on his journey. However, Mercury, Venus, and Mars are in a *kaam rashi*. The realization is not ultimate (i.e., the blissful *moksha*).**

Decision Making Factor #4

For the native in Case Study 1, we have Saturn as the dispositor of Ketu and is located in a *moksha rashi*. We have **Rahu + Saturn + Moon** (trines with each other from the 7th house from Ketu in ascending order of degree) in *moksha rashis*. **Relate this combination to Decision Making Factor #1 earlier, and it is evident why Rahu is a big catalytic factor in the spiritual journey of the native.** The 7th from Saturn has the **Ketu + Sun** connection in *artha rashis*, that has no connection with Rahu (unless with analyze at the *nakshatra* level – the topic of subsequent methods). **The realization isn't ultimate – no blissful *moksha*. Hence, in view of Decision Making Factor #4, Rahu**

Case Study 1: A Political Diplomat and Freedom Fighter 33

influences Ketu gives a significant impetus to the native on his journey to realize spiritual ethos.

Summary: Does the placement of Ketu give a strong spiritual outlook to the native? The answer is an 'yes' from each of the four Decision Making Factors (DMFs). Does Rahu play a major role in the native experiencing spiritual ethos? The answer is an 'yes' from multiple DMFs. The results sync with the *Parashari* analysis. Note that we did not delve into the positivity/negativity with which Rahu influences spiritual ethos. That is not the focus of this research.

1.3.2 Method 2 (BNN with *Nakshatra*)

Since our analysis base is BNN astrology, like in Method 1 we will work with the same DMFs, and be light on the BNN part of the analysis (detailed in Method 1). It is sufficient to see using *nakshatras* **whether and to what extent Rahu influences Ketu to support the native realizing spiritual ethos.** When it comes to doing an analysis using *nakshatra* principles using KP astrology, three KP parameters are relevant for study for each decision making factor: (i) a planet's ***nakshatra* sub-lord**, (ii) the **sub-lord's *nakshatra* lord:** the planet ruling the *nakshatra* in which the sub-lord is situated, and (iii) the **sub-lord's sign lord:** the planet ruling the sign in which the sub-lord is situated. Each *nakshatra* span of 13d20′ is unequally divided into degree space owned by 9 sub-lords proportional to *Vimshottari dasha* duration.

Decision Making Factor #1

For the native in Case Study 1, we have **Ketu +**

Planet	R/C	Sign	Degree	Speed	Nakshatra	Pada	RL	NL	SL	SS	Status	SB
Lagna		Lib	23:21:51		Vishakha	2	Ve	Ju	Sa	Ra		
Sun		Vir	16:57:01	00:59:07	Hasta	3	Me	Mo	Sa	Mo	Frnd.	1.06
Moon		Can	28:46:17	14:27:16	Ashlesha	4	Mo	Me	Sa	Ve	Own	1.19
Mars		Lib	26:24:22	00:41:52	Vishakha	2	Ve	Ju	Ke	Sa	Enemy	1.48
Mercury		Lib	11:46:16	00:36:52	Swati	2	Ve	Ra	Sa	Mo	Neutr.	1.40
Jupiter	R	Ari	28:08:04	-00:04:24	Krittika	1	Ma	Su	Mo	Me	Neutr.	1.13
Venus		Lib	24:28:07	01:11:38	Vishakha	2	Ve	Ju	Me	Ve	Own	1.25
Saturn		Sco	20:19:56	00:04:21	Jyeshtha	2	Ma	Me	Ve	Ra	Neutr.	1.58
Rahu		Can	13:39:27	-00:01:53	Pushya	4	Mo	Sa	Ra	Sa	Neutr.	
Ketu		Cap	13:39:27	-00:01:53	Shravana	2	Sa	Mo	Ra	Mo	Neutr.	

Case Study 1: A Political Diplomat and Freedom Fighter

Sun (trines with each other in ascending order of degree). It is evident **from the analysis in Method 1** that Ketu + Sun combination will enable the native to attain spiritual ethos but via a painful detachment mindset due to a *karmic* call to shed ego and worldly pride, pushing the native toward inner realization.

As part of the 7th house from Ketu analysis, we have **Rahu + Saturn + Moon** (*moksha* trines with each other from the 7th house from Ketu in ascending order of degree) and placed in *moksha rashis*. This combination gives high spiritual impetus to the native though late in life. However, Ketu and Sun being in *artha rashis*, the realization isn't ultimate – no blissful *moksha*. Please refer to BNN details on this combination from Method 1.

Ketu is placed in the *nakshatra* of Moon in the *pada* ruled by Rahu (hence a significant Rahu influence on Ketu significance). Moon is conjunct Rahu in a *moksha rashi*. Using KP, Ketu's sub-lord is Rahu. Rahu's *nakshatra* lord is Saturn who is in trine with Rahu. Rahu's sign lord is Moon which is conjunct Rahu. Sun's sub-lord is Saturn which is in trine with Rahu. Saturn's *nakshatra* lord is Mercury. Rahu's *nakshatra* sub-lord is Saturn. Saturn's *nakshatra* lord is Mercury, and Saturn's sign lord is Mars — none of which is connected with Rahu. Saturn's *nakshatra* sub-lord's *nakshatra* lord is Jupiter. Moon's *nakshatra* sub-lord is Saturn who is in trine with Rahu. Saturn's *nakshatra* lord's sign lord is Mars – not connected with Rahu. **Hence, the spiritual significator Ketu has considerable strength for the native to realize spiritual ethos and is influenced by Rahu considerably.**

If we look at the trine houses from the 2nd house from Ketu, we get **Mercury + Venus + Mars.** Only Mercury is significantly influenced by Rahu as it is in the *nakshatra* of Rahu in the *pada* lorded by Saturn that is in trine with Rahu. Using KP, Mercury's *nakshatra* sub-lord is Saturn that is in trine with Rahu. Saturn's *nakshatra* lord is Mercury (not connected with Rahu) and Saturn's sign lord is Mars (not connected by Rahu). Venus's *nakshatra* sub-lord is Mercury; Mercury's *nakshatra* lord is Rahu; and Mercury's sign lord is Venus. Mars's *nakshatra* sub-lord is Ketu whose *nakshatra* lord is Moon that is conjunct Rahu. Ketu's sign lord is Saturn that is in a trine with Rahu. **In summary, Rahu significantly influences DMF #1 to enable the native experience spiritual ethos.**

Decision Making Factor #2

Since Ketu, in the *nakshatra pada* of Rahu, is the significator of spirituality in BNN astrology one must check for the 12th from Ketu (12th house is the house of *moksha/dissolution* from any signification).

For the native in Case Study 1, we have a retrograde Jupiter as the lord of the 12th house from **Ketu.** Jupiter is placed alone in a trine from the 12th house. It is evident **from the analysis in Method 1** that with Jupiter in a trine from the 12th from Ketu, spiritual fruition is delayed and comes through loss, sacrifice, or detachment via relationships and passions. Nonetheless, the 12th house from Ketu has decent strength to make the native realize spiritual ethos.

Jupiter is placed in a *dharma rashi* in the *nakshatra* of Sun in the *pada* lorded by Moon. Moon is conjunct

Rahu. Using KP, Jupiter is placed in the *nakshatra* of Sun and the *nakshatra* sub-lord is Moon. Moon's *nakshatra* lord is Mercury (not related to Rahu) Moon is conjunct Rahu. Moon is in his own sign with Rahu. The trines from the 7th from Jupiter is **Mercury + Venus + Mars** (in ascending order of degree). The Mercury–Venus–Mars cluster becomes the *karmic* stage where desires are lived out, drained, and finally sublimated. Mercury is in the *nakshatra* of Rahu in the *pada* lorded by Saturn that is in a trine with Rahu. The *nakshatra* placements of Venus and Mars are tangentially influenced by Rahu via a retrograde Jupiter. Mercury's *nakshatra* sub-lord is Saturn that is in trine with Rahu. Saturn's *nakshatra* lord is Mercury (not connected with Rahu) and Saturn's sign lord is Mars (not connected by Rahu). Venus's *nakshatra* sub-lord is Mercury; Mercury's *nakshatra* lord is Rahu; and Mercury's sign lord is Venus. Mars's *nakshatra* sub-lord is Ketu whose *nakshatra* lord is Moon that is conjunct Rahu. Ketu's sign lord is Saturn that is in a trine with Rahu. **Hence the 12th house from Ketu is influenced by Rahu in giving spiritual ethos.**

Decision Making Factor #3

Since Ketu is the significator of spirituality in BNN astrology one must check for the 11th from Ketu (11th house analysis checks for catalytic factors contributing to a significator – in our case Ketu of spirituality). For the native in Case Study 1, we have Mars as the *moksha rashi* lord of the 11th house from **Ketu**. We also have Saturn placed in the 11th from Ketu. **Rahu + Saturn + Moon provides impetus to Ketu to realize spiritual essence.** It is evident from

Method 1 why Rahu is a big catalytic factor in the spiritual journey of the native. This configuration suggests that the native's spiritual awakening is delayed, *karmically* heavy, and emotionally turbulent. Rahu + Moon agitate the mind, while Saturn enforces discipline and *karmic* repayment.

However, Saturn is not in the *nakshatra* of Rahu or in the *pada* lorded by Rahu. Rahu is in the *nakshatra pada* lorded by Rahu, and Moon is conjunct Rahu. Using KP, Saturn's *nakshatra* sub-lord's *nakshatra* lord is Rahu. Moon's *nakshatra* sub-lord is Saturn who is in trine with Rahu. Saturn's *nakshatra* lord's sign lord is Mars — not connected with Rahu.

For the combination **Rahu + Saturn + Moon**, Rahu's *nakshatra* sub-lord is Saturn. Saturn's *nakshatra* lord is Mercury, and Saturn's sign lord is Mars — none of which is connected with Rahu. Moon's *nakshatra* sub-lord is Saturn who is in trine with Rahu. Saturn's *nakshatra* lord's sign lord is Mars – not connected with Rahu. Ketu and Sun (that are in trine to the 7th house from the 11th from Ketu) both have their *nakshatra* lords as Moon that is conjunct Rahu.

If we now consider Mars as the lord of the 11th house from Ketu, we have the combination **Mercury + Venus + Mars** (in ascending order of degree). Mercury is in the *nakshatra* of Rahu in the *pada* lorded by Saturn that is in a trine with Rahu. The *nakshatra* placements of Venus and Mars are tangentially influenced by Rahu via retrograde Jupiter. Using KP, Mercury's *nakshatra* sub-lord is Saturn that is in trine with Rahu. Saturn's *nakshatra* lord is Mercury (not connected with Rahu) and Saturn's sign lord is

Case Study 1: A Political Diplomat and Freedom Fighter 39

Mars (not connected by Rahu). Venus's *nakshatra* sub-lord is Mercury; Mercury's *nakshatra* lord is Rahu; and Mercury's sign lord is Venus. Mars's *nakshatra* sub-lord is Ketu whose *nakshatra* lord is Moon that is conjunct Rahu. Ketu's sign lord is Saturn that is in a trine with Rahu. Hence, **Rahu influences the 11th house from Ketu and promotes it to impart spiritual ethos to the native.**

Decision Making Factor #4

For the native in Case Study 1, we have Saturn as the dispositor of Ketu and is located in a *moksha rashi*. We have **Rahu + Saturn + Moon** (trines with each other from the 7th house from Ketu in ascending order of degree) in *moksha rashis*. It is evident from Method 1 and the analysis thus far in Method 2 that **the spiritual significator in Ketu has strength for the native to realize spiritual ethos.** It is also evident from earlier analysis why Rahu is a big catalytic factor in the spiritual journey of the native. Rahu is in the *nakshatra pada* lorded by Rahu, and Moon is conjunct Rahu.

Using KP, Saturn's *nakshatra* sub-lord's *nakshatra* lord is Rahu. Moon's *nakshatra* sub-lord is Saturn who is in trine with Rahu. Saturn's *nakshatra* lord's sign lord is Mars — not connected with Rahu. We have for the combination **Rahu + Saturn + Moon**, Rahu's *nakshatra* sub-lord as Saturn. Saturn's *nakshatra* lord is Mercury, and Saturn's sign lord is Mars – none of which is connected with Rahu. Moon's *nakshatra* sub-lord is Saturn who is in trine with Rahu. Saturn's *nakshatra* lord's sign lord is Mars – not connected with Rahu. The trines from the 7th from Saturn is **Ketu + Sun**. Both Ketu and Sun are in the *nakshatra* of Moon that is conjunct Rahu. **Overall, Rahu gives a significant impetus to the native on his journey to realize spiritual ethos.**

Summary: Does the placement of Ketu give a strong spiritual outlook to the native? The answer is an 'yes' from each of the four DMFs. Does Rahu play a role in the native experiencing spiritual ethos? The answer is an 'yes' from Decision Making Factors 1-4. The results sync with the *Parashari* analysis. Note that we did not delve into the positivity or negativity with which Rahu influences spiritual ethos. That is not the focus of the research.

1.3.3 Method 3 (BNN with *Karmic* Angles)

We wish to analyse in **three parts** using the *karmic Nadi jyotish* principles the strength of Rahu in influencing each of the mind, body, and soul to realize a spiritual ethos. After all, these are the basic pillars that eventually decide whether a native will be able to realize spiritual ethos in the lifetime. **If the connection is strong in at least two out of the three cases, we can say that Rahu has been significantly instrumental in promoting spirituality within the native.** Unlike in *Parashari jyotish*, there is no need to do a dynamic analysis (e.g., via progressions and transits) of Rahu to establish its quantum of influence on native spiritual ethos. This is because the static *Nadi* analysis is sufficiently causal to judge the quantum of Rahu's effects.

Case Study 1: A Political Diplomat and Freedom Fighter 41

***Dridh-Adridh Karma* Axes** - In *Nadi jyotish*, directions embody the metaphysics of *karma* itself. **East and West** anchor *dridh karma* — duties to father, guru, and ancestors that bind the soul to its inescapable obligations. **East**, aligned with Sun and Jupiter, signifies *dharma*, authority, and righteous beginnings; **West** blends closure and entanglement, largely fixed through Saturn's weight, though softened by Venus's negotiable pleasures. **North and South** anchor *adridh karma* — mutable desires and worldly pursuits shaped by free will. **North**, guided by Mercury and Rahu, points to growth, commerce, and ambition; while **South**, linked with Mars, Ketu, and Moon, carries ancestral debts, *tapas*, and *karmic* reckonings. In summary, East pulls a native towards *dharmic* duty, West toward worldly entanglement, North toward ambition, and South toward purification.

Thus, the four directions mark not mere space but the soul's *karmic* geography: some pathways immovable, others pliable. The horoscope becomes a compass of necessity and possibility, mapping destiny's fixity against the field of conscious striving. One may ask: why not diagonal directions? In *Nadi jyotish*, only the **four cardinal directions** - East, West, North, and South—are used, not the intermediates like Northeast or Northwest. This is because Vedic cosmology is fundamentally **fourfold**, based on sunrise and sunset, solstices and equinoxes, day and night. Each direction is tied to specific *grahas* and *karmic* qualities: East (Sun, Jupiter), West (Saturn, Venus), North (Mercury, Rahu), South (Moon, Mars, Ketu). This framework mirrors the *dik-palas* (directional guardians) of Vedic ritual, which are cardinal. By limiting to four, *Naḍi* emphasizes clarity: destiny is seen through primal axes of *dharma*, desire, past, and closure, without diluting meaning in diagonals.

We provide the planetary directional compass diagram for Case Study 1.

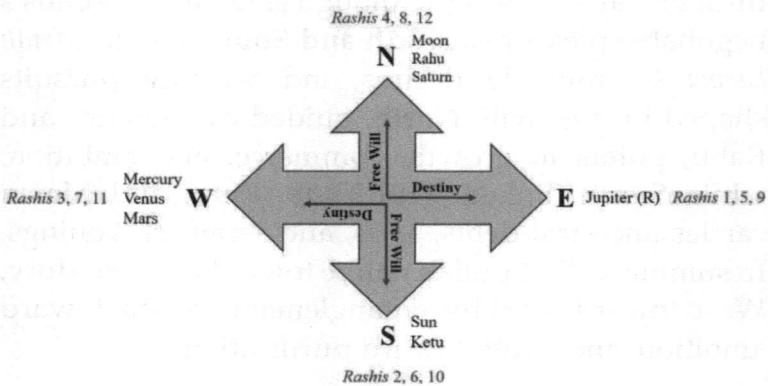

Part 1

We analyze the planet **Moon — the significator of the mind**, to judge whether (a) the mind is spiritual and (b) and how Rahu plays a role in driving the mind towards projecting spirituality.

The combination of **Rahu + Saturn + Moon** in northern signs signifies a restless, illusion-ridden mind bound by *karmic* debts towards homeland and resulting in *adridh karma* towards India. Saturn's weight ensures struggles with delay, duty, and social entanglement, while Rahu and Moon magnify confusion and desire. Opposite this, **Ketu + Sun** in southern signs burns the ego and draws the soul toward detachment and *mokṣha*. This liberation impulse has

Case Study 1: A Political Diplomat and Freedom Fighter

a *dṛidh* element, often showing unavoidable loss or crises with authority and self-identity. Rahu + Saturn + Moon can collapse into suffering or be transmuted into *tapas* (discipline of fasting and non-violence) that which happened for the native, while Sun + Ketu gave the native despair from government (authority) actions. Thus, the chart shows polarity of bondage versus release, where the native's free will steers his struggle for homeland independence and becomes a crucible for his spiritual awakening.

If we now arrange the planets in the eastern direction in ascending order of degree, we have the sequence **Jupiter (R)**. Being retrograde Jupiter directly influences Moon from a *moksha rashi* and contributes to the proxy sequence **Jupiter + Moon**. In addition, according to *Nadi* directionality principles Moon here is influenced by Jupiter with half power (50%+ due to the retrograde effect) from a *dharma rashi* because Jupiter in trine to the second house from Moon. The eastern direction is that of destiny (*dṛidh karma*) and the native is in 'certain sense' simply driven by destiny to do *karma* on significations in these directions towards evolution. Jupiter retrograde with Moon in eastern signs signifies a *karmic* revisitation of wisdom and mind. The *dṛidh karma* lies in unresolved past-life duties around *dharma*, learning, and maternal/emotional (homeland) bonds that must mature through struggle. Retrogression makes knowledge inward, delayed, and self-revising. Hence Jupiter provides a noble and philosophical support to the mindset of the native by destiny built up from past lives – the mindset that is driven through *karma* on homeland towards detachment and spirituality by (Ketu, Sun).

So, **in summary**: is the mind spiritual? The answer is a resounding 'yes'. Does Rahu play a role in driving the mind towards spirituality? The answer is a resounding 'yes'. However, Rahu is not the main contributor — it is simply the compulsive causative factor driving the native to doing *karma* on an object (i.e., the motherland). This *karma* is influenced by (a) Ketu and Sun, and (b) destined philosophical approach carried from past lives given by Jupiter. Hence, the main contributors to the spiritual mindset of the native are Jupiter, Ketu, Saturn, and Sun.

Part 2

We now analyze the planet **Sun — the significator of the soul**, to judge whether (a) the soul is projecting spirituality and (b) and how Rahu plays a role in driving the soul towards projecting spirituality.

We observe that Ketu and Sun occupy the southern direction of the *Kaalpurusha* chart because they are in 1,5,9 positions from each other. In *Nadi* astrology, planets in these positions are related to each other.

Ketu is the significator of spirituality, and Sun is the significator of the soul. We now arrange the planets in the **southern direction** in ascending order of degree. We have the sequence **Ketu + Sun**. It is then evident that Ketu provides spiritual essence to the soul of the native. According to *Nadi* directionality principles Sun is influenced by Ketu in full (100%) because Sun is in trine with Ketu.

Case Study 1: A Political Diplomat and Freedom Fighter

We now arrange the planets in the **northern direction** in ascending order of degree, we have the sequence **Rahu + Saturn + Moon**. According to *Nadi* directionality principles Sun (significator of the soul) here is influenced by Rahu (*karaka* of *karmic* compulsion) Saturn, and Moon in nearly full (75%) because Rahu, Saturn, and Moon are in 7th from Sun. However, Rahu is not the main contributor to spiritual projection of the soul. It is Ketu who influences the soul in full power. Rahu is simply the compulsive causative factor driving the native to doing *karma* on an object (i.e., the motherland) — the *karma* process moulding the spiritual projection in the native.

The Sun + Ketu combination reflects ego-dissolution: the native's repeated humiliations, imprisonments, and self-imposed austerities were trials that stripped pride and pressed him toward renunciation. This was his *dṛidh karma* — unavoidable ego-crises rooted in past-life residues. At the same time, Rahu + Saturn + Moon manifested as restlessness, illusion, and *karmic* burdens: political compromises, inner conflicts, and strained family ties. These bound him to worldly struggle, reflecting fixed *karmic* entanglements. Yet Gandhi's greatness lay in his *adhridh response*: instead of succumbing to despair, he transmuted these struggles into *tapas* — fasting, truth-seeking, and non-violence. In doing so, he offered the Sun's ego into Ketu's fire, making the soul shine as servant-leader.

If we arrange planets in the western direction in ascending order of degree, we have the sequence **Mercury + Venus + Mars**. According to *Nadi* directionality principles Sun (significator of the soul) here is influenced by Mercury (*karaka* of intelligence) Venus (*karaka* of higher knowledge) and Mars (*karaka* of body), in half power (50%) since the planets are in 2nd house from the Sun. **Rahu does not play a role here to influence (Ketu, Sun).**

If we now arrange the planets in the eastern direction in ascending order of degree, we have the sequence **Jupiter (R)**. Being retrograde Jupiter directly influences Sun from a *moksha rashi* and contributing to the proxy north-south thread on the Jupiter-Sun axis. There is also a proxy trine combination between Jupiter (retrograde) and Rahu in *moksha rashis*. In addition, according to *Nadi* directionality principles Sun here is influenced by Jupiter with less power (25% and a bit more due to the retrograde effect) from a *dharma rashi* (this is because Jupiter is in a trine from the 12th house from Sun). The destiny impact of Jupiter on Rahu feeds thinly into Ketu + Sun that projects spirituality in the native.

In this western-eastern configuration, Mercury, Venus, and Mars in the western direction signify the *karmic* field of relationships, persuasion, and action. For the native, these manifested as his eloquence (Mercury), appeal through devotion and aesthetics (Venus), and fiery activism (Mars); qualities that drew him into the arena of worldly struggle. Jupiter retrograde in the eastern direction symbolizes wisdom turned inward, revisited across *karmic* cycles. This retrogression delayed but deepened the native's *dharmic* insight, making him wrestle with contradictions before arriving at clarity. The Sun, as significator of the soul, was thus pulled between outer activism and inner wisdom. His *dridh karma* bound him to conflicts of desire, politics, and relationships; his *adridh karma* lay in transforming these into *tapas* — fasting, non-violence, and truth-seeking. Philosophically, the Sun here is refined through polarity: ego tested by worldly entanglements; illumined by delayed wisdom, with the native converting struggle to spiritual awakening.

So, **in summary**: does the soul project spirituality? The answer is a resounding 'yes'. Does Rahu play a role in driving the mind towards spirituality? The answer is a resounding 'yes'. However, Rahu is not the main contributor – it is simply the compulsive causative factor driving the native to doing *karma* on an object (i.e., the motherland). This *karma* is influenced by (a) Ketu and Sun, and (b) destined philosophical approach carried from past lives given by Jupiter. Hence, the main contributors to the spiritual mindset of the native are Jupiter, Ketu, Saturn, and Sun.

Part 3

We now analyze the planet **Mars — the significator of the body (*deha*) and ego**, to judge whether (a) the body is aligned to be projecting spirituality and (b) and how Rahu plays a role in driving the body towards projecting spirituality.

We observe that Mars, Mercury, and Venus occupy the **western direction** of the *Kaalpurusha* chart because they are in 1, 5, 9 positions from each other. In *Nadi* astrology, planets in these positions are related to each other. Mars (that is influenced by Mercury and Venus) placed in the western direction is modified by planets in the opposite direction, i.e., the east direction. Here in the east, we have a retrograde Jupiter. The eastern and western directions are that of destined *karma* (*dridh karma*) and the native is destined to do *karma* on these directional significations towards evolution.

If we arrange the planets in the western **direction** in ascending order of degree, we have the sequence **Mercury + Venus + Mars** placed in a *kaam rashi*. It is evident from a destined notion that (a) spiritual significators have no direct and full power (100%) influence on the body and (b) Rahu does not have a full power (100%) effect on the body signified by Mars.

If we now arrange the planets in the eastern direction in ascending order of degree, we have the sequence **Jupiter (R)**. In addition, according to *Nadi* directionality principles Mars here is influenced by Jupiter with nearly full power (75%) from a *dharma rashi* (this is because Jupiter is 7th from Mars). Note that Rahu has a proxy trine effect on the retrograde Jupiter that impacts Mars. It is evident from this that Rahu has virtually no direct significant role on the body projecting a religiously philosophical persona — Jupiter indeed plays a major role.

If we arrange planets in the northern direction in ascending order of degree, we have the sequence **Rahu + Saturn + Moon**. According to *Nadi* directionality principles Mars in influenced by these planets in half power (50%) because these planets are placed in the 2nd house or its trine houses from the Mars. Rahu does play a role here to influence Mars (significator of body) via its 50% influence, but it is not strongly

Case Study 1: A Political Diplomat and Freedom Fighter

through the path of spirituality but more on lines of a body whose sustenance that does not rely on excesses (due to the influence of Saturn and Moon on Mars) — merely a pre-condition to achieving spirituality. The native was mostly in loin clothing for nearly 30% of his life.

If we now arrange the planets in the southern direction in ascending order of degree, we have the sequence **Ketu + Sun**. In addition, according to *Nadi* directionality principles Mars here is influenced by spiritual significator Ketu and soul *karaka* Sun with less power (25%) (this is because Ketu and Sun is in a trine from the 12th house from Mars). Hence, there is a connection between the body and spirituality with spiritual tendencies influencing body. Since Rahu is 7th of Ketu, the influence of Rahu on spirituality that further influences the body is even smaller (less than 20%).

So, **in summary**: does the body project spirituality? The answer is a resounding 'yes'. Does Rahu play a role in driving the body towards spirituality? The answer is a non-resounding 'yes'. Rahu is a small driving factor in the body projecting spiritual ethos.

Overall Inference from Parts 1 to 3 – Rahu, in a *karmic* sense, does not strongly influence or cause spiritual essence through either the mind, body, or soul – hence Rahu is only a driving factor but not the main contributor of spirituality in the native. The results sync with the inferences from *Nadi* analysis methods 1, 2, and 3, and the *Parashari* analysis.

Case Study 2
A Religiously Confused and Agnostic Politician

Section 2.1:
A Narrative of Spiritual Philosophy

The native's spiritual life, viewed through the lens of Vedic philosophy, reveals a sincere but troubled quest. Educated under the strong influence of Western rationalism, the native could never entirely detach from the spiritual soil of India. The *Upanishadic* ideals of unity, compassion, and cosmic order were admired and often spoken of with reverence. Yet, unlike those who rooted themselves in *tapas* (discipline) or *sadhana* (practice), the native lacked a stable foundation to live those ideals fully. In truth, his confusion lay in a weak reconciliation between *jnana* (knowledge) and *bhakti* (devotion).

The native was not a cynic. He tried earnestly to harmonize science, reason, and *dharma*, as reflected in writings such as *Discovery of India*, which glow with genuine admiration for the *rishis* and their vision of unity and cosmic order. He praised the *Upanishads* as *"the first outpourings of the human mind,"* showing reverence for India's spiritual heritage even as he confessed his preference for rational inquiry. His attempts to blend the analytic clarity of the West

Case Study 2: A Religiously Confused and Agnostic Politician

with the spiritual intuitions of the East reveal him as a seeker struggling to build a bridge across two civilizational streams. Yet his commitment to secular modernism kept him from embracing the spiritual heritage fully, leaving him in unresolved tension.

As Sri Aurobindo warned of India's elite, there was a danger in *"aping the West while losing the East."* The native embodied this paradox: intellectually brilliant, emotionally bound to tradition, yet spiritually divided. Radhakrishnan, a contemporary philosopher, noted that modern India's leaders often admired the *"spirit of Vedanta"* but lacked the discipline to internalize it; their spirituality remained "philosophical, not experiential." This captures the native's dilemma: a sincere seeker revering the wisdom of the *rishis*, but whose practice was incomplete, leaving a spiritual identity suspended between admiration and realization.

Philosophically, his shortfall was existential, not moral. He sought to be both a *yogi* of reason and a leader of *dharma* but ended as neither fully. Thus, the native remains a figure of greatness tinged with incompletion: a seeker who tried, faltered, and left behind a legacy of unresolved spiritual questions.

अविद्यायामन्तरे वर्तमाना:
स्वयं धीरा: पण्डितं मन्यमाना: ।
दन्द्रम्यमाणा: परियन्ति मूढा
अन्धेनैव नीयमाना यथान्धा: ॥

Living in ignorance but thinking themselves wise, the deluded wander about, driven here and there, like the blind led by the blind. **Katha Upanishad (1.2.5)**

Rahu and Spirituality

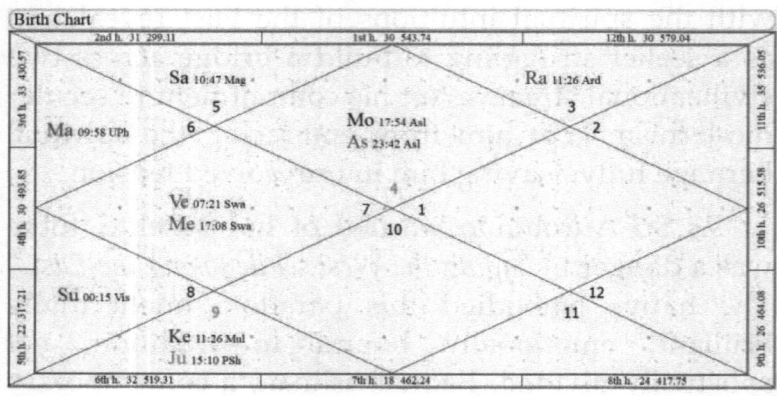

D9 Navamsha (spouse)

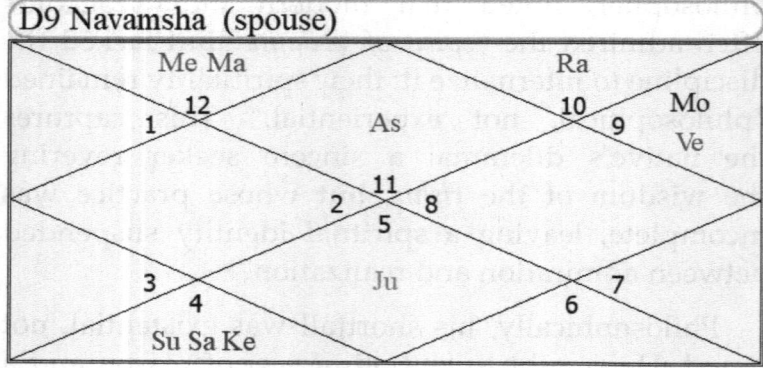

Birth Chart

As	23:42:00		Ashlesha	Day	3,Me/Ma/Sa
Su	00:15:59		Vishakha	Toh	4,Ju/Mo/Ke
Mo	17:54:21		Ashlesha	Dee	1,Me/Me/Ra
Ma	09:58:52		U.Phalg.	Pee	4,Su/Ve/Ke
Me	17:08:29	c	Swati	Tah	4,Ra/Ve/Me
Ju	15:10:28		P.Shad.	Bho	1,Ve/Ve/Me
Ve	07:21:26		Swati	Roo	1,Ra/Ra/Sa
Sa	10:47:40		Magha	May	4,Ke/Sa/Ma
Ra	11:26:41		Ardra	Gha	2,Ra/Sa/Ve
Ke	11:26:41		Moola	Bhe	4,Ke/Me/Me

DOB - 14th November 1889, Time - 11 PM, Allahabad, India

Section 2.2:
A *Parashari-Nakshatra* Analysis

We first study the basic potential of the native to inculcate spiritual ethos through a body, mind, soul study of how the trio provides the basic strength needed to develop a spiritual ethos.

2.2.1 Examining a Mind-Body-Soul Synchrony

The lord of the Lagna (significator of body) is placed in the Lagna in a *moksha rashi*. Both the Lagna and the lord of the Lagna are in the *Ashlesha nakshatra* of transformation. The Moon (significator of mind) that is also the Lagna lord is placed in the first house (its own house) that is a *moksha rashi*, but in a *paapakartari* position (hemmed between Rahu and Saturn). Hence, the significator of the body and mind are the same planet and support transformational events in the native, but not without challenging situations. The Moon is also in the 5/9 axis with the Sun (significator of the soul) that is also placed in a *moksha rashi* in the 5th house.

In addition, the *Manasa nakshatra* (24th *nakshatra* from the *Janma nakshatra* in the 27 *nakshatra* scheme) that signifies the nature of thoughts in the mind, is *Mrigashira* and lorded by Mars who is the 5th lord and placed in the *nakshatra* of Sun. Hence, the Moon placement of the native together with the *Manasa nakshatra* influence drives the natives towards a spiritual bent of mind.

In addition, the *Janma nakshatra* (*Ashlesha*) is an *manda nakshatra* (a *nakshatra* type in the *andhadi nakshatra* set) gives this native a slow and hardworking mindset towards achieving the goal. However, Mercury is lord of *upachaya* (gain) houses, and orthogonal to *dharmic* purity - though also being lord of the 12th lord, though Mercury is not the significator of spirituality. The *Manasa nakshatra* is also a *manda nakshatra* (a *nakshatra* type in the *andhadi nakshatra* set) and denotes that the native will have to work hard to obtain his goals of achieving a spiritual bent of mind. Hence, the nature of the *Janma* and *Manasa nakshatras* together contribute to the "gain"-driven, slow, and hardworking progress towards imbibing a spiritual ethos in life.

Sun (the significator of the soul) is placed in the 5th house in a *moksha rashi* and is in the 5/9 axis from the Moon. Sun is also placed in the *Vishakha nakshatra* that is lorded by Jupiter (9th lord), who is placed with Ketu (significator of spirituality) in a *dharma rashi* but a bad (6th) house. Hence, in the D1, the mind, body, and soul are working together to support the native in experiencing transformation and spiritual upheavals if they occur during the lifetime - but with significant challenges along the way.

In the D9, the lord of Lagna (Saturn) is also the 12th lord and is in a *moksha rashi*, with Ketu and Sun. In D1 this Saturn is in a *dharma rashi* in the *nakshatra* of spiritual significator Ketu and aspected by Jupiter who is ninth lord of D1 and placed in a *dharma rashi*. Returning to D9, the Moon is in a *dharma rashi* with *Vargottam* Venus (9th lord in D9, and 4th lord in D1) and is aspected by Jupiter who is placed in a *dharma rashi*.

Case Study 2: A Religiously Confused and Agnostic Politician

Given the above analysis, there is decent potential in the native to experience spiritual ethos based on the mind-body-soul synchrony.

2.2.2 Influence of Rahu on Spiritual Potential

To reason out why the native was agnostic, despite having significant potential of spiritual ethos, note that since the 9th lord is on the Rahu/Ketu axis - a *Guru Chandala Yoga* is formed in the 6th house (with no benefic influence on Jupiter either in D1 or D9) of the D1 chart that resulted in the native not being religious/skeptical about his religion, and mocking the saints of his religion in a public manner. However, this combination also adds enough hypocrisy in the native wherein the native goes to saints and astrologers for material and spiritual help knowing very well that there is merit in their philosophy but does not want to acknowledge this in public.

Rahu is placed in the Ardra *nakshatra* that is a *kana nakshatra* (a type of *nakshatra* in the *andhadi nakshatra* set) — hence the Rahu aspect of the native would prefer him working for large organizations/masses and take up social responsibilities, when compared to investing one's body and mind in achieving high levels of spiritual ethos. The native has Rahu in the 12th house in Gemini - a *kaam rashi,* placed in its own *nakshatra*. Hence it acts like the 12th lord and exhibits properties of Mercury that is itself in the *Swati nakshatra* owned by Rahu. Rahu is aspected by 9th lord Jupiter who is conjunct Ketu. Rahu is also on the 1/7 axis in the D9 chart and sitting in a *moksha rashi*. Hence, *Rahu as a planet will promote spiritual ethos* in the native but not without the touch of hypocrisy and a preference towards materialistic and social/business goals.

2.2.3 *Dasha* Analysis

Take note that the dispositors of the birth ascendant and Sun - Moon and Mars, respectively are mutual friends. All of the three dispositors of Lagna, Sun, and Moon are mutual friends. Hence, while analyzing *dasha* periods, and in accordance with the *Sudarshan Paddhati* (SP) principles from the *Parashari* code of *dasha* analysis, we need not perform a logical analysis from all the three reference points (Lagna, Sun, Moon) to arrive at conclusions/inferences.

The native during the middle of the Venus MD was in prison for freedom fighting activities and read religious books and devotional songs from all religions. This was during the Venus-Rahu and Venus-Jupiter periods, with Venus and Rahu being in 5/9 axis from one another. Not only that, the native enjoyed these activities very much even though publicly he claimed himself as an agnostic. Note that Venus is the 4th lord and 11th lord, forming the *Malavya Yoga*, and conjunct with the 12th lord who is in the *nakshatra* of Rahu that is part of a *Guru-Chandal Yoga* in this chart on the 6/12 axis. The native was guided in prison by a person who was his political Guru and someone with a spiritual bent of mind. Both exchanged multiple letters where it is documented that the native lovingly enjoyed the religious and devotional readings (as baby steps to evolving spiritually). *This period was the native's tangential experience of spiritual evolution due to the positive influence of Venus.* Though there is inherent

Case Study 2: A Religiously Confused and Agnostic Politician

hypocrisy about religious and spiritual matters, it is in the positive direction for self-growth as the native was 'spiritually' growing inside irrespective of what religious image he projected outside in public.

However, the Sun and the Moon periods, i.e., their MDs, vacillated the native's growth on the spiritual lines, simply because of their malefic positioning in the chart with respect to spiritual evolution. However, in terms of career and materialistic growth such periods were excellent. Sun having two benefics on either side gave a *shubhkartari yoga* and the *Ubhayachari Yoga* conferring great leadership prowess. Moon is forming tha *Raja Lakshana Yoga* being in kendra with natural benefics Venus and Mercury gave an exuberance of aristocracy and mass appeal as the native held political power. However, in relation to 12th house matters Moon was in *paapakartari* with Sun and Saturn are in mutual *kendras* from one another. The mind of the native was too confused to think and experience spirituality. In the D9, Sun joins Saturn in the 6th house that forms the Rahu-Ketu axis with the 12th house, leading to repeated imprisonments of the native due to clashes with the government during the Sun MD. The Sun and Moon periods saw the native mentally disturbed and confused with ideas of secularism that clashed with socialist principles that did not allow his inherent spiritual potential to grow in a linear fashion.

It was only in the Rahu MD, and especially after the Rahu/Saturn period that the native fell to ground from the successful Moon and Mars (*yogakaraka*) MDs with respect to career. *It was from here that the native started* to ascend on the path of spirituality. Note that Saturn is the 7th lord (*maraaka*) and 8th lord (lord of disgraceful events) in the D1 chart, Rahu is in the 12th house and aspected by Jupiter from 6th house of enemies and war. The administrative charisma diminished in the native and so did his popularity. The native lost a major war with an enemy country, being the leader of the nation, and being led down by his advisors. It is around the last five years of his life (that ended in the Rahu MD) that the native was in constant touch with spiritual giants and philosophers and was leading a lifestyle that was grossly non-materialistic.

Summarizing Inference

The only experience of a small degree of spirituality in the native was planted and inculcated in the Venus MD as Venus is positively placed in the horoscope (without much affliction and forming good *yogas*) with respect to treading in the spirituality space. However, the *Vimshottari dasha* sequence was such that the native achieved fame and power and the spirituality potential became latent and hidden to the public and also to the native for most of his life.

The native was mostly confused about religion, and its impact on society throughout his life, and the spiritual potential in the native could never overpower this confusion and hypocrisy. It is only in the Rahu MD that the native was battered and bruised in his career and knocked on the doors of spirituality. We establish for this native that **Rahu did not give him spiritual ethos; it only gave the primary seed during its MD for the native to attain spirituality** later, but the native passed away. It is possible that if the native would have lived on, he could have gotten more spiritual in periods after Rahu (likely in the Jupiter MD).

Section 2.3:
A *Nadi* Commentary

We provide THREE alternative, concise, and precise methods of analysis — based on *Bhrigu-Nandi Nadi* (BNN) astrology complementing the *Parashari* analysis of Case Study 2. **The goal is to establish the *Parashari* inference from Case Study 2 independently for each of the alternative methods of analysis.**

The essence of a good astrological analysis is the necessity for it to be validated from multiple schools of Vedic astrological thought. We choose the BNN approach as the alternative school of thought in this book — however, we smoothly integrate and blend an in-depth *nakshatra jyotish* analysis with the BNN framework, as we did with the *Parashari* analysis. While a strong *Parashari* education and a unique predictive *nakshatra jyotish* course are the pillars of the *Dev Jyotish* school of astrology, the BNN analysis was self-learned by Ranjan Pal under the personal guidance of Richa Shukla and then imparted to Ekta Jain by both.

2.3.1 Method 1 (*Bhrigu-Nandi Nadi*)

The significator of spirituality is Ketu. In BNN astrology, only this planet can grant spiritual realization to a native. Hence, unlike in the *Parashari* analysis we need not check whether Rahu provides a spiritual ethos. It cannot. Simply put, BNN saves us effort to test this that takes a significant effort to test via *Parashari jyotish*. It is sufficient to see **(a) whether the placement of Ketu is of sufficient strength to provide a spiritual outlook to the native** and **(b) whether and to what extent Rahu influences Ketu to support the native realizing spiritual ethos.** Unlike in *Parashari jyotish*, there is no need to do a dynamic analysis in BNN astrology (e.g., via progressions and transits) of Rahu to establish its quantum of influence on native spiritual ethos. This is because the static *Nadi* analysis is sufficiently causal to judge the quantum of Rahu's effects.

Decision Making Factor #1

For the native in Case Study 2, we have **Saturn + Ketu + Jupiter** (trines with each other in ascending order of degree) in *dharma rashis*. As part of the 7th house from Ketu analysis, we have **Venus + Rahu + Mercury** (trines with each other from the 7th house from Ketu in ascending order of degree) in *kaam rashis*. The Saturn + Ketu + Jupiter combination in a fiery sign makes the native famous (Ketu is the flag that stands out) via governance and administration in a moral way. Why? because Ketu lies between Saturn and Jupiter. Saturn, Ketu, and Jupiter form a powerful trine where discipline, detachment, and wisdom join forces to press the soul toward renunciation and higher truth. In other words, the combination leads the native to do *karma* via the influence of ethical, moral, and legal philosophies. This does not necessarily imply the native practices austere spirituality, but adhering to *dharmic* philosophy is the

Case Study 2: A Religiously Confused and Agnostic Politician

first step to such austerity. In *Discovery of India*, the naïve praised the *rishis*, Vedanta, and India's spiritual heritage, echoing Jupiter–Ketu's higher call. Yet these were filtered through Saturn's weight of duty and rationalism, leaving spirituality more philosophical than experiential.

Venus + Rahu + Mercury in *kaam rashis* indicate social networking and communication in foreign lands (or with foreigners) and with women. **It is evident that this latter trine combination that influences Saturn + Ketu + Jupiter distracts the native from going deep into spiritual practice or realizing the purity of spiritual ethos.** Together the combinations represent the soul's battlefield: austerity versus indulgence, *mokṣha* versus bondage. The native embodied this through charm, refined tastes, and political ambition, often rationalizing worldly pursuits in the language of modernity. Hence, he was drawn toward the austerity of India's *dharmic* wisdom, yet entangled in the allures of power, admiration, and sensual refinement.

The elements in the same trine from the 7th house from Ketu has a strong modifying/influencing effect to the significance impact of Ketu of making a native realizing (or not) spiritual ethos. Rahu is always part of this trine to no surprise, the interesting thing to see is how the other planets together with Rahu shape the quantum of impact, as we have done above. It might be tempting to also check for the trines from the 2nd to the placement of Ketu — however, since we are interested in the role of Rahu, we skip this step for now and will return to the analysis of such trines when we integrate *nakshatra* astrology with BNN astrology.

Decision Making Factor #2

For the native in Case Study 2, we have Mars as the lord of the watery 12th house from **Ketu**. Since Ketu is the significator of spirituality in BNN astrology one must check for the 12th from Ketu (12th house is the house of *moksha/dissolution* from any signification). We have a **Sun + Moon** standing on the trines from the 12th house from Ketu in a *moksha rashi* – hence, the luminaries that makes the native move throughout (i.e., oscillate) his life between ego (rational duty) and emotions influence Ketu, and **such a dichotomy creates a barrier towards sustained spiritual evolution**. The combination reflects an inner aspiration toward liberation, intuition, and higher consciousness. Being trinal from the 12th to Ketu intensifies *karmic* ties with spirituality, suggesting latent tendencies of *jnana* (knowledge) and inward quest. The trines from the 7th from Sun is **Mars** that introduces struggle: Mars signifies dynamism, conflict, and worldly assertion. This placement often externalizes the inner spiritual current into activism, debate, and outward engagement rather than renunciatory stillness. **Rahu has no role to play here based on sign placement (if we do not include a *nakshatra* analysis here that is left for subsequent Methods 2 and 3).**

Decision Making Factor #3

For the native in Case Study 2, we have Venus as the lord of the 11th house from **Ketu**. We also have Venus and Mercury placed in the 11th from Ketu. Since Ketu is the significator of spirituality in BNN astrology one must check for the 11th from

Case Study 2: A Religiously Confused and Agnostic Politician

Ketu (11th house analysis checks for catalytic factors contributing to a significator — in our case Ketu of spirituality). We have **Venus + Rahu + Mercury** (in ascending order of degree). **Relate this combination to DMF #1 earlier, and it is evident why Rahu is a not a big catalytic factor in the spiritual journey of the native.** The Venus + Rahu + Mercury cluster signifies a *karmic* pull toward desire, intellectualism, and worldly engagement. Venus infuses aesthetics, Rahu magnifies ambition and disruption, while Mercury sharpens rationality and communication. This made the native deeply drawn to knowledge, beauty, and progress, yet always entangled with material and political currents.

If we now consider the trine houses from the 7th to the 11th house from Ketu, we have the combination **Saturn + Ketu + Jupiter** (in ascending order of degree). In opposition, Saturn + Ketu + Jupiter in symbolizes restraint, detachment, and higher wisdom. Saturn imposes discipline, Ketu dissolves ego, and Jupiter points toward *dharma* and spiritual philosophy. This trinal pull reflects an inner dialogue: worldly *kama* impulses constantly met with the corrective force of *dharma*. **Rahu does not play a role here based on its sign placement (unless we deal with a *nakshatra* analysis).**

Venus being lord (dispositor) of the 11th from Ketu is forming the combination Venus + Rahu + Mercury in trines and the reader is referred back to the point above, leading back to the inference from DMF #1. In other words, the **native projects ethics, morality, and austerity in his work life but is distracted from** going deep into spiritual practice or realizing the purity of spiritual ethos.

Decision Making Factor #4

For the native in Case Study 2, we have Jupiter as the dispositor of Ketu and is located in a *moksha rashi*. We have **Saturn + Ketu + Jupiter** (trines with each other in ascending order of degree) in *dharma rashis*. This combination forms a powerful trine where discipline, detachment, and wisdom join forces to press the soul toward renunciation and higher truth. It leads the native to do *karma* via the influence of ethical, moral, and legal philosophies. This does not necessarily imply the native practices austere spirituality, but adhering to *dharmic* philosophy is the first step to such austerity. The trine houses from the 7th house of Jupiter is the combination **Venus + Rahu + Mercury** (in ascending order of degree). The Venus + Rahu + Mercury cluster signifies a *karmic* pull toward desire, intellectualism, and worldly engagement. Venus infuses aesthetics, Rahu magnifies ambition and disruption, while Mercury sharpens rationality and communication. This made the native deeply drawn to knowledge, beauty, and progress, yet always entangled with material and political currents. Relate this combination to **DMF #1** earlier, and it is evident why Rahu is a not a big catalytic factor in the spiritual journey of the native. The native is **distracted from going deep into spiritual practice or realizing the purity of spiritual ethos.**

Summary: Does the placement of Ketu give a strong spiritual outlook to the native? The answer is

Case Study 2: A Religiously Confused and Agnostic Politician

Planet	R/C	Sign	Degree	Speed	Nakshatra	Pada	RL	NL	SL	SS	Status	SB
Lagna		Can	23:42:00		Ashlesha	3	Mo	Me	Ma	Sa		
Sun		Sco	00:15:59	01:00:29	Vishakha	4	Ma	Ju	Mo	Ke	Grt.Fr.	0.74
Moon		Can	17:54:21	11:54:42	Ashlesha	1	Mo	Me	Me	Ra	Own	1.31
Mars		Vir	09:58:52	00:36:13	Uttara Phalg.	4	Me	Su	Ve	Ke	Neutr.	1.19
Mercury	C	Lib	17:08:29	01:34:09	Swati	4	Ve	Ra	Ve	Me	Neutr.	1.07
Jupiter		Sag	15:10:28	00:11:44	Poorvashadha	1	Ju	Ve	Ve	Me	Own	1.07
Venus		Lib	07:21:26	01:14:50	Swati	1	Ve	Ra	Ra	Sa	Moolt.	1.30
Saturn		Leo	10:47:40	00:03:11	Magha	4	Su	Ke	Sa	Ma	Neutr.	1.32
Rahu		Gem	11:26:41	00:01:17	Ardra	2	Me	Ra	Sa	Ve	Moolt.	
Ketu		Sag	11:26:41	00:01:17	Moola	4	Ju	Ke	Me	Me	Moolt.	

a 'somewhat yes' from each of the four DMFs. Does Rahu play a positive role in the native experiencing spiritual ethos? The answer is a 'no' from DMF #s 1-4. The results sync with the *Parashari* analysis.

2.3.2 Method 2 (BNN with *Nakshatra*)

Since our analysis base is BNN astrology, like in Method 1 we will work with the same DMFs, and be light on the BNN part of the analysis (detailed in Method 1). It is sufficient to see using *nakshatras* **whether and to what extent Rahu influences Ketu to support the native realizing spiritual ethos.** When it comes to doing an analysis using *nakshatra* principles using KP astrology, three KP parameters are relevant for study for each decision making factor: (i) a planet's ***nakshatra* sub-lord**, (ii) the **sub-lord's *nakshatra* lord:** the planet ruling the *nakshatra* in which the sub-lord is situated, and the (iii) the **sub-lord's sign lord:** the planet ruling the sign in which the sub-lord is situated. Each *nakshatra* span of 13d20' is unequally divided into degree space owned by 9 sub-lords proportional to *Vimshottari dasha* duration.

Decision Making Factor #1

For the native in Case Study 2, we have **Saturn + Ketu + Jupiter** (trines with each other in ascending order of degree) in *dharma rashis*. Saturn is in the *nakshatra* of Ketu in the *pada* of Saturn. Ketu is in the *nakshatra* of Ketu in the *pada* of Mercury. Jupiter is in the *nakshatra* of Venus in the *pada* of Venus. As per KP principles, Saturn is in the *nakshatra* of Ketu and has Saturn as its sub-lord. Saturn's *nakshatra* lord is Ketu, and Jupiter is the lord of Ketu. Ketu is in the *nakshatra* of Ketu and has Mercury as its sub-lord. Mercury's sub-lord is Rahu. Rahu's sign lord is Mercury. Jupiter is in the *nakshatra* of Venus and has Venus as its sub-lord. Rahu is Venus's sub-lord and Venus is in own house and in trine with Rahu. This leads the native to do *karma* via the influence of ethical, moral, and legal philosophies. This does not necessarily imply the native practices austere spirituality, but adhering to *dharmic* philosophy is the first step to such austerity.

As part of the 7th house from Ketu analysis, we have **Venus + Rahu + Mercury** (trines with each other from the 7th house from Ketu in ascending order of degree) and placed in *kaam rashis*. Venus is placed in *nakshatra* of Rahu in the *pada* of Rahu. Rahu is in the *nakshatra* of Rahu and in the *pada* of Saturn. Mercury is in the *nakshatra* of Rahu and in the *pada* of Venus. It is evident that Rahu in a *kaam rashi* is considerably influencing the Ketu trine. As per KP principles, Venus is placed in *nakshatra* of Rahu and has Rahu as its sub-lord. Rahu is in the *nakshatra* of Rahu and its sign lord is Mercury. Mercury is in the trine of Rahu. It is evident that Rahu in a *kaam rashi* is considerably influencing the Ketu trine by influencing each of Venus and Mercury. **Hence, this latter trine combination that influences Saturn + Ketu + Jupiter distracts the native from going deep into spiritual practice or realizing the purity of spiritual ethos.**

If we now look at the trine houses from the 2nd house from Ketu, we get **Mars**. It is in the *nakshatra* of Sun and in the *pada* of Venus (that is in trine with Rahu).

As per KP principles, Mars has sub-lord Venus. Venus is in the *nakshatra* of Rahu and in own house.

Rahu influences Ketu significance and leads to the confusion of the native's spiritual ethos.

Decision Making Factor #2

For the native in Case Study 2, we have Mars as the lord of the watery 12th house from **Ketu**. Since Ketu is the significator of spirituality in BNN astrology one must check for the 12th from Ketu (12th house is the house of *moksha/dissolution* from any signification). We have a **Sun + Moon** standing on the trines from the 12th house from Ketu in a *moksha rashi* — hence, the luminaries that makes the native move throughout (i.e., oscillate) his life between ego (rational duty) and emotions influence Ketu, and **such a dichotomy creates a barrier towards sustained spiritual evolution**. The combination reflects an inner aspiration toward liberation, intuition, and higher consciousness. Being trinal from the 12th to Ketu intensifies *karmic* ties with spirituality, suggesting latent tendencies of *jnana* (knowledge) and inward quest.

Sun is in the *nakshatra* of Jupiter and in the *pada* of the Moon. Moon is in the *nakshatra* of Mercury in the *pada* of Mercury. Mercury is in trine with Rahu. As per KP principles, Sun's *nakshatra* sub-lord is Moon. Moon's sub-lord is Mercury and is in trine with Rahu. Moon is in its own *rashi*.

The trine houses from the 7th from Sun (and the 12th house from Ketu) is only comprised of **Mars**. Mars is in the *nakshatra* of Sun and in the *pada* of

Case Study 2: A Religiously Confused and Agnostic Politician

Venus that forms a trine with Rahu. The 7th from Mars has in trine the Sun and the Moon. As per KP principles, Mars has the sub-lord of Venus (that is in trine with Rahu). Venus's *nakshatra* lord is Rahu, and Rahu's sign lord is Mercury that is in trine with Rahu. Sun's *nakshatra* sub-lord is Moon. Moon's sub-lord is Mercury and is in trine with Rahu. Moon is in its own *rashi*. **Hence Rahu influences Ketu significance and contributes to the confusion and dichotomy of the native's spiritual ethos.**

Decision Making Factor #3

For the native in Case Study 2, we have Venus as the lord of the 11th house from **Ketu**. We also have Venus and Mercury placed in the 11th from Ketu. Since Ketu is the significator of spirituality in BNN astrology one must check for the 11th from Ketu (11th house analysis checks for catalytic factors contributing to a significator – in our case Ketu of spirituality). We have **Venus + Rahu + Mercury** (in ascending order of degree). Venus is in the *nakshatra* of Rahu and in the *pada* of Rahu. Rahu is in the *nakshatra* of Rahu and in the *pada* of Saturn. Mercury is in the *nakshatra* of Rahu and in the *pada* of Venus. However, Rahu is in between Venus and Mercury in a *kaam rashi* – see implication in DMF #1. As per KP principles, Venus is placed in *nakshatra* of Rahu and has Rahu as its sub-lord. Rahu is in the *nakshatra* of Rahu and its sign lord is Mercury. Mercury is in the trine of Rahu. It is evident that Rahu in a *kaam rashi* is considerably influencing the Ketu trine by influencing each of Venus and Mercury. However, Rahu is in between Venus and Mercury in a *kaam rashi* — see implication in DMF #1. **Rahu** plays a pivotal role towards distracting the native in realizing the true spiritual potential of Ketu.

If we now consider the trine houses from the 7th to the 11th house from Ketu, we have the combination **Saturn + Ketu + Jupiter** (in ascending order of degree). Saturn is in the *nakshatra* of Ketu and in the *pada* of Saturn. Ketu is in the *nakshatra* of Ketu and in the *pada* of Mercury (in trine with Rahu). Jupiter is in the *nakshatra* of Venus and in the *pada* of Venus (in trine with Rahu). As per KP principles, Saturn is in the *nakshatra* of Ketu and has Saturn as its sub-lord. Saturn's *nakshatra* lord is Ketu, and Jupiter is the lord of Ketu. Ketu is in the *nakshatra* of Ketu and has Mercury as its sub-lord. Mercury's sub-lord is Rahu. Rahu's sign lord is Mercury. Jupiter is in the *nakshatra* of Venus and has Venus as its sub-lord. Rahu is Venus's sub-lord and Venus is in own house and in trine with Rahu. Thus, Rahu has a significant influence on the Saturn + Ketu + Jupiter combination that **leads the native towards an austere and ethically moral work life but distracts him from going deep into spiritual practice or realizing the purity of spiritual ethos.**

Decision Making Factor #4

For the native in Case Study 2, we have Jupiter as the dispositor of Ketu and is located in a *moksha rashi*. We have **Saturn + Ketu + Jupiter** (trines with each other in ascending order of degree) in *dharma rashis*. Saturn is in the *nakshatra* of Ketu and in the *pada* of Saturn. Ketu is in the *nakshatra* of Ketu and in the *pada* of Mercury (in trine with Rahu). Jupiter is in the *nakshatra* of Venus and in the *pada* of Venus

Case Study 2: A Religiously Confused and Agnostic Politician 71

(in trine with Rahu). As per KP principles, Saturn is in the *nakshatra* of Ketu and has Saturn as its sub-lord. Saturn's *nakshatra* lord is Ketu, and Jupiter is the lord of Ketu. Ketu is in the *nakshatra* of Ketu and has Mercury as its sub-lord. Mercury's sub-lord is Rahu. Rahu's sign lord is Mercury. Jupiter is in the *nakshatra* of Venus and has Venus as its sub-lord. Rahu is Venus's sub-lord and Venus is in own house and in trine with Rahu. Hence Rahu that **considerably influences this combination leads the native to do *karma* via the influence of ethical, moral, and legal philosophies. This does not necessarily imply the native practices austere spirituality, but adhering to *dharmic* philosophy is the first step to such austerity.**

The trine houses from the 7th house of Jupiter is the combination **Venus + Rahu + Mercury** (in ascending order of degree). Venus is in the *nakshatra* of Rahu and in the *pada* of Rahu. Rahu is in the *nakshatra* of Rahu and in the *pada* of Saturn. Mercury is in the *nakshatra* of Rahu and in the *pada* of Venus. However, Rahu is in between Venus and Mercury in a *kaam rashi* — see implication in DMF #1. Venus is placed in *nakshatra* of Rahu and has Rahu as its sub-lord. Rahu is in the *nakshatra* of Rahu and its sign lord is Mercury. Mercury is in the trine of Rahu. It is evident that Rahu in a *kaam rashi* is considerably influencing the Ketu trine by influencing each of Venus and Mercury. **Hence, Rahu is influential in distracting the native from going deep into spiritual practice or realizing the purity of spiritual ethos.**

Summary: Does the placement of Ketu give a strong spiritual outlook to the native? The answer is a 'somewhat yes' from each of the four DMFs. Does Rahu play a positive role in the native experiencing spiritual ethos? The answer is a 'no' from DMF #s 1-4. The results sync with the *Parashari* analysis.

2.3.3 Method 3 (BNN with *Karmic* Angles)

We wish to analyse in **three parts** using the *karmic Nadi jyotish* principles the strength of Rahu in influencing each of the mind, body, and soul to realize a spiritual ethos. After all, these are the basic pillars that eventually decide whether a native will be able to realize spiritual ethos in the lifetime. **If the connection is strong in at least two out of the three cases, we can say that Rahu has been significantly instrumental in promoting spirituality within the native.** Unlike in *Parashari jyotish*, there is no need to do a dynamic analysis (e.g., via progressions and transits) of Rahu to establish its quantum of influence on native spiritual ethos. This is because the static *Nadi* analysis is sufficiently causal to judge the quantum of Rahu's effects.

Dridh-Adridh Karma **Axes:** In *Naḍi jyotish*, directions embody the metaphysics of *karma* itself. **East and West** anchor *dridh karma* — duties to father, guru, and ancestors that bind the soul to its inescapable obligations. **East**, aligned with Sun and Jupiter, signifies *dharma*, authority, and righteous beginnings; **West** blends closure and entanglement, largely fixed through Saturn's weight, though softened by Venus's negotiable pleasures. **North and South** anchor *adridh karma* — mutable desires and worldly pursuits shaped by free will. **North**, guided by Mercury and

Case Study 2: A Religiously Confused and Agnostic Politician 73

Rahu, points to growth, commerce, and ambition; while **South**, linked with Mars, Ketu, and Moon, carries ancestral debts, *tapas*, and *karmic* reckonings. In summary, East pulls a native towards *dharmic* duty, West toward worldly entanglement, North toward ambition, and South toward purification.

Thus, the four directions mark not mere space but the soul's *karmic* geography: some pathways immovable, others pliable. The horoscope becomes a compass of necessity and possibility, mapping destiny's fixity against the field of conscious striving. One may ask: why not diagonal directions? In *Nadi jyotish*, only the **four cardinal directions** - East, West, North, and South—are used, not the intermediates like Northeast or Northwest. This is because Vedic cosmology is fundamentally **fourfold**, based on sunrise and sunset, solstices and equinoxes, day and night. Each direction is tied to specific *grahas* and *karmic* qualities: East (Sun, Jupiter), West (Saturn, Venus), North (Mercury, Rahu), South (Moon, Mars, Ketu). This framework mirrors the *dik-palas* (directional guardians) of Vedic ritual, which are cardinal. By limiting to four, *Naḍi* emphasizes clarity: destiny is seen through primal axes of *dharma*, desire, past, and closure, without diluting meaning in diagonals.

We provide the planetary directional compass diagram for Case Study 2.

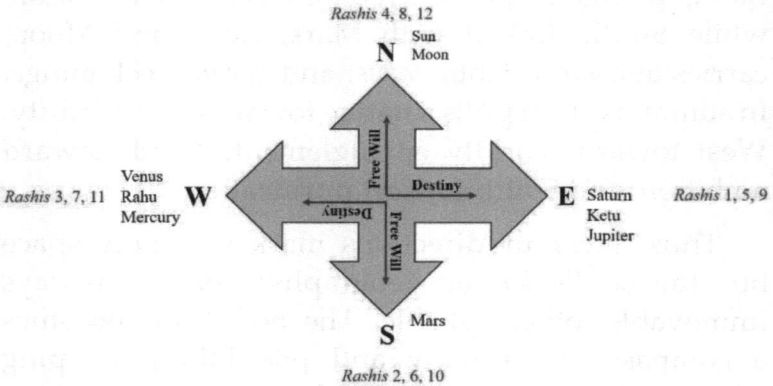

Part 1

We first analyze the planet **Moon — the significator of the mind**, to judge whether (a) the mind is inherently spiritual and (b) and how Rahu plays a role in driving the mind towards spirituality.

We observe that Sun and Moon occupy the northern direction (the watery signs) of the *Kaalpurusha* chart because they are in 1,5,9 positions from each other. In *Nadi* astrology planets in these positions are related to each other. Moon (that is influenced by Sun) placed in the northern direction is modified by planets in the opposite direction, i.e., the south direction. Here in the south, we have Mars. The northern and southern directions are that of free will (*adridh karma*) and the native is in 'certain sense' free to do *karma* on significations in these directions towards evolution.

If we arrange the planets in the **northern direction** in ascending order of degree, we have the sequence **Sun, Moon** — a friendly combination. Moon (*karaka* of mind) and Sun (*karaka* of *soul*) are both in *moksha*

Case Study 2: A Religiously Confused and Agnostic Politician 75

rashis. According to *Nadi* directionality principles Moon here is influenced by Sun in full (100%) because Moon and Sun are in trine with one another. The native's mind and soul are latently in sync and influenced by spiritual essence. However, Ketu is the significator of spirituality and we do not see a strong connection of Ketu with the Moon because Ketu is in trine with the 2nd house from Moon and contributes 50% of its significance power to Moon. At the same time Moon is influenced with 75% power with the significance of Mars because Mars lies in trine to 7th house from Moon in a **southern direction**. Mars is in an earthy and *artha rashi* and this placement influences the mind to ego and power. The native was a popular leader of a nation (Sun signifying government) with a charitable and motherly disposition. The *adridh karma* of the native wasn't in the direction of spiritual realization.

Overall, the placement of Sun and Moon in the northern direction and Mars in the southern direction captures the native's spiritual and *karmic* paradox. The Sun–Moon in the north signifies *adṛidha karma* — mutable, experiential, and shaped by choice. The native's soul (Sun) and mind (Moon) were restless, always experimenting with reconciling rationality and tradition. His embrace of secularism and scientific modernity reflected this mutable search for meaning. Yet, Mars in the south embodied destiny that demanded vigorous action, leadership, and struggle. Mars bound him to conflict and nation-building, tasks from which he could not escape. Philosophically, this created a tension between a searching, unsettled spirit and an unyielding *karmic* duty to act. His brilliance lay in channeling doubt into constructive leadership, yet his spirituality remained incomplete, caught between free will's experiments and destiny's compulsions. The native epitomized a leader whose soul sought transcendence but was anchored in worldly responsibility.

If we arrange planets in the **eastern direction** (the direction of *dridh karma* or destiny) in ascending order of degree we have the sequence **Saturn, Ketu, Jupiter** — friendly combination for spiritual essence. According to *Nadi* directionality principles Moon here is influenced by these planets with half power (50%) because they are in trine with one another from the 2nd house of Moon. The *karma* (signified by Saturn) of the native (towards his country and motherland) formed the channel towards understanding spirituality (signified by Ketu) and philosophy (signified by Jupiter). The native went to prison for freedom fighting activities, and it is then that he picked up spiritual practices of austerity and delved into ancient Indian history and philosophy. In addition, the 12th from Ketu has Sun that is in trine with Moon in *moksha rashis*. This re-validates the native's mind and soul being latently influenced by spiritual essence and his destiny leads him to experience spiritual undercurrents.

If we arrange planets in the **western direction** (the direction of *dridh karma* or destiny) in ascending order of degree we have the sequence **Venus, Rahu, Mars**. According to *Nadi* directionality principles Moon here is influenced by these planets with minimum power

Case Study 2: A Religiously Confused and Agnostic Politician

(25%) because they are in trine with one another from the 12th house from Moon. Note here that the sequence does not show a comfortable sequence as Venus mutually likes Rahu, but Mars does not like Rahu, and all three planets are in *kaam rashis*.

It is evident that Rahu has little to no power to influence the Moon on spiritual angles.

Overall, the alignment of Saturn + Ketu + Jupiter in the eastern direction and Venus + Rahu + Mars in the western direction reveals a deep *karmic* polarity within the native's life and mind. The eastern direction (Saturn, Ketu, Jupiter) reflects *dṛḍha karma*: fixed tendencies toward *dharma*, discipline, detachment, and higher wisdom. Saturn imposes restraint, Ketu dissolves ego, and Jupiter points toward philosophy and justice. This anchored the native in an inherited call to spirituality, ethics, and the responsibility of leadership. The western direction (Venus, Rahu, Mars) leads to *karma* that is mutable pulls toward desire, ambition, aesthetics, and restless action. Rahu magnified worldly engagement and Venus-Mars drew him into passion and political drive. Philosophically, this opposition manifested as the native's divided psyche: a mind pulled between *dharma* and *kama*, wisdom and desire, discipline and indulgence. His public life leaned westward—modernist, ambitious, restless—while the east whispered an unfulfilled spiritual longing. Thus, his soul's light was brilliant yet incomplete, suspended between destiny and choice.

So, **in summary**: is the mind spiritual? The answer is not a resounding 'yes' (partly). Does Rahu play a positive role in driving the mind towards spirituality? The answer is a 'no'.

Part 2

We want to analyze the planet **Sun — the significator of the soul**, to judge whether (a) the mind is inherently spiritual and (b) and how Rahu plays a role in driving the mind towards spirituality. However, since Moon and Sun are in the same direction, the analysis and inference for Part 2 is exactly same as that in Part 1. **Sun + Moon in the northern direction** reflects *adṛdha karma* — mutable, experiential forces shaping the soul. For the native, this created a restless pursuit of ideals, a constant search for balance between rational modernity and India's spiritual inheritance. The Sun (soul) illuminated vision, while the Moon (mind) absorbed influences, leaving him open yet unsettled. **Mars in the southern direction** denotes the *karmic* duty toward action and leadership. Thus, the native's soul carried brilliance shaped by experimentation yet was bound to destiny through political struggle and nation-building.

Saturn + Ketu + Jupiter in the east symbolizes *dṛdha karma* — fixed tendencies toward *dharma*, discipline, detachment, and higher wisdom. These planets infused the native's soul with responsibility, restraint, and a latent pull toward spiritual ethics. Yet in the **west, Venus + Rahu + Mars** reflect mutable forces of desire, ambition, and restless passion. This opposition shaped his soul into a paradox: *dharmic* insights constantly countered by worldly drives. Thus, the native's brilliance carried spiritual

Case Study 2: A Religiously Confused and Agnostic Politician 79

aspiration yet was overshadowed by ambition and material engagement.

It is evident that Rahu has little to no power to influence the Sun on spiritual angles.

In **summary** is the soul projecting spiritual essence? The answer is not a resounding 'yes' (partly). Does Rahu play a positive role in driving the soul towards spirituality? The answer is a 'no'.

Part 3

We now analyze the planet **Mars – the significator of the body (*deha*) and ego**, to judge whether (a) the body is aligned to be projecting spirituality and (b) and how Rahu plays a role in driving the body towards projecting spirituality.

We observe that **Mars** alone occupies the **southern direction** of the *Kaalpurusha*. Mars (that is influenced by Sun and Moon) placed in the southern direction is modified by planets in the opposite direction, i.e., the north direction by 75% of the power of the planets. Here in the **north**, we have Sun and Moon placed in *moksha rashis*. The northern direction is that of free will *karma* (*adridh karma*) and the native is in 'certain sense' free to do *karma* on significations in these directions towards evolution. The native aligned his ego and body with leadership and charitable *karma* towards his motherland (home country). The native had a mindset more of *rajasic* in nature though within there was sense of detachment (from materialistic gains) towards activities performed towards his motherland. Why? The dispositor of the 12th house from Ketu is ruled by Mars. **Mars in the southern** direction signifies *adṛidh karma* rooted in the body and action: unyielding drive, vitality, and conflict-oriented leadership. The southern and northern polarity meant that the native's ego was restless, seeking ideals, while his body was *karmically* bound to struggle and worldly engagement, shaping him as a statesman torn between spiritual longing and political duty. **It is evident that Rahu has little to no power to influence Mars on spiritual angles.**

If we arrange the planets in the **western direction** in ascending order of degree, we have the sequence **Venus, Rahu, Mercury** — a friendly combination and placed in *kaam rashis*. The native had significant materialistic and obsessive desires with women, and this *karma* was destined. According to *Nadi* directionality principles Mars here is influenced by these planets with half power (50%) because they are in trine with one another from the 2nd house of Mars. The native has materialized his desires in a physical sense. If we arrange the planets in the **eastern direction** in ascending order of degree, we have the sequence **Saturn, Ketu, Jupiter** — a non-materialistic combination and placed in *dharma rashis*. According to *Nadi* directionality principles Mars here is influenced by these planets with minimum power (25%) because they are in trine with one another from the 12th house of Mars. It is evident then that **Rahu has very little power to influence Mars on spiritual angles.**

Saturn + Ketu + Jupiter in the eastern direction signify *dridha karma* anchoring the ego in *dharma*, discipline, detachment, and higher wisdom. These forces impressed upon the native a *karmic* weight

Case Study 2: A Religiously Confused and Agnostic Politician

of responsibility, restraint, and an inherited pull toward philosophy and justice. Yet, **Venus + Rahu + Mars in the western direction** represent a counterflow of ambition, desire, and restless drive, shaping his body and outward action. The west's influences fueled passion, charisma, and political engagement but often pulled him into worldly entanglements. Philosophically, this polarity left the native's ego suspended: shaped by *dharmic* ideals yet compromised by *karmic* pursuits. His body became the instrument of action, bound by destiny to nation-building, while his inner self carried the tension of unrealized spiritual depth. Thus, his life reflects the struggle between higher wisdom's call and worldly ambition's compulsion.

So, **in summary**: is the body projecting spirituality? The answer is somewhat 'yes' (partly). Does Rahu play a positive role in driving the mind towards spirituality? The answer is 'no'.

Overall Inference from Parts 1 to 3 — Rahu does not strongly influence spiritual essence through either the mind, body, or soul. The results sync with the *Parashari* angle of analysis and even get more fine-grained with the *Nadi* analysis that says the body, mind, and soul are each aligned partly with a spiritual essence that is good, but not very strong towards realizing spirituality. Moreover, Rahu does not have much of a role to play in the native's spiritual ethos.

Case Study 3
A Controversial Spiritual Leader

Section 3.1:
A Narrative of Spiritual Philosophy

The native's spiritual arc unfolded as a dialectic of illumination and entanglement. Rising in the 1960s, the native dismantled institutional religion yet invoked the *Upanishadic* spirit of direct realization. His vision of *Zorba the Buddha* — a fusion of sensual embodiment with meditative transcendence — was both a challenge and a reinterpretation of the Vedic ethos. Unlike the classical path of *tapas* and renunciation, he celebrated life's energies as gateways to awareness: *"Existence is not a problem to be solved but a mystery to be lived."*

Yet this tantric exuberance inevitably bled into controversy. His affirmation of sexuality, rejection of Gandhian austerity, and indulgence in wealth clashed with orthodox ideals of *yama* (restraint) and *niyama* (discipline), which form the ethical foundation of yoga in the Vedic tradition. For classical Vedanta, the purification of desire is a prerequisite for realization; but for him, desire itself became a potential pathway. The Oregon commune — adorned with Rolls Royces, yet marred by political intrigue — dramatized this tension, raising a quintessential Vedantic question: had the *jiva* (individual self) dissolved into the *atma* (universal Self), or had the ego merely expanded under the mask of spirituality? Philosophically, this raised the issue of *adhikara* (spiritual eligibility). Was the native's radicalism a true *upaya* — a skillful method to purge repression and liberate consciousness — or a dangerous concession to *avidya* (ignorance) that mistook indulgence for transcendence? Critics dismissed him as a *"merchant of mysticism,"* seducing seekers with spectacle. Admirers, however, interpreted his methods as a paradoxical *tantric sadhana*: confronting desire directly so that its energy could be transmuted into silence.

Philosophically, the native embodied a tension between *vidya* and *avidya*. He voiced luminous insights on consciousness yet often remained implicated in spectacle. J. Krishnamurti dismissed him as *"entertaining but not liberating,"* while Radhakrishnan's warning that modern leaders admire Vedanta but fail to internalize it seems apt. Raimon Panikkar saw in him a spark of Vedantic intuition but not the integration of a realized *ṛishi*. Other thinkers added nuance. Heinrich Zimmer cautioned that modern gurus risk *"confusing the mythic with the personal,"* a trap the native often fell into. Alan Watts admired his irreverence as the *"honesty of a Zen master in a modern dress,"* though doubted its ripening into realization. Agehananda Bharati viewed him as a *"countercultural sage,"* radiant but unanchored in Vedic restraint.

Thus, the native stands as a paradox: a seeker of brilliance suspended between illumination and

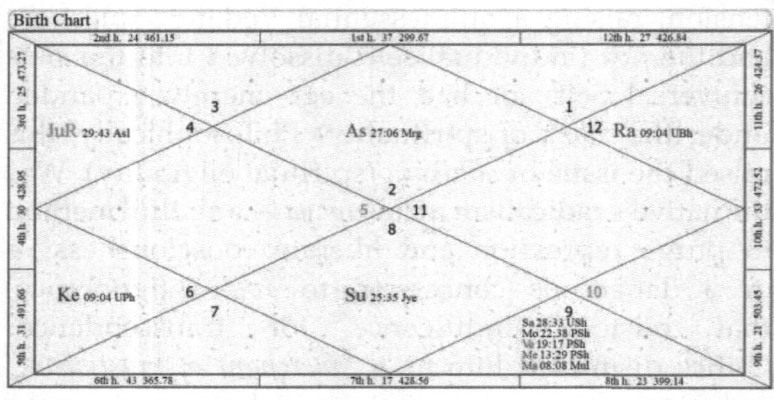

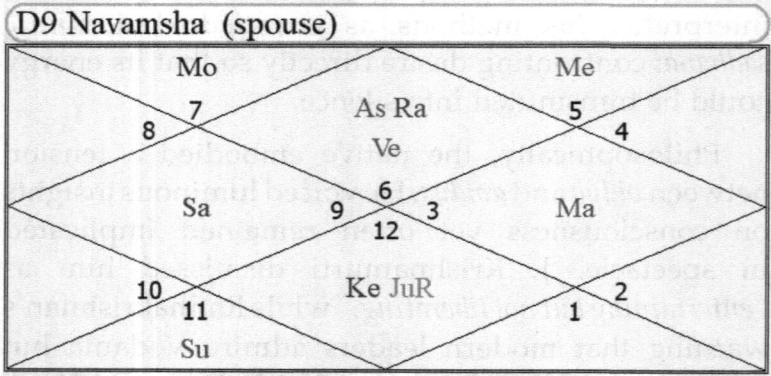

Birth Chart

As	29:57:48		Mrigashi	Vo	2,Ma/Sa/Ju
Su	25:35:30		Jyeshtha	Yee	3,Me/Ra/Ve
Mo	22:38:08		P.Shad.	Pah	3,Ve/Sa/Ke
Ma	08:08:20	c	Moola	Bha	3,Ke/Ju/Me
Me	13:29:04		P.Shad.	Bho	1,Ve/Ve/Ve
Ju	29:43:33	R	Ashlesha	Doh	4,Me/Sa/Ju
Ve	19:17:16		P.Shad.	Dah	2,Ve/Ra/Ke
Sa	28:33:27		U.Shad.	Bay	1,Su/Ma/Ra
Ra	09:04:36		U.Bhadra.	Th	2,Sa/Ve/Ra
Ke	09:04:36		U.Phalg.	Pee	4,Su/Ve/Ju

DOB - 11 December 1931, Time - 5:45 PM, Kuchwada, India

excess, reflecting the unresolved tension of modern Vedantic life.

यस्यामतं तस्य मतं मतं यस्य न वेद सः ।
अविज्ञातं विजानतां विज्ञातमविजानताम् ॥

He who thinks he knows, knows not; he who knows he knows not, truly knows.　　**Kena Upanishad (2.3)**

Section 3.2: A *Parashari-Nakshatra* Analysis

We first study the basic potential of the native to inculcate spiritual ethos through a body, mind, and soul study of how the trio provides the basic strength needed to develop a spiritual ethos.

3.2.1 Examining a Mind-Body-Soul Synchrony

The lord of the Lagna (significator of body) Venus is placed in the 8th house in a *dharma rashi*. The Lagna is in the *nakshatra* of 12th lord Mars, whereas the Lagna lord is in the *nakshatra* of the Lagna lord. The Lagna lord is conjunct 9th lord, 3rd lord (the lord of the *bhavat bhavam* of the 8th house), Lagna lord, 5th lord, and 12th lord. The 8th house of transformations in a *dharma rashi* is heavily packed to deliver loads of potential for spiritual evolution.

The Moon (significator of mind) is placed in the 8th house of transformations in a *dharma rashi* along with the Lagna lord establishing a mind-body connection in relation to spiritual transformations. The Moon is also conjunct Saturn (who is 9th lord) who is a separative planet, supporting the native to have a detached mindset (forms a *sannyas yoga*). Moon is also conjunct Mars (12th lord) who is placed in the *Mula nakshatra* lorded by Ketu (a significator of spirituality). In addition, the *Manasa nakshatra* (24th *nakshatra* from the *Janma nakshatra*) that signifies the nature of thoughts in the mind, is *Vishakha* and lorded by Jupiter (8th lord) who is placed in the transformative *Ashlesha nakshatra* (ruled by Mercury acting as 5th lord) and is aspected by 12th lord Mars. Hence, the Moon placement of the native; it being conjunct with the Lagna lord; together with the *Manasa nakshatra* influence supports a mind-body synchronization for the native for a spiritual bent of mind.

In addition, the *Janma nakshatra (Purvaashada)* is an *andha nakshatra* (a *nakshatra* type in the *andhadi nakshatra* set) gives this this native a "lost in their own world and blind to materialistic things" mindset where they do not care about the surroundings but only about focusing and achieving a world duty goal but will be gain-minded (as Venus is 6th lord) to an extent in a 'balanced' way. The *Manasa nakshatra* is *Vishakha* also an *andha nakshatra* (a *nakshatra* type in the *andhadi nakshatra* set) and denotes that the native will be very focused and gifted enough to obtain his goals of achieving a spiritual bent of mind (Jupiter being the *nakshatra lord* who is the 8th lord and aspected by the 12th lord) without much hard work. Hence, the nature of the *Janma* and *Manasa nakshatras* together implies that the mind is extremely focused ("blind" to surroundings) on achieving *spirituality*-related goals.

Sun (the significator of the soul) is placed in a *moksha rashi* in the 7th house and is aspected by a retrograde and exalted Jupiter from a *moksha rashi*

Case Study 3: A Controversial Spiritual Leader

who is the 8th lord (retrograde Jupiter giving the native a God-complex in terms of knowing it all in matters of spirituality). Note that Jupiter is also in a *gandanta* position placed in the *Ashlesha nakshatra* of transformation, aspected by 12th lord Mars placed in *nakshatra* of Ketu. Sun is also placed in the *Jyestha nakshatra* that is lorded by Mercury (5th lord), who is placed in the heavily loaded 8th house. Hence, in the D1, the mind, body, and soul are working together to support the native in experiencing transformation and spiritual upheavals if they occur during the lifetime.

In the D9, the Lagna lord of D1 is aspected by Jupiter who is conjunct Ketu. Mercury - the Lagna lord of D9 is in the 12th house in a *dharma rashi* and aspected by 12th lord and soul significator Sun, establishing a soul-body connection in D9 on spiritual matters. The Moon is on the 5/9 axis with the 8th lord (Mars) of D9 — both being in *kaam rashis*. This Moon combination indicates a spiritual propensity via the channel of desires.

Given the above analysis, there is strong potential in the native to experience spiritual ethos rooted upon a mind-body-soul synchrony.

3.2.2 Influence of Rahu on Spiritual Potential

The native has Rahu in the 11th house in Pisces that is a *moksha rashi*. Hence it acts like the 11th lord and exhibits the properties of an exalted Jupiter (who is the 8th lord of transformation and aspected by 12th lord Mars who is placed in the *Mula nakshatra* ruled by Ketu). Rahu is in the *Uttarabhadrapada nakshatra* (ruled by 9th and 10th lord Saturn in the 8th house who is placed in 12th from his own place — hence *dharma* is *karma* for such a native who does not distinguish between high and low and is fiery in temper but has outlier-ish *dharma* principles characteristic of Rahu). Jupiter aspects soul *karaka* Sun and is in the 5/9 mutual axis of *moksha rashis*. In addition, according to the classical text *Jataka Tatvam* that considers Rahu aspects, Rahu and Jupiter (8th lord) mutually aspect each other. However, *Uttarabhadrapada* is a *sulochana nakshatra* and takes away some sheen of Rahu being able to give the single-minded focus to achieve the highest form of spiritual ethos, appended by the fact that Rahu is in the 11th house (signifying gains). In the D9, Rahu in an *arth rashi* is aspected by Jupiter from a *moksha rashi*, and is aspected by 8th lord Mars placed in a *kaam rashi*. It is also aspected by 5th lord Saturn who is in a *dharma rashi*. Moreover, Rahu is hemmed between benefics forming a *shubh kartari yoga*. Rahu can give spiritual ethos to the native but not without a touch of materialism.

3.2.3 *Dasha* Analysis

Take note that the dispositor of the Sun (Mars) and Moon (Jupiter) are mutual friends, and enemies of the ascendant dispositor (Venus). The majority of the dispositors are enemies of the ascendant lord. Hence, while analyzing dasha periods, and in accordance with the *Sudarshan Paddhati* (SP) principles from *Parashari* code of *dasha* analysis, we need to perform a logical analysis from all the three reference points (Lagna, Sun, Moon) to arrive at conclusions/inferences.

Mars is the 12th lord from the birth ascendant and placed in the 8th house (house of transformation)

Case Study 3: A Controversial Spiritual Leader 89

and is conjunct Saturn (9th lord, 10th lord and *yogakaaraka*), Moon (3rd lord), Mercury (2nd lord, 5th lord), and Venus (Lagna lord, 6th lord). The dispositor of Mars is placed 8th from itself and aspects Sun (the significator of the soul). The native publicly admitted that he got spiritually enlightened when he was 21 years old (at the advent of the Mars MD), in a mystical experience while sitting under a garden tree in northwest India. Mars is the 12th lord in the 8th house in the *Mula nakshatra* (ruled by Ketu – hence MD of Mars went into creating a new-rooted/revolutionary philosophy). Prior to the Mars MD, the Moon MD was going on for the native, where the Moon, the 3rd lord is conjunct Saturn (9th lord) and is a strong astrological indicator of spiritual enlightenment. The native had to experience a lot of mental turbulence (due to an afflicted and much impression-ed Moon) and that eventually led to his spiritual enlightenment at the advent of the Mars MD. The Moon MD seeded spiritual evolution. Moon is in 6/8 position from its own house.

In the Mars MD, the native extensively traveled throughout India and teaching/preaching on topics related to institutional religions and the likes. Note that Mars is placed in the sign of Jupiter that is 8th lord and 11th lord along with Mercury (a significator of communication). Mars is also conjunct Saturn and Moon and represents mass influence through his teaching/preaching. Making Mars as Lagna (being MD lord), Sun (significator of soul) is in the 12th house with Lagna lord going 8th from his own house and aspected by the 12th lord implies mind and body and soul together invested in spirituality and sustaining it throughout the MD period. Now considering Moon as the ascendant, Mars is the 12th lord, with the dispositor of the 12th lord placed 8th from its own house. In D9, Mars is the 8th lord, mutually aspected by Saturn (5th lord), and in the 5/9 trine axis of Sun (the 12th lord). *Hence in the MD of Mars, and in accordance with consensus achieved from Lagna and Moon ascendant based on the SP principles, the native is justified in attaining and cultivating high spiritual ethos.*

In the Rahu MD, the native's name spread far and wide throughout the country and in the west in terms of spiritual preaching, but not without extreme controversy (10th lord from Rahu, i.e., retrograde Jupiter, in 8th from own house and aspected by 12th lord of foreign/faraway lands and aggressive Mars from 8th house that is conjunct with 2nd lord of speech and 6th lord of controversy; in addition Saturn as 9th lord conjunct Mars and in the 10th house from Rahu – MD lord). Also note that making Rahu as Lagna, Jupiter is 10th lord, Mars is 2nd lord, and Saturn is 12th lord. The preceding analysis adds in weight. The native spoke and preached about anti-capitalism, anti-socialism, the orthodoxy of Indian religions, the free acceptance of sex, and the pitfalls of the Indian caste system. Venus and Mars in 8th house along with Mercury (in a fiery sign) made the native speak on the controversial subject of sex in public with confidence and vocal fire, much to the wrath of the religious elite in India (exalted Jupiter that represents Gurus placed 8th from itself). Given Mars and Moon are in the same house, we have consensus on the native maintaining/

Case Study 3: A Controversial Spiritual Leader   91

sustaining a controversial spiritual ethos/outlook (whose peak was attained in the Mars MD) and lifestyle in the Rahu MD according to SP principles.

Summarizing Inference

The seed of a significant degree of detachment and spiritual enlightenment in the native was planted and inculcated in the MD of Moon because of the connection of Moon with Saturn and the very heavy (with planets) transformative 8th house. Mars MD, where Mars is 12th lord and 8th lord in D1 and D9 respectively, enabled the native to reach the heights of attaining spiritual ethos. Rahu MD only had the role of him controversially preaching to the world of his 'self-realized' philosophy. Hence, Rahu cannot be taken as the primary contributor to the genesis of spiritual ethos in the native. **Rahu sustained/amplified the effects that were generated and materialized in earlier MD periods of Mars and Moon.**

Section 3.3:
A *Nadi* Commentary

We provide THREE alternative, concise, and precise methods of analysis – based on *Bhrigu-Nandi Nadi* (BNN) astrology complementing the *Parashari* analysis of Case Study 2. **The goal is to establish the *Parashari* inference from Case Study 3 independently for each of the alternative methods of analysis.**

The essence of a good astrological analysis is the necessity for it to be validated from multiple schools of Vedic astrological thought. We choose the BNN approach as the alternative school of thought in this book – however, we smoothly integrate and blend an in-depth *nakshatra jyotish* analysis with the BNN framework, as we did with the *Parashari* analysis. While a strong *Parashari* education and a unique predictive *nakshatra jyotish* course are the pillars of the *Dev Jyotish* school of astrology, the BNN analysis was self-learned by Ranjan Pal under the personal guidance of Richa Shukla and then imparted to Ekta Jain by both.

3.3.1 Method 1 (*Bhrigu-Nandi Nadi*)

The significator of spirituality is Ketu. In BNN astrology, only this planet can grant spiritual realization to a native. Hence, unlike in the *Parashari* analysis we need not check whether Rahu provides a spiritual ethos. It cannot. Simply put, BNN saves us effort to test this that takes a significant effort to test via *Parashari jyotish*. It is sufficient to see **(a) whether the placement of Ketu is of sufficient strength to provide a spiritual outlook to the native** and **(b) whether and to what extent Rahu influences Ketu to support the native realizing spiritual ethos.** Unlike in *Parashari jyotish*, there is no need to do a dynamic analysis in BNN astrology (e.g., via progressions and transits) of Rahu to establish its quantum of influence on native spiritual ethos. This is because the static *Nadi* analysis is sufficiently causal to judge the quantum of Rahu's effects.

Decision Making Factor #1

For the native in Case Study 3, we have **Ketu** as the only planet in trine in an *artha rashi*. This signals detachment from material structures, a *karmic* push

Case Study 3: A Controversial Spiritual Leader

to transcend worldly gain. As part of the 7th house from Ketu analysis, we have **Rahu + Sun + Jupiter** (trines with each other from the 7th house from Ketu in ascending order of degree) in *moksha rashis*. This combination reflects a paradoxical polarity. Rahu magnifies desire, Sun symbolizes the soul's radiance, and Jupiter embodies higher wisdom. In *mokṣha* signs, this trio turns worldly ambition into a restless quest for liberation.

Though the native was immersed in controversy, wealth, and unorthodox practices, his inner trajectory pointed toward dismantling convention and awakening seekers. The Rahu–Sun–Jupiter blend made his teaching disruptive yet radiant with *Vedantic* and *Upaniṣhadic* insight, reframing desire and knowledge as paths to transcendence. Ketu's placement ensured renunciation lingered beneath the spectacle. Spiritually, this combination reveals the native's essence: a seeker whose soul (Sun) and wisdom (Jupiter), intensified by Rahu, transformed material contradictions into a radical, if unsettling, pursuit of *mokṣha*.

Rahu influences the spirituality significator in a positive way with this combination of Ketu and the trine of planets 7th from it, suggesting someone who becomes a **public figure** (signified by Sun), **spiritual teacher** (Jupiter in *moksha rashi*), with a *karmic* mission tied to guiding large groups of people in foreign countries or of foreign nature (signified by Rahu). Ketu being influenced by Rahu, Sun, and Jupiter in *moksha rashis* promotes spiritual outlook in the native.

Decision Making Factor #2

For the native in Case Study 3, we have Sun as the lord of the fiery 12th house from **Ketu**. Since Ketu is the significator of spirituality in BNN astrology one must check for the 12th from Ketu (12th house is the house of *moksha/dissolution* from any signification). We have a **Mars + Mercury + Venus + Moon + Saturn** standing on the trines from the 12th house from Ketu in a *dharma rashi*.

It is evident that the native's mind does *karma* motivated by higher knowledge, intelligence and an aggressive projecting ego. This also highlights the soul's (Sun) deep *karmic* connection with *moksha* - the dissolution of individuality through fire, sacrifice, and transcendence. This aligns well with the role of the spiritual significator Ketu. The trines from the 7th from the 12th house of Ketu is empty – not influencing the above planet-heavy combination. Standing in trines from this house, the combination of **Mars + Mercury + Venus + Moon + Saturn in** a *dharma rashi* creates a vast spiritual complexity. **Mars** infuses dynamism and restless energy, **Mercury** lends intellectual brilliance, **Venus** draws aesthetics and sensuality, **Moon** brings emotional flux, and **Saturn** imposes restraint and *karmic* tests. In *dharma* signs, these planets redirect their forces toward a higher ideal: the purification of desire, intellect, and action into spiritual discipline.

For the native, this mirrors his life: fiery Sun as *moksha*-lord fueled his radical teachings, while the *dharma-rashi* trine expressed through charisma, eloquence, sensual philosophy, and *karmic* trials. His controversial path turned worldly energies into

Case Study 3: A Controversial Spiritual Leader 95

paradoxical vehicles of awakening, dramatizing the *Vedantic* truth that even desire and intellect, when transmuted, can point toward liberation. **Rahu has no role to play here based on sign placement (if we do not include a *nakshatra* analysis here that is left for Methods 2 and 3).**

Decision Making Factor #3

For the native in Case Study 3, we have Moon as the lord of the 11th house from **Ketu**. This shows how desire (*kama*) and aspiration are tied to mutable, emotional, and social currents. The Moon's rulership here reflects an ever-changing quest for fulfillment, yet in a fiery house, it can also spiritualize aspirations into larger collective ideals. We also have a retrograde Jupiter placed in the 11th from Ketu. Since Ketu is the significator of spirituality in BNN astrology one must check for the 11th from Ketu (11th house analysis checks for catalytic factors contributing to a significator – in our case Ketu of spirituality). The native's restless desires were transfigured into collective spiritual experiments.

We have **Rahu + Sun + Jupiter** (in ascending order of degree). Placed in trines in a *dharma rashi*. The combination creates a striking paradox. Rahu intensifies and disrupts, the Sun signifies the soul's radiance, and retrograde Jupiter forces wisdom to unfold inwardly through struggle. In *dharma* signs, this becomes the tug-of-war between worldly disruption and transcendent insight. Rahu gave radical, disruptive methods; the Sun illuminated the native's charisma and vision; retrograde Jupiter made his wisdom unconventional, drawn from self-exploration rather than tradition. Spiritually, this reflects a native compelled to challenge orthodoxy, turning the volatile pursuit of desire into an experimental *dharmic* quest for liberation, even if surrounded by controversy. **It is evident that Rahu influences the spirituality significator in a positive way with this combination** suggesting a public figure in spirituality with a *karmic* mission tied to guiding groups of people in foreign countries.

If we now consider the trine houses from the 7th to the 11th house from Ketu, we have the combination of **Ketu** sitting alone. This combination signifies an uncompromising spiritual impulse — a rootless seeker, unwilling to conform to traditional structures.

The dispositor Saturn forms the trine combination of **Mars + Mercury + Venus + Moon + Saturn**. Hence, spirituality is influenced by intelligence and higher knowledge. This combination complicates spiritual purity with worldly drives. Spiritually, this means the native's evolution would emerge not from serene detachment but through turbulent interplay — desire, passion, intellect, and struggle all feeding into the *karmic* cauldron. This is precisely the paradox of the native. His teachings radiated Ketu's rootlessness - dissolving tradition, breaking categories — yet the Saturn-led cluster brought embodiment through wealth, sexuality, discourse, and controversy. Rather than renunciation alone, his spirituality expressed itself as a radical reworking of worldly energies, turning Venusian aesthetics and Mercurial intellect into gateways toward awareness. **Rahu does not play a role here based on its sign placement.**

Case Study 3: A Controversial Spiritual Leader

Decision Making Factor #4

For the native in Case Study 3, we have Mercury as the dispositor of Ketu and is located in a *dharma rashi* as part of the combination **Mars + Mercury + Venus + Moon + Saturn**. Since Mercury controls Ketu here, the soul's detached quest (Ketu) is expressed through intellectual articulation, philosophical discourse, and communicative brilliance. We reemphasize that the native's mind does *karma* motivated by higher knowledge, intelligence and an aggressive projecting ego. This aligns well with the role of the spiritual significator Ketu. This alignment shows that the native's spirituality was never silent asceticism but an eloquent deconstruction of tradition through Mercury's tongue. Ketu dissolves boundaries, but Mercury verbalizes that dissolution, producing paradoxical teachings — playful yet profound. The trinal cluster embodies an intense *karmic* drama: Venus pulls toward sensual beauty, Moon toward emotionality, Mars toward fiery disruption, and Saturn toward *karmic* discipline. The trinal resonance suggests that the native's teachings would fuse sensuality, intellect, and detachment into a *dharmic* framework, albeit one controversial by orthodox standards. The trine houses from the 7th house of Mercury is influenced by a retrograde Jupiter with partial power (Jupiter having a part in Gemini). The native's mind and ego is influenced by a self-advertised philosophy that he promotes in a grandiose fashion. **Rahu does not play a role here based on its sign placement (unless we deal with a *nakshatra* analysis).**

Summary: Does the placement of Ketu give a strong spiritual outlook to the native? The answer is a 'yes' from each of the four DMFs. Does Rahu play a positive role in the native experiencing spiritual ethos? The answer is a 'yes' from Decision Making Factors 1-2 which form 50% of the DMFs, in addition to the fact that Rahu is influencing by sitting in a *moksha rashi* in trine with Jupiter. The results sync with the *Parashari* analysis. Note, that we did not delve into the positivity or negativity with which Rahu influences spiritual ethos. That is not the focus of the research.

3.3.2 Method 2 (BNN with *Nakshatra*)

Since our analysis base is BNN astrology, like in Method 1 we will work with the same DMFs, and be light on the BNN part of the analysis (detailed in Method 1). It is sufficient to see using *nakshatras* **whether and to what extent Rahu influences Ketu to support the native realizing spiritual ethos.** When it comes to doing an analysis using *nakshatra* principles using KP astrology, three KP parameters are relevant for study for each decision making factor: (i) a planet's ***nakshatra* sub-lord**, (ii) the **sub-lord's *nakshatra* lord:** the planet ruling the *nakshatra* in which the sub-lord is situated, and the (iii) the **sub-lord's sign lord:** the planet ruling the sign in which the sub-lord is situated. Each *nakshatra* span of 13d20' is unequally divided into degree space owned by 9 sub-lords proportional to *Vimshottari dasha* duration.

Decision Making Factor #1

For the native in Case Study 3, we have **Ketu** alone

Case Study 3: A Controversial Spiritual Leader

Planet	R/C	Sign	Degree	Speed	Nakshatra	Pada	RL	NL	SL	SS	Status	SB
Lagna		Tau	27:06:33		Mrigasira	2	Ve	Ma	Ju	Ve		
Sun		Sco	25:35:30	01:01:01	Jyeshtha	3	Ma	Me	Ra	Ve	Grt.Fr.	1.17
Moon		Sag	22:38:08	13:36:59	Poorvashadha	3	Ju	Ve	Sa	Ke	Enemy	1.22
Mars	C	Sag	08:08:20	00:45:32	Moola	3	Ju	Ke	Ju	Me	Neutr.	1.23
Mercury		Sag	13:29:04	00:03:52	Poorvashadha	1	Ju	Ve	Ve	Ve	Enemy	1.13
Jupiter	R	Can	29:43:33	-00:00:21	Ashlesha	4	Mo	Me	Sa	Ju	Exalt.	0.99
Venus		Sag	19:17:16	01:14:46	Poorvashadha	2	Ju	Ve	Ra	Ke	Enemy	0.95
Saturn		Sag	28:33:27	00:06:22	Uttarashadha	1	Ju	Su	Ma	Ra	Enemy	1.50
Rahu		Pis	09:04:36	-00:11:22	Uttarabhadra	2	Ju	Sa	Ve	Ra	Neutr.	
Ketu		Vir	09:04:36	-00:11:22	Uttara Phalg.	4	Me	Su	Ve	Ju	Neutr.	

in its trine in an *artha rashi*. Ketu is in the *nakshatra* of Sun in the *pada* of Venus. Sun is in trine with Rahu in a *moksha rashi*. The dispositor of Venus (who is in a *dharma rashi*) is in the trine of Rahu. Hence, Ketu significance of spirituality is boosted, and is significantly influenced by Rahu. From a KP viewpoint, Ketu is in the *nakshatra* of Sun and has Venus as its sub-lord. Sun is in trine with Rahu in a *moksha rashi*. The dispositor of Venus (who is in a *dharma rashi*) is in the trine of Rahu. Venus has Venus as its *nakshatra* lord and is placed in the *rashi* of Jupiter that is in trine with Rahu. **Hence, Ketu significance of spirituality is boosted, and is significantly influenced by Rahu.**

As part of the 7th house from Ketu analysis, we have **Rahu + Sun + Jupiter** (trines with each other from the 7th house from Ketu in ascending order of degree) and placed in *moksha rashis*. Rahu is placed in *nakshatra* of Saturn in the *pada* of Venus. The dispositor of Venus and Saturn are in the trine of Rahu. Sun is in the *nakshatra* of Mercury and in the *pada* of Rahu. The dispositor of Mercury is in trine with Rahu. Jupiter is in the *nakshatra* of Mercury and in the *pada* of Saturn. The dispositor of Mercury and Saturn is in trine with Rahu. From a KP viewpoint, Rahu is placed in *nakshatra* of Saturn and has sub-lord Venus. Venus has Venus as its *nakshatra* lord and is placed in the *rashi* of Jupiter that is in trine with Rahu. The dispositor of Venus and Saturn are in the trine of Rahu. Sun is in the *nakshatra* of Mercury and has sub-lord Rahu. Rahu's *nakshatra* lord is Saturn and its sign lord is Jupiter that is in trine with Rahu. The dispositor of Mercury is in trine with Rahu. Jupiter is in the *nakshatra* of Mercury

Case Study 3: A Controversial Spiritual Leader

and has sub-lord Saturn. Saturn's *nakshatra* lord is Sun and its sign lord is Jupiter. Sun is in trine with Rahu and Jupiter. The dispositor of Mercury and Saturn is in trine with Rahu. **It is evident Rahu significantly influences the spiritual Ketu significance of the native in a positive way.**

If we now look at the trine houses from the 2nd house from Ketu, we get a leg of retrograde Jupiter. Jupiter is in the *nakshatra* of Mercury and in the *pada* of Saturn. The dispositor of Mercury and Saturn is in trine with Rahu. From a KP viewpoint, Jupiter is in the *nakshatra* of Mercury and has Saturn as its sub-lord. Saturn's *nakshatra* lord is Sun and its sign lord is Jupiter. Sun is in trine with Rahu and Jupiter. The dispositor of Mercury and Saturn is in trine with Rahu.

Decision Making Factor #2

For the native in Case Study 3, we have Sun as the lord of the fiery 12th house from **Ketu**. Since Ketu is the significator of spirituality in BNN astrology one must check for the 12th from Ketu (12th house is the house of *moksha/dissolution* from any signification). We have a **Mars + Mercury + Venus + Moon + Saturn** standing on the trines from the 12th house from Ketu in a *dharma rashi*. The dispositors of all of these planets are in trine with Rahu. Mars is in the *nakshatra* of Ketu and in the *pada* of Jupiter. Jupiter is in trine with Rahu. Mercury is the *nakshatra* of Venus and in the *pada* of Venus whose dispositor is in trine with Rahu. Venus is in the *nakshatra* of Venus and in the *pada* of Rahu. Moon is in the *nakshatra* of Venus and in the *pada* of Saturn – the dispositors of which are in the trine of Rahu. Saturn is in the *nakshatra* of Sun and in the *pada* of Mars. Sun is the trine of Rahu whereas the dispositor of Mars is in trine with Rahu. From a KP viewpoint, Mars is in the *nakshatra* of Ketu and has Jupiter as its sub-lord. Jupiter is in trine with Rahu. Jupiter's *nakshatra* lord is Mercury and Jupiter's sign lord is Moon. Mercury and Moon's dispositor is in trine with Rahu. Mercury is the *nakshatra* of Venus and has Venus as its sub-lord. Venus is in the *nakshatra* of Venus and in in the sign of Jupiter. The dispositor of Venus is in trine with Rahu. Jupiter is in trine with Rahu. Venus is in the *nakshatra* of Venus and has a sub-lord of Rahu. Rahu is in Saturn's *nakshatra* and lies in the sign of Jupiter. The dispositor of Saturn is Jupiter that is in trine with Rahu. Moon is in the *nakshatra* of Venus and has Saturn as its sub-lord – the dispositors of which are in the trine of Rahu. Saturn's *nakshatra* lord is Sun that is in trine with Rahu. Saturn is in the *nakshatra* of Sun and has a sub-lord of Mars. Mars is in the *nakshatra* of Ketu and in the sign of Jupiter. Sun is the trine of Rahu whereas the dispositor of Mars is in trine with Rahu. It is surprising that **Rahu has no role to play here based on sign placement (see Method 1), but a very significant role to play in influencing Ketu significance when we go deeper into a *nakshatra* analysis.**

The trines from the 7th from the 12th house of Ketu is empty — not influencing the above planet-heavy combination.

Decision Making Factor #3

For the native in Case Study 3, we have Moon as

Case Study 3: A Controversial Spiritual Leader

the lord of the 11th house from **Ketu**. We also have a retrograde Jupiter placed in the 11th from Ketu. Since Ketu is the significator of spirituality in BNN astrology one must check for the 11th from Ketu (11th house analysis checks for catalytic factors contributing to a significator — in our case Ketu of spirituality). We have **Rahu + Sun + Jupiter** (in ascending order of degree). Rahu is placed in *nakshatra* of Saturn in the *pada* of Venus. The dispositor of Venus and Saturn are in the trine of Rahu. Sun is in the *nakshatra* of Mercury and in the *pada* of Rahu. The dispositor of Mercury is in trine with Rahu. Jupiter is in the *nakshatra* of Mercury and in the *pada* of Saturn. The dispositor of Mercury and Saturn is in trine with Rahu. From a KP viewpoint, Rahu is placed in *nakshatra* of Saturn and has sub-lord Venus. Venus has Venus as its *nakshatra* lord and is placed in the *rashi* of Jupiter that is in trine with Rahu. The dispositor of Venus and Saturn are in the trine of Rahu. Sun is in the *nakshatra* of Mercury and has sub-lord Rahu. Rahu's *nakshatra* lord is Saturn and its sign lord is Jupiter that is in trine with Rahu. The dispositor of Mercury is in trine with Rahu. Jupiter is in the *nakshatra* of Mercury and has sub-lord Saturn. Saturn's *nakshatra* lord is Sun and its sign lord is Jupiter. Sun is in trine with Rahu and Jupiter. The dispositor of Mercury and Saturn is in trine with Rahu. **It is evident Rahu significantly influences the spiritual Ketu significance of the native in a positive way.**

If we now consider the trine houses from the 7th to the 11th house from Ketu, we have the combination of **Ketu** sitting alone. Ketu is in the *nakshatra* of Sun and the pada of Venus. Sun is in trine with Rahu and the dispositor of Venus is in trine with Rahu. The dispositor Saturn (of the 7th to the 11th house from Ketu) forms the trine combination of **Mars + Mercury + Venus + Moon + Saturn**. The dispositors of all of these planets are in trine with Rahu. Mars is in the *nakshatra* of Ketu and in the *pada* of Jupiter. Jupiter is in trine with Rahu. Mercury is the *nakshatra* of Venus and in the *pada* of Venus whose dispositor is in trine with Rahu. Venus is in the *nakshatra* of Venus and in the *pada* of Rahu. Moon is in the *nakshatra* of Venus and in the pada of Saturn — the dispositors of which are in the trine of Rahu. Saturn is in the *nakshatra* of Sun and in the *pada* of Mars. Sun is the trine of Rahu whereas the dispositor of Mars is in trine with Rahu.

From a KP viewpoint, Ketu is in the *nakshatra* of Sun and has Venus as its sub-lord. Sun is in trine with Rahu in a *moksha rashi*. The dispositor of Venus (who is in a *dharma rashi*) is in the trine of Rahu. Venus has Venus as its *nakshatra* lord and is placed in the *rashi* of Jupiter that is in trine with Rahu. Hence, Ketu significance of spirituality is boosted, and is significantly influenced by Rahu. Mars is in the *nakshatra* of Ketu and has Jupiter as its sub-lord. Jupiter is in trine with Rahu. Jupiter's *nakshatra* lord is Mercury and Jupiter's sign lord is Moon. Mercury and Moon's dispositor is in trine with Rahu. Mercury is the *nakshatra* of Venus and has Venus as its sub-lord. Venus is in the *nakshatra* of Venus and in in the sign of Jupiter. The dispositor of Venus is in trine with Rahu. Jupiter is in trine with Rahu. Venus is in the *nakshatra* of Venus and has a sub-lord of Rahu. Rahu is in Saturn's *nakshatra* and lies in the sign of

Case Study 3: A Controversial Spiritual Leader 105

Jupiter. The dispositor of Saturn is Jupiter that is in trine with Rahu. Moon is in the *nakshatra* of Venus and has Saturn as its sub-lord — the dispositors of which are in the trine of Rahu. Saturn's *nakshatra* lord is Sun that is in trine with Rahu. Saturn is in the *nakshatra* of Sun and has a sub-lord of Mars. Mars is in the *nakshatra* of Ketu and in the sign of Jupiter. Sun is the trine of Rahu whereas the dispositor of Mars is in trine with Rahu. It is surprising that **Rahu has no role to play here based on sign placement (see Method 1), but a very significant role to play in influencing Ketu significance when we go deeper into a *nakshatra* analysis.**

Decision Making Factor #4

For the native in Case Study 3, we have Mercury as the dispositor of Ketu and is located in a *dharma rashi* as part of the combination **Mars + Mercury + Venus + Moon + Saturn**. The dispositors of all of these planets are in trine with Rahu. Mars is in the *nakshatra* of Ketu and in the *pada* of Jupiter. Jupiter is in trine with Rahu. Mercury is the *nakshatra* of Venus and in the *pada* of Venus whose dispositor is in trine with Rahu. Venus is in the *nakshatra* of Venus and in the *pada* of Rahu. Moon is in the *nakshatra* of Venus and in the pada of Saturn − the dispositors of which are in the trine of Rahu. Saturn is in the *nakshatra* of Sun and in the *pada* of Mars. Sun is the trine of Rahu whereas the dispositor of Mars is in trine with Rahu. We reemphasize that the native's mind does *karma* motivated by higher knowledge, intelligence and an aggressive projecting ego. This aligns well with the spiritual significance of Ketu. The trine houses from the 7th house of Mercury is influenced by a retrograde

Jupiter with partial power (Jupiter having a part in Gemini). Jupiter is in the *nakshatra* of Mercury and in the *pada* of Saturn. The dispositor of Mercury and Saturn is in trine with Rahu.

As per KP, Mars is in the *nakshatra* of Ketu and has Jupiter as its sub-lord. Jupiter is in trine with Rahu. Jupiter's *nakshatra* lord is Mercury and Jupiter's sign lord is Moon. Mercury and Moon's dispositor is in trine with Rahu. Mercury is the *nakshatra* of Venus and has Venus as its sub-lord. Venus is in the *nakshatra* of Venus and in in the sign of Jupiter. The dispositor of Venus is in trine with Rahu. Jupiter is in trine with Rahu. Venus is in the *nakshatra* of Venus and has a sub-lord of Rahu. Rahu is in Saturn's *nakshatra* and lies in the sign of Jupiter. The dispositor of Saturn is Jupiter that is in trine with Rahu. Moon is in the *nakshatra* of Venus and has Saturn as its sub-lord — the dispositors of which are in the trine of Rahu. Saturn's *nakshatra* lord is Sun that is in trine with Rahu. Saturn is in the *nakshatra* of Sun and has a sub-lord of Mars. Mars is in the *nakshatra* of Ketu and in the sign of Jupiter. Sun is the trine of Rahu whereas the dispositor of Mars is in trine with Rahu.

Rahu has a significant role to play in influencing Ketu significance when we go deeper into a *nakshatra* analysis.

Summary: Does the placement of Ketu give a strong spiritual outlook to the native? The answer is a 'yes' from each of the four DMFs. Does Rahu play a positive role in the native experiencing spiritual ethos? The answer is a 'yes' from Decision Making Factors 1-4. The results sync with the *Parashari* analysis. Note that we did not delve into the positivity or negativity with which Rahu influences spiritual ethos. That is not the focus of the research.

3.3.3 Method 3 (BNN with *Karmic* Angles)

We wish to analyse in **three parts** using the *karmic Nadi jyotish* principles the strength of Rahu in influencing each of the mind, body, and soul to realize a spiritual ethos. After all, these are the basic pillars that eventually decide whether a native will be able to realize spiritual ethos in the lifetime. **If the connection is strong in at least two out of the three cases, we can say that Rahu has been significantly instrumental in promoting spirituality within the native.** Unlike in *Parashari jyotish*, there is no need to do a dynamic analysis (e.g., via progressions and transits) of Rahu to establish its quantum of influence on native spiritual ethos. This is because the static *Nadi* analysis is sufficiently causal to judge the quantum of Rahu's effects.

Dridh-Adridh Karma **Axes:** In *Naḍi jyotish*, directions embody the metaphysics of *karma* itself. **East and West** anchor *dridh karma* — duties to father, guru, and ancestors that bind the soul to its inescapable obligations. **East**, aligned with Sun and Jupiter, signifies *dharma*, authority, and righteous beginnings; **West** blends closure and entanglement, largely fixed through Saturn's weight, though softened by Venus's negotiable pleasures. **North and South** anchor *adridh karma* - mutable desires and worldly pursuits shaped by free will. **North**, guided by Mercury and Rahu, points to growth, commerce, and ambition; while

South, linked with Mars, Ketu, and Moon, carries ancestral debts, *tapas*, and *karmic* reckonings. In summary, East pulls a native towards *dharmic* duty, West toward worldly entanglement, North toward ambition, and South toward purification.

Thus, the four directions mark not mere space but the soul's *karmic* geography: some pathways immovable, others pliable. The horoscope becomes a compass of necessity and possibility, mapping destiny's fixity against the field of conscious striving. One may ask: why not diagonal directions? In *Nadi jyotish*, only the **four cardinal directions** — East, West, North, and South—are used, not the intermediates like Northeast or Northwest. This is because Vedic cosmology is fundamentally **fourfold**, based on sunrise and sunset, solstices and equinoxes, day and night. Each direction is tied to specific *grahas* and *karmic* qualities: East (Sun, Jupiter), West (Saturn, Venus), North (Mercury, Rahu), South (Moon, Mars, Ketu). This framework mirrors the *dik-palas* (directional guardians) of Vedic ritual, which are cardinal. By limiting to four, *Naḍi* emphasizes clarity: destiny is seen through primal axes of *dharma*, desire, past, and closure, without diluting meaning in diagonals.

We provide the planetary directional compass diagram for Case Study 3.

Case Study 3: A Controversial Spiritual Leader

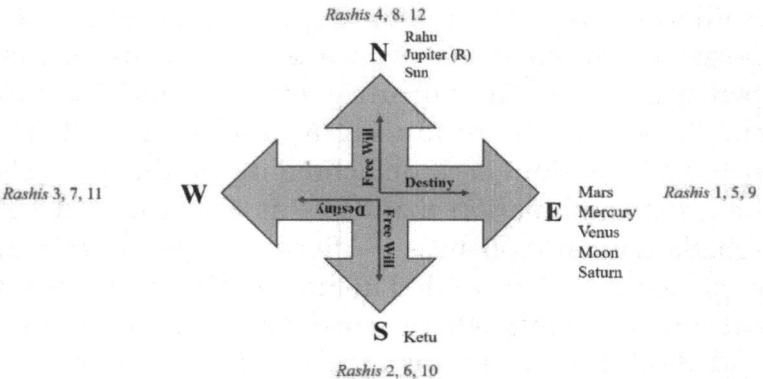

Part 1

We first analyze the planet **Moon** — the **significator of the mind**, to judge whether (a) the mind is inherently spiritual and (b) and how Rahu plays a role in driving the mind towards spirituality.

We observe that Moon occupies the eastern direction (a fiery sign) of the *Kaalpurusha* chart. If we arrange the planets in the **eastern direction** in ascending order of degree, we have the sequence **Mars, Mercury, Venus, Moon, Saturn** — a potent combination of planets in a *dharma rashi*. This combination fuses intellect, emotion, discipline, sensuality, and drive into one evolutionary field. For the native, this reflects the intense interplay of passion and restraint seen in his life: a fiery Mars fueling transformation, a reflective Moon seeking union, and a meditative Saturn grounding insight into disciplined teaching. In *Nadi* astrology, Mars, Mercury, Venus, Moon, and Saturn forming a *dharmic* trine in the eastern direction signify *dridh karma* expressing through disciplined action, intellectual brilliance, and emotional depth. Mars energizes purpose, Mercury sharpens intellect, Venus refines perception, Moon nurtures feeling, and Saturn stabilizes it all — producing a mind that oscillates between passion and detachment. In the native's life, this combination manifests as a disciplined yet rebellious consciousness — fiery in logic, poetic in expression, and grounded in inner stillness. His mind became a crucible where sensual experience, reason, and discipline fused, birthing a spiritual revolution that was intellectual yet transcendental. According to *Nadi* directionality principles Moon here is influenced by Mars, Mercury, Venus, and Saturn in full (100%) because these planets are in trine with one another.

Note that retrograde Jupiter (significator of philosophy and religious learning) is in trines with the 7th house from Moon because of the retrograde effect from the previous *rashi* of Jupiter that is in the **western direction**. In *Nadi* astrology, a retrograde Jupiter forming trines with the 7th from the Moon in the western direction signifies *dridh karma* rooted in introspective philosophy. Retrogression internalizes Jupiter's wisdom, making spiritual understanding self-realized rather than inherited. The mind, influenced by this, questions orthodoxy and transforms doubt into insight. For the native, this aspect produced an intellect that dissected tradition while seeking transcendence — turning rebellion into revelation. His thought became the meeting point of reason and mysticism, a philosophical awakening born of *karmic* reflection. According to *Nadi* directionality principles Moon here is influenced by Jupiter in nearly full

Case Study 3: A Controversial Spiritual Leader

power (75%). Since the eastern and western directions in *Nadi* astrology is the axis of *dridh karma* (destiny), the native is destined to be on the path of higher knowledge that is influenced by higher knowledge, intelligence, and ego.

Ketu is the significator of spirituality and we see that the dispositor to the 11th of Ketu is Moon and is in trine with Mars, Mercury, Venus, and Saturn. Hence there is a strong connection of the mind with spirituality in the native. This mind is philosophically knowledgeable (due to the influence of Jupiter and Venus from *moksha* and *dharma rashis*), intelligent, and aggressive. In *Nadi* astrology, when Ketu—significator of spirituality—occupies the southern (*adridh karma*) direction and its 11th dispositor, the Moon, forms trines with Mars, Mercury, Venus, and Saturn, it indicates a mind shaped by flexible *karmic* currents rather than fixed destiny. The Moon here channels fluctuating yet profound intuitive insights, while the trinal planets refine intellect, passion, and discipline toward spiritual experimentation. In the native's life, this produced a restless yet visionary consciousness—one that questioned conventions, turned sensual experience into meditation, and transformed *karmic* uncertainty into creative spiritual evolution.

Ketu (in the **southern direction**) also influences Moon with 50% power as the former is in trines with the second house from Moon. The *karma* pushed by Ketu here is the free will *karma*.

If we arrange planets in the **northern direction** (the direction of *adridh karma* or free will) in ascending order of degree we have the sequence **Rahu, Sun, Jupiter**. These planets are lying in the *moksha rashis*. In *Nadi* astrology, Rahu, Sun, and Jupiter aligned in *moksha rashis* in the northern direction — signifying *adridh karma* or the realm of free will — suggest a spiritual evolution achieved through conscious effort and experiential transformation. Rahu's disruptive curiosity propels inquiry; the Sun symbolizes the awakening of soul-awareness; and Jupiter, as divine wisdom, harmonizes the chaos into revelation. This trio signifies liberation through rebellion, where enlightenment is self-forged rather than inherited. In the native's life, this manifested as a bold pursuit of truth through intellect, sensuality, and meditation—transcending dogma to discover inner divinity. His *adridh karmic* journey turned free will into the crucible of awakening, making spirituality an act of deliberate self-realization rather than passive surrender. According to *Nadi* directionality principles Moon here is influenced by these planets with minimum power (25%) because they are in trine with one another from the 12th house from Moon. This combination shows the native practice philosophical and spiritual teachings in a foreign country. **However, the role of Rahu in spiritual realization is not significant by any means.**

So, **in summary**: is the mind spiritual? The answer is a resounding 'yes'. Does Rahu play a role in driving the mind towards spirituality? The answer is a 'no' (non-significant).

Part 2

We want to analyze the planet **Sun — the significator of the soul**, to judge whether (a) the soul

Case Study 3: A Controversial Spiritual Leader   113

is inherently spiritual and (b) and how Rahu plays a role in driving the soul towards spirituality.

We observe that Rahu, Sun, and Jupiter lie in the **northern direction** in *moksha rashis* and are in mutual trines with one another. According to *Nadi* directionality principles Sun here is influenced by these planets with maximum power (100%). This combination shows the native practice philosophical and spiritual teachings in a foreign country (signified by Rahu). In *Nadi* astrology, Rahu, Sun, and Jupiter forming mutual trines in *moksha rashis* in the northern (*adridh karma*) direction reflects a soul that evolves through conscious engagement with illusion, power, and wisdom. Rahu propels the soul into unconventional exploration; the Sun awakens divine individuality; and Jupiter harmonizes both through higher understanding. This trinal flow directs *adridh karma*—free will—toward spiritual awakening. In the native's life, this manifested as a radiant soul that sought liberation not through renunciation, but through experience, awareness, and integration. His enlightenment was a self-directed ascent — an act of will transmuting desire into divine realization.

Ketu is the significator of spirituality, and Sun is the significator of the soul. It is then evident that Ketu (in the **southern direction**) provides spiritual essence to the soul of the native because it is in trine with the 7th house from Sun. According to *Nadi* directionality principles Sun is influenced by Ketu with nearly full power (75%) because Sun is in trine with Ketu. In *Nadi* astrology, Ketu in trine with the 7th from the Sun signifies *adridh karma* — a destiny guided by free will and inner detachment. The Sun, as the soul's light, represents identity and purpose, while Ketu dissolves egoic boundaries, turning experience into transcendence. Their trinal harmony reflects a soul liberated through introspection rather than external control. In the native's life, this alignment manifested as the awakening of an independent spiritual consciousness—one that transformed individuality into illumination, merging selfhood with universal awareness. As Ketu influences Rahu that is in trine with Sun, **Rahu does have an influence on the soul projecting spirituality.**

If we arrange planets in the **eastern direction** (the direction of *dridh karma* or destiny) in ascending order of degree we have the sequence **Saturn, Moon, Mercury, Venus, Mars**. These planets are lying in the *dharma rashis*. In *Nadi* astrology, this combination signifies a destiny deeply anchored in spiritual evolution through disciplined awareness. Saturn grants endurance and detachment; the Moon refines emotional sensitivity; Mercury brings analytical clarity; Venus adds harmony and love; and Mars provides the will to act. Together, they form a soul pattern inclined toward inner mastery through worldly engagement. In the native's life, this constellation mirrors a predestined unfolding where the soul's *karmic* maturity expressed itself through profound intellect, emotional intensity, and sensual transcendence. His teachings—bridging reason and devotion—reflect a *dridh karmic* calling to spiritualize human experience, transforming desire and thought into tools of liberation. According to *Nadi* directionality

Case Study 3: A Controversial Spiritual Leader

principles Sun here is influenced by these planets with nearly half power (50%) because they are in trine with one another from the 2nd house from Sun. There is a sufficient influence power of Saturn and Moon (a combination of detachment) on Rahu (in a foreign setting) to be able to infer that **Rahu does not have non-significant role to play on the soul projecting spirituality.** In addition, Moon is the dispositor of the 11th house from Ketu indicating the stringed connection of Moon and Sun in realizing spirituality.

The **western direction** only consists of the retrograde effect of Jupiter with a non-significant 25% power influence on Sun.

So, **in summary**: is the soul projecting spirituality? The answer is a resounding 'yes'. Does Rahu play a role in driving the mind towards spirituality? The answer is a 'yes'.

Part 3

We want to analyze the planet **Mars — the significator of the body and ego,** to judge whether (a) the body is inherently spiritual and (b) and how Rahu plays a role in driving the body and ego towards spirituality. However, since Moon and Mars are in the same direction, the analysis and inference for Part 3 is exactly same as that in Part 1. In other words, is the body projecting spiritual essence? The answer is not a resounding 'yes'. **Does Rahu play a role in driving the body towards spirituality? The answer is a 'no' (non-significant).**

Overall Inference from Parts 1 to 3: Rahu does not strongly influence spiritual essence through the mind and body, though it significantly influences the soul projecting spirituality. The results sync with the *Parashari* angle of analysis that Rahu does not generate spiritual realization in the native. However, the results get even more fine-grained with the *Nadi* analysis that says the body, mind, are not aligned with Rahu in projecting spirituality but the soul is aligned with Rahu in this regard. Since two out of the three (Sun, Moon, and Mars) are not being influenced by Rahu on the lines of spiritual realization, we can say that Rahu does not generate spiritual ethos in the native.

Case Study 4
A Renowned Holy Saint

Section 4.1:
A Narrative of Spiritual Philosophy

The native stands as a luminous figure whose spiritual journey reflected a deep synthesis of Vedic insight, *bhakti* devotion, and radical reformist vision. Born in Punjab at a time of socio-religious fragmentation, the native's early questioning of ritual and caste echoes the *Upanishadic* spirit of inquiry: *"Neti, neti"* — "not this, not this" — pointing beyond form to essence. A mystical experience at the river Beas, where the native disappeared for three days and returned proclaiming *"Na ko Hindu, na ko Musalman"* (*"There is no Hindu, there is no Muslim"*), marked the moment of transcendence beyond duality into the universal ground of *Ik Onkar*, the One Reality.

Philosophically, this insight parallels the Vedic dictum from the **Rig Veda (1.164.46)**: *"Ekam sat vipra bahudha vadanti"* — "Truth is One, the wise call it by many names." The native universalized this vision, rejecting sectarianism and asserting the unity of humanity. The teachings embodied *bhakti-yoga* as described in the **Bhagavad Gita (9.22)**: *"To those who are devoted, I carry what they lack and preserve what they have."* In the *Guru Granth Sahib*, the native emphasizes *nama-simran* (remembrance of the Divine Name) as the path to liberation, echoing the *Upanishadic* emphasis on *sabda-brahman*, the Word as the eternal vibration of Truth.

Philosophers recognized this radical synthesis. Radhakrishnan noted: *"The native gave India a fresh orientation—spirituality without dogma, devotion without exclusion."* Heinrich Zimmer described Sikhism as *"a bridge religion, affirming the One while sustaining the human need for loving devotion."*

Jain and Buddhist resonances also echo in the rejection of blind ritual and in the insistence on compassion and right livelihood. Yet, the native's insistence on the householder's path distinguished this vision: spirituality was not to be confined to renunciates but to be lived amidst the world — *"ghal khae kichh hathon de, rahu pachhane se"* (*"One who earns by honest labor and shares with others, knows the true way"*).

The native's evolution culminated not in abstract doctrine but in a living realization of *moksha* — liberation while embodied. Unlike the renunciatory model of salvation, this vision reflected the Vedic and *Upanishadic* ideal of *jivanmukti*, freedom attained amidst worldly duties. By anchoring in *nama-simran*, the ego-self dissolved into *Ik Onkar*, the One Reality, fulfilling the *Upanishadic* dictum: *"Brahmavid apnoti param"* **(*Taittiriya Upanishad 2.1*)** — *"The knower of Brahman attains the Supreme."* For the native, *moksha* was not escape, but abidance in Truth while serving creation. Egalitarian ethics — work, share, remember — are the embodied expression of this freedom. As Radhakrishnan noted, the native showed that

Case Study 4: A Renowned Holy Saint

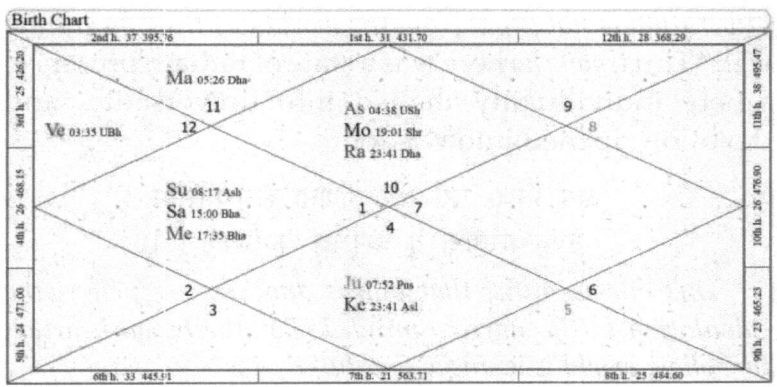

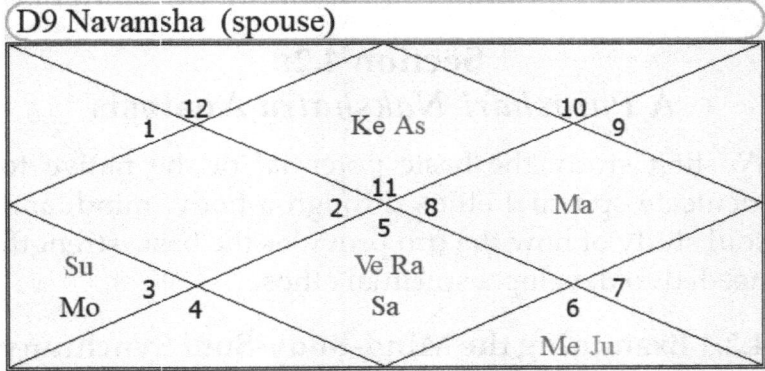

Birth Chart					
As	04:36:15	U.Shad.	Jah	3,Su/Sa/Ra
Su	08:17:04	Ashwini	Cho	3,Ke/Ju/Me
Mo	19:01:54	Shravana	Khe	3,Mo/Me/Ra
Ma	05:26:30	Dhanish.	Gay	4,Ma/Su/Ke
Me	17:35:01 c	Bharani	Loo	2,Ve/Ma/Ju
Ju	07:52:24	Pushya	Hay	2,Sa/Ke/Ju
Ve	03:35:11	U.Bhadra.	Doo	1,Sa/Sa/Sa
Sa	15:00:24 c	Bharani	Lee	1,Ve/Ve/Sa
Ra	23:41:45	Dhanish.	Gah	1,Ma/Ma/Sa
Ke	23:41:45	Ashlesha	Day	3,Me/Ma/Sa

DOB - 15 April 1469, Time - 12:55 AM, Talwandi, Pakistan

"liberation is not flight from the world but transfiguration of it." Thus, *moksha* here was a state of radiant presence, where individuality melted into universality, and devotion ripened into wisdom.

अयं निजः परो वेति गणना लघुचेतसाम् ।
उदारचरितानां तु वसुधैव कुटुम्बकम् ॥

This one is mine, that one is another — such is the calculation of the narrow-minded. For the broad-hearted, the whole world is a single family.

(Maha Upanishad, VI.71)

Section 4.2:
A *Parashari-Nakshatra* Analysis

We first study the basic potential of the native to inculcate spiritual ethos through a body, mind, and soul study of how the trio provides the basic strength needed to develop a spiritual ethos.

4.2.1 Examining the Mind-Body-Soul Synchrony

We first study the basic potential of the native to inculcate spiritual ethos through a body, mind, soul study of how the trio provides the basic strength needed to develop a spiritual ethos.

The lord of the Lagna (significator of body) Saturn is placed in the 4th house conjunct with 8th lord Sun, and 9th lord Mercury in a *dharma rashi*. The Lagna is in the *nakshatra* of 8th lord Sun who is conjunct 9th lord Mercury, whereas the Lagna lord is in the *Bharani nakshatra* that is ruled by the 5th lord Venus. The Moon (significator of mind) is placed in the first house on the Rahu/Ketu axis and aspected by an

Case Study 4: A Renowned Holy Saint 121

exalted Jupiter who is conjunct Ketu and is the 12th lord. Moon is in the *Shravan nakshatra* whose lord is aspected by 12th lord Jupiter.

The Moon is also aspected by Saturn who is Lagna lord and placed in a *dharma rashi*, and in the *nakshatra* of Venus who is the 5th lord. Saturn's aspect on the Moon forms a *sannyas yoga*. Hence, with the placement of the Lagna lord and the Moon, we establish a mind-body connection in relation to spiritual transformations. In addition, the *Manasa nakshatra* (24th *nakshatra* from the *Janma nakshatra*) that signifies the nature of thoughts in the mind, is *Jyestha* and lorded by 9th lord Mercury who is conjunct the 8th lord Sun, and Lagna lord Saturn and placed in a *dharma rashi*. Hence, the Moon placement of the native; it being aspected by the Lagna lord; together with the *Manasa nakshatra* influence supports a mind-body synchronization for the native for a spiritual bent of mind.

Sun (the significator of the soul) is placed in a *dharma rashi* in the 4th house, is conjunct the Lagna lord, and the 9th lord Mercury. Sun is in the transformative *Ashlesha nakshatra* ruled by the 9th lord Mercury that itself is in the *nakshatra* of the 5th lord Venus who is aspected by Jupiter who is lord of the 12th house. Jupiter mutually aspects the Moon from a *moksha rashi*. Hence, in the D1, the mind, body, and soul are working together to support the native in experiencing transformation and spiritual upheavals if they occur during the lifetime.

In the D9, Ketu is present in the Lagna. The Lagna lord has gone to 8th from his own house and placed in a *dharma rashi*, and conjunct the 9th lord in the *rashi* owned by Sun who is conjunct the Moon. Ketu is in mutual 5/9 trine with both the Sun and the Moon. Hence, in the D9, the mind, body, and soul are working together to support the native in experiencing spiritual transformations.

4.2.2 Influence of Rahu on Spiritual Potential

The native has Rahu in the first house in Capricorn. Hence it acts like the Lagna lord and exhibits the properties of Saturn (in the 4th house conjunct with the 8th lord of transformation). Rahu is aspected by Jupiter as 12th lord and Lagna lord Saturn. Rahu is in the *Dhanishta nakshatra* that is a *andha nakshatra* (a *nakshatra* type in the *andhadi nakshatra* set) and denotes that the Rahu will support the native in being focused and gifted enough to obtain his goals of achieving a spiritual bent (via the properties of its dispositors and aspects from other planets) of mind without much hard work or without facing much challenges. In addition, according to the classical text *Jataka Tatvam* that considers Rahu aspects, Rahu (acting as Lagna lord and conjunct the 8th lord of transformation) aspects the 5th and 9th houses of the native that promote spirituality. In the D9, Rahu is in a *dharma rashi* and is conjunct the 12th lord and the 9th lord. Hence, *Rahu has significant potential to give spiritual ethos to the native.*

4.2.3 *Dasha* Analysis

The dispositor of the Sun (Mars) is a mutual enemy to the dispositor of Moon (Venus) and the dispositor of birth lagna (Saturn). Hence, while analyzing *dasha* periods, and in accordance with the *Sudarshan Paddhati*

Case Study 4: A Renowned Holy Saint

(SP) principles from *Parashari* code of *dasha* analysis, we need to perform a logical analysis from only the Lagna to arrive at conclusions/inferences. Note that the chart is blessed with multiple *Mahapurusha Yogas* of Jupiter. The native also has a *Kaal Sarpa Yoga* that is of the *Kaal Amrit* form.

In the Rahu MD, the native made very significant progress in spiritual life. Rahu is aspected by exalted Jupiter as 12th lord who is also with Ketu. Rahu is also aspected by the Lagna lord Saturn who is with the 8th lord Sun (spiritual significator). The native early in the Rahu MD was spoken about in his neighborhood of being the protagonist of miraculous religion and God related events (3rd lord Jupiter exalted in 7th house of public fame/popularity – 7th house is 10th from 10th via *Parashari Bhavat Bhavam* principles). These events showcased the fact that the native was born an evolved soul. If we make Rahu as lagna being the MD lord, we get the same analysis as the birth lagna is conjunct Rahu. During the Rahu MD, the native got married (In Rahu/Ketu period; Ketu is in 7th house with Jupiter) and had two children. If we make Rahu as the MD lord in the D9 chart, we see Rahu is conjunct 7th lord and 10th lord and is not aspected by any other planet. Hence, though Rahu period can give external manifestation of the prodigy nature of the native in terms of spiritual evolution, the period itself does not have sufficient potential to make the native attain spiritual heights.

However, evolved souls such as the native with prodigious potential still need to experience the act of getting *moksha* (the highest possible spiritual ethos) in the current birth. The native is said to have attained enlightenment (as per historical data) in the beginning of the Jupiter MD (the official confirmation of achieving *moksha*). Exalted Jupiter as 12th lord is with Ketu, the significator of *moksha*, with dispositor Moon exalted in the Lagna. Jupiter aspects the lagna and is in *kendra* to Sun and Lagna lord. Hence, the mind, body, and soul were all united in the native getting divine *moksha* in the Jupiter MD. The fame of the native as a spiritual Guru spread far and wide in the Jupiter MD and established the native as a *mahapurusha* in the *dharma* and religious space. The native has the third house hosting an exalted Venus (5th lord) aspected by exalted Jupiter from the seventh house, showing his exquisite, immortal poetical compositions of unparalleled spiritual merit, in the Jupiter MD. The native traveled far and wide in the Jupiter MD (Jupiter is the 12th lord) to preach his teachings. The native traveled and preached the philosophy of a new religion in Jupiter MD. The 11th house is networking and the spread of new ideas, and the 11th lord from Jupiter is exalted in the 9th house from Jupiter and is aspected by Jupiter. Making Jupiter as Lagna being the MD lord makes Sun exalted in the 10th house of fame, giving the native popularity far and wide through communication of his teachings.

Summarizing Inference

The native was born an evolved soul. The concept of a seed of spirituality does not arise in this case study. However, an absolute degree of detachment and spiritual enlightenment (*moksha* as attained by saints) in the native (who started a cult religious

Case Study 4: A Renowned Holy Saint

following) was planted and inculcated in the MD of Jupiter. Jupiter aspects the Lagna and is in *kendra* to Sun and Lagna lord, mutually aspects the Moon. Hence, the mind, body, and soul were all united in the native getting divine *moksha* in the Jupiter MD. This case is a classic example where even though the native was born an evolved soul and faced Rahu MD before the Jupiter MD, showed enough traits of being an evolved soul in the Rahu MD, absolute *moksha* was only attained by the native in the Jupiter MD Hence, **Rahu cannot be taken as the contributor to the native attaining *moksha*.**

Section 4.3:
A *Nadi* Commentary

We provide THREE alternative, concise, and precise methods of analysis — based on *Bhrigu-Nandi Nadi* (BNN) astrology complementing the *Parashari* analysis of Case Study 2. **The goal is to establish the *Parashari* inference from Case Study 4 independently for each of the alternative methods of analysis.**

The essence of a good astrological analysis is the necessity for it to be validated from multiple schools of Vedic astrological thought. We choose the BNN approach as the alternative school of thought in this book — however, we smoothly integrate and blend an in-depth *nakshatra jyotish* analysis with the BNN framework, as we did with the *Parashari* analysis. While a strong *Parashari* education and a unique predictive *nakshatra jyotish* course are the pillars of the *Dev Jyotish* school of astrology, the BNN analysis was self-learned by Ranjan Pal under the personal guidance of Richa Shukla and then imparted to Ekta Jain by both.

4.3.1 Method 1 (*Bhrigu-Nandi Nadi*)

The significator of spirituality is Ketu. In BNN astrology, only this planet can grant spiritual realization to a native. Hence, unlike in the *Parashari* analysis we need not check whether Rahu provides a spiritual ethos. It cannot. Simply put, BNN saves us effort to test this that takes a significant effort to test via *Parashari jyotish*. It is sufficient to see **(a) whether the placement of Ketu is of sufficient strength to provide a spiritual outlook to the native** and **(b) whether and to what extent Rahu influences Ketu to support the native realizing spiritual ethos.** Unlike in *Parashari jyotish*, there is no need to do a dynamic analysis in BNN astrology (e.g., via progressions and transits) of Rahu to establish its quantum of influence on native spiritual ethos. This is because the static *Nadi* analysis is sufficiently causal to judge the quantum of Rahu's effects.

Decision Making Factor #1

For the native in Case Study 4, we have **Venus + Jupiter + Ketu** (ordered in ascending order of degree) in trines in *moksha rashis*. Venus grants devotional love, Jupiter expands philosophical understanding, and Ketu dissolves ego—together symbolizing a soul perfected through compassion and detachment.

As part of the 7th house from Ketu analysis, we have **Moon + Rahu** (trines with each other from the

Case Study 4: A Renowned Holy Saint

7th house from Ketu in ascending order of degree) in *artha rashis*. This combination reflects the worldly mind's engagement with illusion and human emotion, yet ultimately channeling them toward realization. The higher knowledge and devotional arts (Venus), philosophy (Jupiter) and spirituality (Ketu) significators are influenced by the mind (signified by the Moon) that is briming with revolutionary ideas (signified by Rahu) on religion and spirituality. The native tastes wealth and love but is *karmically* redirected toward spiritual growth, often through loss, dissatisfaction, or an inner call beyond luxury. This dual polarity—spiritual detachment on one side and emotional involvement on the other—mirrors the native's divine mission. His enlightenment fused inner renunciation with outer compassion, transforming worldly experience into sacred insight. The native turned to *satsang* and service-oriented *bhakti* – channeling the artsy side of Venus into creating and singing devotional songs (devotion signified by *dharma* and devotion). The native struggled between indulgence and renunciation. Life events (marriage, children, wealth) had become vehicles of detachment rather than enjoyment and led to renunciation of the native from *sansara* via instability in marriage, and causing emotional highs and lows driven by the push–pull between wisdom and illusion, restraint and indulgence. Thus, his soul's evolution revealed the harmony of *bhakti* (devotion), *jnana* (wisdom), and *vairagya* (detachment)—a perfect synthesis of divine love and spiritual liberation.

Decision Making Factor #2

For the native in Case Study 4, we have Mercury as the lord of the 12th house from **Ketu**. Since Ketu is the significator of spirituality in BNN astrology one must check for the 12th from Ketu (12th house is the house of *moksha/dissolution* from any signification). We have only **Mars** standing on the trines from the 12th house from Ketu in a *kaam rashi*. In *Nadi* astrology, Mars alone standing on the trines from the 12th house from Ketu in a *kaam rashi* reflects the transformation of desire into divine action. Mars here represents the disciplined energy that sublimates passion into purpose, while its trinal connection to Ketu's *moksha* impulse channels worldly drive toward service. For the native, this signifies the soul's mastery over impulse—turning vitality into compassion. His missionary journeys embodied this principle: *karmic energy spiritualized through fearless devotion, expressing divine love through dynamic engagement with the world.*

The trines from the 7th from the 12th house of Ketu has **Sun + Saturn + Mercury** (in ascending order of degree). This combination symbolizes the *karmic refinement of consciousness* through disciplined wisdom. The Sun represents the soul's radiance and divine purpose; Saturn, detachment and humility born of endurance; Mercury, discrimination and expression. Together, they signify the illumination of truth through trial and understanding. For the native, this alignment mirrors his spiritual realization through experience — divine intellect (*Buddhi*) awakened by discipline and devotion. Saturn's restraint balanced

Case Study 4: A Renowned Holy Saint 129

the Sun's illumination, while Mercury gave voice to revelation — producing hymns that merged philosophy with devotion. Mars under Sun + Saturn + Mercury is a *karmic* crucible: Mars's fiery ambition is caught between Sun's soulfulness and Saturn's discipline and uplifted by Mercury's intelligence and communication brilliance to realize the ambition despite obstacles. Spiritually, this combination teaches the native that raw energy (Mars) must be illumined by wisdom (Sun), disciplined by *karma* (Saturn), and expressed through clarity (Mercury). Now if consider the dispositor of the 12th house from Ketu we have **Sun + Saturn + Mercury** and this is influenced by **Mars** from the trine houses from the 7th house from Mercury.

Rahu has no role to play based on sign placement (if we do not include a *nakshatra* analysis here that is left for Methods 2 and 3).

Decision Making Factor #3

For the native in Case Study 4, we have Venus as the lord of the 11th house from **Ketu**. Since Ketu is the significator of spirituality in BNN astrology one must check for the 11th from Ketu (11th house analysis checks for catalytic factors contributing to a significator – in our case Ketu of spirituality). In *Nadi* astrology, Venus as the lord of the 11th from Ketu placed in a *moksha rashi* signifies the refinement of desire (*kama*) into devotion (*bhakti*). The 11th from Ketu governs spiritual gains, and Venus here transforms material longing into divine love. This configuration reflects *karma* evolving toward liberation through aesthetic and emotional purity. In the native's life, it manifests as his radiant compassion and musical devotion - his hymns expressing beauty as a bridge to truth, where love itself became the instrument of realization and union with the Divine.

We have **Moon + Rahu** (in ascending order of degree). This combination suggests the native's mind is prone to obsession, confusion, or illusion. Mental peace is hard to stabilize. This is because Rahu pulls the Moon toward the unusual, foreign, or socially disruptive and foreign thoughts. The combination represents transformation of material consciousness into spiritual service where worldly engagement becomes a field for inner awakening. The Moon governs sensitivity and emotional awareness, while Rahu intensifies desire and expands perception beyond convention. This is often a pre-requisite for a native to pioneer disruption in society, if influenced by the right forces. For the native, this configuration mirrors his life's synthesis of the sacred and the social: he attained realization not by withdrawal but by infusing divinity into daily existence. Rahu's expansive impulse universalized his compassion, while the Moon's empathy grounded it in love. Thus, through balancing material purpose (*artha*) with spiritual realization (*moksha*), his consciousness transcended duality, revealing the truth that the Divine permeates both the temporal and the eternal.

If we now consider the trine houses from the 7th to the 11th house from Ketu, we have the combination of **Venus + Jupiter + Ketu**. The higher knowledge and devotional arts (Venus), philosophy (Jupiter) and spirituality (Ketu) significators influenced

Case Study 4: A Renowned Holy Saint 131

this disruptive mind (signified by the Moon) that is briming with revolutionary ideas (signified by Rahu) on religion and spirituality. This combination represents the perfect synthesis of love, wisdom, and renunciation — the triadic essence of spiritual liberation. Venus bestows devotion and aesthetic sensitivity, Jupiter grants divine knowledge and *dharma*, and Ketu dissolves ego-bound identity into transcendence. In the native's life, this configuration manifests as the merging of *bhakti* (devotion) and *jnana* (wisdom) into a universal vision of oneness. His compassion flowed through Venus, his divine insight through Jupiter, and his detachment through Ketu — creating a consciousness that embraced the world while transcending it. This union turned his spiritual realization into service, teaching that liberation arises not from withdrawal but from seeing the Divine pervading all creation — *Ik Onkar*, the One Reality beyond all distinctions. If we analyze using the dispositor of the 11th house from Ketu we get a similar outcome in analysis.

Decision Making Factor #4

For the native in Case Study 4, we have Moon as the dispositor of Ketu and is located in an *artha rashi* as part of the combination **Moon + Rahu**. This planetary pattern shows a mind unsettled by intensity. The Moon, when entangled with Rahu, inclines toward obsession, disorientation, and restless illusion. This combination symbolizes the transformation of worldly consciousness into spiritual awareness through emotional and *karmic* intensity. The Moon represents mind and empathy, while Rahu amplifies perception and challenges conventional boundaries. Inner calm is difficult to secure because Rahu drags the lunar nature into realms of the unusual, the foreign, and the socially disruptive. Yet, this very disturbance often becomes the seedbed for innovation: when rightly guided, such a mind can pioneer radical change. For the native, this combination mirrors his compassionate engagement with the material world, transforming emotion into universal love. His realization emerged not by rejecting life, but by sanctifying it, finding the Divine within human existence itself.

Now, consider the trinal influence — from the 7th to the dispositor of Ketu where **Venus + Jupiter + Ketu** converge. Here we find the *karakas* of higher learning and devotional arts (Venus), philosophy and wisdom (Jupiter), and renunciation and spiritual insight (Ketu). These forces impress themselves upon the restless Moon-Rahu axis. The trinal harmony in this combination creates a triad of spiritual perfection — love, knowledge, and renunciation balanced in divine proportion. For the native, this alignment mirrors the soul's journey from desire to transcendence. His devotion was radiant but free of attachment; his wisdom vast yet rooted in compassion. Ketu's presence dissolved ego, while Venus and Jupiter infused divine beauty and moral order. This configuration expresses the essence of his realization — that true liberation arises when love and knowledge merge in self-surrender. Through this synthesis, the native embodied the *Upanishadic* truth: *"Brahmavid apnoti param"* — the knower of Brahman becomes one with the Supreme. The result is a native whose emotionally turbulent, Rahu-

Case Study 4: A Renowned Holy Saint

fueled imagination is filled with unconventional and revolutionary visions about religion and spirituality. In other words, the turbulence of the Moon-Rahu conjunction, when influenced by Venus-Jupiter-Ketu, redirects its disruptive potential into spiritual philosophy, creative devotion, and reformist ideas.

Summary: Does the placement of Ketu give a strong spiritual outlook to the native? The answer is a 'yes' from each of the four Decision Making Factors (DMFs). Does Rahu play a positive role in the native experiencing spiritual ethos? The answer is a 'yes' from DMFs 1,2, and 4 which form 75% of the DMFs. The results sync with the *Parashari* analysis. Note, that we did not delve into the positivity or negativity with which Rahu influences spiritual ethos. That is not the focus of the research.

4.3.2 Method 2 (BNN with *Nakshatra*)

Since our analysis base is BNN astrology, like in Method 1 we will work with the same DMFs, and be light on the BNN part of the analysis (detailed in Method 1). It is sufficient to see using *nakshatras* **whether and to what extent Rahu influences Ketu to support the native realizing spiritual ethos.** When it comes to doing an analysis using *nakshatra* principles using KP astrology, three KP parameters are relevant for study for each decision making factor: (i) a planet's ***nakshatra* sub-lord**, (ii) the **sub-lord's *nakshatra* lord:** the planet ruling the *nakshatra* in which the sub-lord is situated, and the (iii) the **sub-lord's sign lord:** the planet ruling the sign in which the sub-lord is situated. Each *nakshatra* span of 13d20′

Planet	R/C	Sign	Degree	Speed	Nakshatra	Pada	RL	NL	SL	SS	Status	SB
Lagna		Cap	04:38:22		Uttarashadha	3	Sa	Su	Sa	Ra		
Sun		Ari	08:17:04	00:58:27	Ashwini	3	Ma	Ke	Ju	Me	Exalt.	1.35
Moon		Cap	19:01:58	12:04:57	Shravana	3	Sa	Mo	Me	Ra	Frnd.	1.35
Mars		Aqu	05:26:30	00:44:40	Dhanishta	4	Sa	Ma	Su	Ke	Frnd.	1.64
Mercury	C	Ari	17:35:02	02:04:13	Bharani	2	Ma	Ve	Ma	Ju	Frnd.	1.09
Jupiter		Can	07:52:24	00:04:41	Pushya	2	Mo	Sa	Ke	Ju	Exalt.	0.82
Venus		Pis	03:35:12	01:11:43	Uttarabhadra	1	Ju	Sa	Sa	Sa	Exalt.	1.41
Saturn	C	Ari	15:00:24	00:07:42	Bharani	1	Ma	Ve	Ve	Sa	Debil.	1.24
Rahu		Cap	23:41:45	00:00:13	Dhanishta	1	Sa	Ma	Ma	Sa	Neutr.	
Ketu		Can	23:41:45	00:00:13	Ashlesha	3	Mo	Me	Ma	Sa	Neutr.	

Case Study 4: A Renowned Holy Saint 135

is unequally divided into degree space owned by 9 sub-lords proportional to *Vimshottari dasha* duration.

Decision Making Factor #1

For the native in Case Study 4, we have **Venus + Jupiter + Ketu** (ordered in ascending order of degree) in trines in *moksha rashis*. Venus is in the *nakshatra* of Saturn and in the *pada* of Saturn. Rahu acts like Saturn. Jupiter (12th lord) is in the *nakshatra* of Saturn and in the *pada* of Ketu. Ketu is in the *nakshatra* of Mercury and in the *pada* of Mars – a *moksha rashi* lord. As per KP principles, Venus is in the *nakshatra* of Saturn and has sub-lord Saturn. Saturn's *nakshatra* lord is Venus and it is in the sign of Mars. Rahu acts like Saturn. Jupiter (12th lord) is in the *nakshatra* of Saturn and has sub-lord of Ketu (dispositor of Ketu is with Rahu). Ketu is in the *nakshatra* of Mercury (conjunct Saturn that Rahu imitates) and in the sign of Moon (conjunct Rahu). Ketu is in the *nakshatra* of Mercury and has sub-lord Mars – a *moksha rashi* lord. Mars is in the *nakshatra* of Mars and in the sign of Saturn.

As part of the 7th house from Ketu analysis, we have **Moon + Rahu** (trines with each other from the 7th house from Ketu in ascending order of degree) in *artha rashis*. Moon is in the *nakshatra* of Moon in the *pada* of Mercury. Rahu is in the *nakshatra* of Mars (a *moksha rashi* lord) and in the *pada* of Mars.

As per KP principles, Moon is in the *nakshatra* of Moon (conjunct Rahu) and has a sub-lord of Mercury (conjunct Saturn that Rahu imitates). Mercury is in the *nakshatra* of Venus (that is placed in a *moksha rashi*) and is in the sign of Mars. Rahu is in the *nakshatra* of

Mars (a *moksha rashi* lord) and has a sub-lord of Mars. Mars is in the *nakshatra* of Mars and is in the sign of Saturn.

If we now look at the trine houses from the 2nd house from Ketu, we get **Sun + Saturn + Mercury** in a trine and then **Mars** as the only planet in the trine from the 7th house from the 2nd house from Ketu. Sun is in the *nakshatra* of Ketu and in the *pada* of Jupiter (12th lord). Saturn is in the *nakshatra* of Venus and in the *pada* of Venus. Mercury is in the *nakshatra* of Venus and in the *pada* of Mars – a *moksha rashi* lord. Mars is in the *nakshatra* of Mars and in the *pada* of Sun. As per KP, Sun is in the *nakshatra* of Ketu (having dispositor Rahu) and has sub-lord of Jupiter (12th lord). Jupiter is in the *nakshatra* of Saturn and is in the sign of Moon (conjunct Rahu). Saturn is in the *nakshatra* of Venus and has sub-lord of Venus. Venus is in the *nakshatra* of Saturn and is in the sign of Jupiter (12th lord). Mercury is in the *nakshatra* of Venus and has sub-lord of Mars – a *moksha rashi* lord. Mars is in the *nakshatra* of Mars, has a sub-lord of Sun (conjunct Rahu's dispositor), and in the sign of Saturn. Sun is in the *nakshatra* of Ketu and is in the house of Mars.

Hence, the native has a strong spiritual ethos and Rahu contributes to it.

Decision Making Factor #2

For the native in Case Study 4, we have Mercury as the lord of the 12th house from **Ketu**. Since Ketu is the significator of spirituality in BNN astrology one must check for the 12th from Ketu (12th house is the house of *moksha/dissolution* from any signification). We have

Case Study 4: A Renowned Holy Saint 137

only **Mars** standing on the trines from the 12th house from Ketu in a *kaam rashi*. Mars is in the *nakshatra* of Mars and in the *pada* of Sun. As per KP, Mars, has a sub-lord of Sun (conjunct Rahu's dispositor), and in the sign of Saturn. Sun is in the *nakshatra* of Ketu and is in the house of Mars.

The trine from the 7th from the 12th house of Ketu has **Sun + Saturn + Mercury** (in ascending order of degree). Sun is in the *nakshatra* of Ketu (whose dispositor is Rahu) and in the *pada* of Jupiter (12th lord). Saturn is in the *nakshatra* of Venus and in the *pada* of Venus. Mercury is in the *nakshatra* of Venus and in the *pada* of Mars — a *moksha rashi* lord. As per KP, Sun is in the *nakshatra* of Ketu (having dispositor Rahu) and has sub-lord of Jupiter (12th lord). Jupiter is in the *nakshatra* of Saturn and is in the sign of Moon (conjunct Rahu). Saturn is in the *nakshatra* of Venus and has sub-lord of Venus. Venus is in the *nakshatra* of Saturn and is in the sign of Jupiter (12th lord). Mercury is in the *nakshatra* of Venus and has sub-lord of Mars – a *moksha rashi* lord. Mars is in the *nakshatra* of Mars, has a sub-lord of Sun (conjunct Rahu's dispositor), and in the sign of Saturn. Sun is in the *nakshatra* of Ketu and is in the house of Mars.

Now if we consider the dispositor of the 12th house from Ketu we have **Sun + Saturn + Mercury** and this is influenced by **Mars** from the trine houses from the 7th house from Mercury.

Rahu has not much role to play based on sign placement and *nakshatra* analysis – though a high spiritual ethos of the native is established.

Decision Making Factor #3

For the native in Case Study 4, we have Venus as the lord of the 11th house from **Ketu**. Since Ketu is the significator of spirituality in BNN astrology one must check for the 11th from Ketu (11th house analysis checks for catalytic factors contributing to a significator – in our case Ketu of spirituality).

We have **Moon + Rahu** (in ascending order of degree). Moon is in the *nakshatra* of Moon in the *pada* of Mercury. Rahu is in the *nakshatra* of Mars (a *moksha rashi* lord) and in the *pada* of Mars. As per KP principles, Mercury is in the *nakshatra* of Venus (that is placed in a *moksha rashi*) and is in the sign of Mars. Rahu is in the *nakshatra* of Mars (a *moksha rashi* lord) and has a sub-lord of Mars. Mars is in the *nakshatra* of Mars and is in the sign of Saturn.

If we now consider the trine houses from the 7th to the 11th house from Ketu, we have the combination of **Venus + Jupiter + Ketu**. Venus is in the *nakshatra* of Saturn and in the *pada* of Saturn. Rahu acts like Saturn. Jupiter (12th lord) is in the *nakshatra* of Saturn and in the *pada* of Ketu. Ketu is in the *nakshatra* of Mercury and in the *pada* of Mars — a *moksha rashi* lord. The higher knowledge and devotional arts (Venus), philosophy (Jupiter) and spirituality (Ketu) significators influenced this disruptive mind (signified by the Moon) that is briming with revolutionary ideas (signified by Rahu) on religion and spirituality. As per KP, Venus is in the *nakshatra* of Saturn and has sub-lord Saturn. Saturn's *nakshatra* lord is Venus and it is in the sign of Mars. Rahu acts like Saturn. Jupiter (12th lord) is in the *nakshatra* of Saturn and has sub-lord of Ketu (dispositor of Ketu is with Rahu). Ketu is in the *nakshatra* of Mercury (conjunct Saturn that Rahu imitates) and in the sign of Moon (conjunct Rahu). Ketu is in the *nakshatra* of Mercury and has sub-lord Mars – a *moksha rashi* lord. Mars is in the *nakshatra* of Mars and in the sign of Saturn. The higher knowledge and devotional arts (Venus), philosophy (Jupiter) and spirituality (Ketu) significators influenced this disruptive mind (signified by the Moon) that is briming with revolutionary ideas (signified by Rahu) on religion and spirituality. If we analyze using the dispositor of the 11th house from Ketu we get a similar outcome. If we analyze using the dispositor of the 11th house from Ketu we get a similar outcome.

Decision Making Factor #4

For the native in Case Study 4, we have Moon as the dispositor of Ketu and is located in a *artha rashi* as part of the combination **Moon + Rahu**. This planetary pattern shows a mind unsettled by intensity. The Moon, when entangled with Rahu, inclines toward obsession, disorientation, and restless illusion. Inner calm is difficult to secure because Rahu drags the lunar nature into realms of the unusual, the foreign, and the socially disruptive. Yet, this very disturbance often becomes the seedbed for innovation: when rightly guided, such a mind can pioneer radical change). Moon is in the *nakshatra* of Moon in the *pada* of Mercury. Rahu is in the *nakshatra* of Mars (a *moksha rashi* lord) and in the *pada* of Mars. As per KP, Moon is in the *nakshatra* of Moon (conjunct Rahu) and has a sub-lord of Mercury (conjunct Saturn that Rahu imitates). Mercury is in the *nakshatra* of Venus (that is placed in a *moksha rashi*) and is in the sign of Mars. Rahu is in the *nakshatra* of Mars (a *moksha rashi* lord) and has a sub-lord of Mars. Mars is in the *nakshatra* of Mars and is in the sign of Saturn.

Now, consider the trinal influence — from the 7th to the dispositor of Ketu where **Venus + Jupiter + Ketu** converge. Venus is in the *nakshatra* of Saturn and in the *pada* of Saturn. Rahu acts like Saturn. Jupiter (12th lord) is in the *nakshatra* of Saturn and in the *pada* of Ketu. Ketu is in the *nakshatra* of Mercury and in the *pada* of Mars — a *moksha rashi* lord. Here we find the *karakas* of higher learning and devotional arts (Venus), philosophy and wisdom (Jupiter), and renunciation and spiritual insight (Ketu). These forces impress themselves upon the restless Moon-Rahu axis. The result is a native whose emotionally turbulent, Rahu-fueled imagination is filled with unconventional and revolutionary visions about religion and spirituality. As per KP principles, Venus is in the *nakshatra* of Saturn and has sub-lord Saturn. Saturn's *nakshatra* lord is Venus and it is in the sign of Mars. Rahu acts like Saturn. Jupiter (12th lord) is in the *nakshatra* of Saturn and has sub-lord of Ketu (dispositor of Ketu is with Rahu). Ketu is in the *nakshatra* of Mercury (conjunct Saturn that Rahu imitates) and in the sign of Moon (conjunct Rahu). Ketu is in the *nakshatra* of Mercury and has sub-lord Mars — a *moksha rashi* lord. Mars is in the *nakshatra* of Mars and in the sign of Saturn.

Summary: Does the placement of Ketu give a strong spiritual outlook to the native? The answer is a 'yes' from each of the four decision making factors (DMFs). Does Rahu play a positive role in the native experiencing spiritual ethos? The answer is a 'yes' from DMFs 1,2, and 4 which form 75% of the DMFs. The results sync with the *Parashari* analysis. Note, that we did not delve into the positivity or negativity with which Rahu influences spiritual ethos. That is not the focus of the research.

4.3.3 Method 3 (BNN with *Karmic* Angles)

We wish to analyze in **three parts** using the *karmic Nadi jyotish* principles the strength of Rahu in influencing each of the mind, body, and soul to realize a spiritual ethos. After all, these are the basic pillars that eventually decide whether a native will be able to realize spiritual ethos in the lifetime. **If the connection is strong in at least two out of the three cases, we can say that Rahu has been significantly instrumental in promoting spirituality within the native.** Unlike in *Parashari jyotish*, there is no need to do a dynamic analysis (e.g., via progressions and transits) of Rahu to establish its quantum of influence on native spiritual ethos. This is because the static *Nadi* analysis is sufficiently causal to judge the quantum of Rahu's effects.

***Dridh-Adridh Karma* Axes:** In *Nadi jyotish*, directions embody the metaphysics of *karma* itself. **East and West** anchor *dridh karma* — duties to father, guru, and ancestors that bind the soul to its inescapable obligations. **East**, aligned with Sun and Jupiter, signifies *dharma*, authority, and righteous beginnings; **West** blends closure and entanglement, largely fixed through Saturn's weight, though softened by Venus's negotiable pleasures. **North and South** anchor *adridh karma* - mutable desires and worldly pursuits shaped by free will. **North**, guided by Mercury and Rahu, points to growth, commerce, and ambition; while **South**, linked with Mars, Ketu, and Moon, carries ancestral debts, *tapas*, and *karmic* reckonings. In summary, East pulls a native towards *dharmic* duty, West toward worldly entanglement, North toward ambition, and South toward purification.

Thus, the four directions mark not mere space but the soul's *karmic* geography: some pathways immovable, others pliable. The horoscope becomes a compass of necessity and possibility, mapping destiny's fixity against the field of conscious striving. One may ask: why not diagonal directions? In *Nadi jyotish*, only the **four cardinal directions** — East, West, North, and South—are used, not the intermediates like Northeast or Northwest. This is because Vedic cosmology is fundamentally **fourfold**, based on sunrise and sunset, solstices and equinoxes, day and night. Each direction is tied to specific *grahas* and *karmic* qualities: East (Sun, Jupiter), West (Saturn, Venus), North (Mercury, Rahu), South (Moon, Mars, Ketu). This framework mirrors the *dik-palas* (directional guardians) of Vedic ritual, which are cardinal. By limiting to four, *Nadi* emphasizes clarity: destiny is seen through primal axes of *dharma*, desire, past, and closure, without diluting meaning in diagonals.

We provide the planetary directional compass diagram for Case Study 4.

Case Study 4: A Renowned Holy Saint

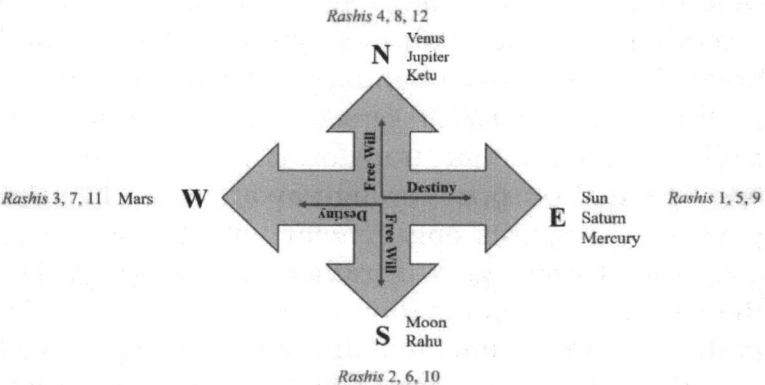

Part 1

We first analyze the planet **Moon – the significator of the mind**, to judge whether (a) the mind is inherently spiritual and (b) and how Rahu plays a role in driving the mind towards spirituality.

We observe that Moon occupies the southern direction (a fiery sign) of the *Kaalpurusha* chart. If we arrange the planets in the **southern direction,** in ascending order of degree, we have **Moon, Rahu** placed in an *artha rashi*. We will leave it till a bit later to analyze what this means for the native. According to *Nadi* directionality principles Moon here is influenced by Rahu in full (100%) because these planets are in trine with one another. The northern and southern directions are that of free will (*adridh karma*) and the native is in 'certain sense' free to do *karma* on significations in these directions towards evolution.

In *Nadi* astrology, Moon and Rahu placed together in an *artha rashi* in ascending order of degree reveal a complex yet fertile ground for spiritual evolution. The

Moon governs the mind, sensitivity, and emotional receptivity, while Rahu magnifies desires and breaks conventional boundaries. Their conjunction in the realm of *adridh karma*—free will—indicates a consciousness that transforms material pursuit into spiritual purpose through awareness. The *artha* placement suggests engagement with the world as a means of inner growth rather than bondage. For the native, this combination mirrors his experiential path: a mind illuminated through worldly contact yet detached in essence. Rahu's expansive nature universalized his compassion beyond sectarian lines, while the Moon's empathy infused it with tenderness. His realization that *Ik Onkar*—the One Divine—pervades all arose from this dynamic interplay between longing and illumination, showing how even desire, when spiritualized, becomes a path to liberation.

If we arrange the planets in the **northern direction,** in ascending order of degree, we have **Venus, Jupiter, Ketu** placed in a *moksha rashi*. According to *Nadi* directionality principles Moon here is influenced by these planets in nearly full (75%) because these planets are in trine with one another from the 7th house of Moon. The higher knowledge and devotional arts (Venus), philosophy (Jupiter) and spirituality (Ketu) significators influence the mind (signified by the Moon) and that further influences Rahu to project revolutionary ideas on religion and spirituality. The combination alternatively represents a native evolving through conscious choice rather than fixed destiny. Venus brings the sweetness of *bhakti* (devotion), Jupiter radiates *jnana* (divine wisdom), and Ketu dissolves worldly attachment—together refining the mind toward transcendence. Their northern placement shows spiritual freedom unfolding through experience and insight. Hence, Rahu is the product of this influence from Moon, Venus, Jupiter, and Ketu rather than the generator of spiritual essence of the mind. The native did free-willed *karma* on the significators of Venus, Jupiter, Ketu that influenced the mind on spirituality. For the native, this configuration signifies the awakening of a liberated consciousness that embraced love, reason, and renunciation in harmony. His teachings of *Ik Onkar* reflected Jupiter's truth, Venus's compassion, and Ketu's detachment—melding intellect and devotion into universal spirituality. The *adridh karmic* aspect denotes his role as a conscious instrument of the Divine, choosing awareness over inheritance. Thus, the mind became both the seeker and the vessel of realization—reflecting the native's journey from human empathy to divine union, transforming free will into enlightened grace.

If we arrange the planets in the **western direction,** in ascending order of degree, we have **Mars** placed in a *kaam rashi*. According to *Nadi* directionality principles Moon (and Rahu) here is influenced by Mars (significator of body and ego) with medium influence (50%) because it is in trine with the latter from the 2nd house from Moon. The western and eastern directions are that of destiny (*dridh karma*) and the native is in 'certain sense' destined to do *karma* on significations in these directions towards (spiritual) evolution.

In *Nadi* astrology, the Moon–Rahu conjunction in an *artha rashi* and Mars in the western (*dridh karma*) direction symbolize the integration of material action and spiritual awakening through destiny. The Moon and Rahu together heighten emotional depth and visionary perception, while Mars channels this intensity into purposeful energy. This reflects the native's *karmic* design — a soul destined to act in the world while transcending it. His spiritual awakening emerged through engagement, not withdrawal; his teachings transformed desire (*artha*) and will (*kriya*) into instruments of divine service, expressing enlightenment through compassionate action.

If we arrange the planets in the **eastern direction,** in ascending order of degree, we have **Sun, Saturn, Mercury** placed in a *dharma rashi*. According to *Nadi* directionality principles Moon (and Rahu) here is influenced by these planets with small influence (25%) because they are in trine from the 12th house from Moon. In *Nadi* astrology, Moon–Rahu in an *artha rashi* with Sun, Saturn, and Mercury aligned in a *dharma rashi* in the eastern (*dridh karma*) direction signifies a predestined evolution of the mind from worldly awareness to divine illumination. Moon–Rahu intensifies emotional perception and intellectual restlessness, pushing the native to question social and spiritual norms. The eastern trine—Sun, Saturn, Mercury—grounds this turbulence into disciplined understanding: Sun brings illumination, Saturn instills endurance, and Mercury refines expression. For the native, this pattern mirrors a soul fated to merge reason with revelation. His *dridh karma* lay in

Case Study 4: A Renowned Holy Saint 147

transforming inquiry into divine communication—turning emotional intensity into spiritual poetry, and intellect into compassionate wisdom. Through discipline and insight, his mind transcended illusion to experience unity with *Ik Onkar*—the eternal One—revealing how divine destiny manifests through inner balance between light, restraint, and thought.

So, **in summary**: is the mind spiritual? The answer is a resounding 'yes'. Does Rahu play a role in driving the mind towards spirituality? The answer is a 'no'. Rather, it is the product of a spiritual mind manifested into revolutionary religious and spiritual thinking.

Part 2

We now analyze the planet **Sun — the significator of the soul**, to judge whether (a) the soul is projecting spiritual and (b) and how Rahu plays a role in driving the soul towards spirituality.

If we arrange the planets in the **eastern direction**, in ascending order of degree, we have **Sun + Saturn + Mercury** placed in a *dharma rashi*. Mars influences Sun from the **western direction** with 75% power as it is trine with the 7th house from Sun. In *Nadi* astrology, the combination of Sun, Saturn, and Mercury in a *dharma rashi* in the eastern (*dridh karma*) direction, influenced by Mars from the west, represents a soul forged through divine discipline and purposeful action. The Sun illuminates higher truth, Saturn anchors it through restraint and humility, while Mercury refines it into clear understanding and expression. Mars from the west adds dynamic will and courage, transforming knowledge into living practice. This synergy signifies a *dridh karmic* destiny of enlightened service — the soul's evolution through work guided by wisdom. In the native's life, this alignment manifests as spiritual illumination grounded in disciplined compassion. His radiant insight (Sun), patience and equality (Saturn), and eloquent teaching (Mercury) found expression through active compassion and fearless reform (Mars). Thus, his soul's journey exemplified the union of light and labor — embodying *dharma* through selfless action rooted in divine awareness.

If we arrange the planets in the **southern direction**, in ascending order of degree, we have **Moon, Rahu** placed in an *artha rashi*, and influencing Sun with 50% power as they are placed in trines from the 2nd house from Sun. The dispositor of Rahu is with Sun.

In *Nadi* astrology, when Moon and Rahu occupy an *artha rashi* in the southern (*adridh karma*) direction and influence the Sun by trinal aspect from the 2nd house, it reflects a soul engaged in transforming worldly awareness into spiritual illumination through experience and free will. The Moon represents emotional receptivity, Rahu intensifies perception beyond boundaries, and their influence on the Sun—significator of the soul—creates inner conflict that ultimately leads to awakening. The dispositor of Rahu being conjoined with the Sun binds material experience to spiritual purpose. For the native, this signifies a *karmic* journey of conscious transcendence: his worldly sensitivity and compassion (Moon), universal outlook breaking dogma (Rahu), and divine realization (Sun) coalesced into enlightenment achieved through life, not renunciation. His *adridh*

Case Study 4: A Renowned Holy Saint

karmic path demonstrated how illusion, when integrated with awareness, becomes a mirror for truth—the soul awakening through engagement with creation rather than retreat from it.

If we arrange the planets in the **northern direction**, in ascending order of degree, we have **Venus, Jupiter, Ketu** placed in a *moksha rashi*. According to *Nadi* directionality principles Sun here is influenced by these planets via a small degree (25%) because these planets are in trine with one another from the 12th house of Sun. The dispositor of the 12th from house from the spiritual significator Ketu is placed in a *dharma rashi* with Sun, whereas the promoter of spirituality is the dispositor of the 11th house from Ketu which is Venus. In *Nadi* astrology Venus, Jupiter, and Ketu positioned in the northern (*adridh karma*) direction in *moksha rashis*, forming mutual trines from the 12th house of the Sun, signify a soul that consciously directs its free will toward divine realization. Ketu, the significator of liberation, receives spiritual reinforcement from Venus—the promoter of devotion—and Jupiter, the beacon of divine wisdom. The Sun, with its dispositor in a *dharma rashi*, illuminates this alignment with righteous purpose and inner clarity. This constellation reflects the native's soul journey—his enlightenment emerging not from fate-bound renunciation but from awakened will. His *adridh karmic* evolution united love (Venus), wisdom (Jupiter), and detachment (Ketu) into radiant harmony. The dispositor's *dharmic* strength ensured his spiritual illumination manifested through compassionate action, while Venus's devotional impulse spiritualized worldly engagement. Thus, his soul realized liberation through conscious synthesis where devotion, wisdom, and renunciation became the instruments of divine union and service to humanity.

So, **in summary**: is the soul projecting a spiritual essence? The answer is a resounding 'yes'. Does Rahu play a role in driving the mind towards spirituality? The answer is considerably non-significant 'yes'.

Part 3

We now analyze the planet **Mars — the significator of the body and ego,** to judge whether (a) the body is projecting spiritual and (b) and how Rahu plays a role in driving the body towards projecting spirituality.

We observe that Mars occupies the **western direction** and is not influenced by any planet in trines to its placement. In *Nadi* astrology, Mars positioned alone in the western (*dridh karma*) direction in a *kaam rashi* symbolizes the destiny-bound transformation of physical energy into disciplined spiritual action. Mars governs vitality, courage, and assertion; when unafflicted by trinal influences, its focus turns inward, refining passion into purposeful restraint. This placement marks a *karmically* fixed path of channeling desire toward divine service. In the native's life, it reflects his fearless activism - transmuting physical vigor into spiritual leadership, expressing divine truth through action rather than ascetic withdrawal.

If we arrange the planets in the **eastern direction,** in ascending order of degree, in ascending order of degree, we have **Sun, Saturn, Mercury** placed in a *dharma rashi*, and influence Mars with a 75% power

Case Study 4: A Renowned Holy Saint 151

as they are placed in trines from the 7th house from Mars. The body has a significant influence of non-excessiveness that is one of the primary requirements towards spirituality. The dispositor of Mars is also in a *dharma rashi* and is the significator of *karma* and non-excessiveness and conjunct with Sun – the significator of the soul, and Mercury – the significator of intelligence and communication. The combination of Sun, Saturn, and Mercury placed in a *dharma rashi* in the eastern (*dridh karma*) direction and forming trines to Mars indicate a predestined synthesis of disciplined intellect, spiritual illumination, and purposeful action. The Sun represents vitality and divine will, Saturn lends endurance and humility, while Mercury refines understanding and communication. Their trinal influence on Mars transforms raw physical energy into sacred service. For the native, this configuration reflects a body governed by divine discipline - his strength channeled toward spiritual work. The native's *dridh karma* ensured that his actions expressed higher truth; physical vigor and intellect united in compassionate reform, turning bodily dynamism into an instrument of divine purpose. It is evident that the body embodies intelligence, soulfulness, and *karma* is *dharma* philosophy. This gift is destined for the native.

The dispositor of Rahu is also the dispositor of Mars, hence the body is non-significantly influenced by Rahu on the significations of Saturn. The dispositor of the 12th house from Ketu is Mercury and so even here Rahu non-significantly influences the body on spiritual projections as Saturn (Rahu's dispositor) is in trine with Mercury (Ketu's dispositor).

If we arrange the planets in the **northern direction**, in ascending order of degree, we have **Venus, Jupiter, Ketu** placed in a *moksha rashi*. According to *Nadi* directionality principles Mars here is influenced by these planets via almost half power (50%) because these planets are in trine with one another from the 2nd house of Mars. Hence the body and ego are blessed to project higher qualities of learning and philosophy with a considerable amount of spirituality. Venus, Jupiter, and Ketu aligned in *moksha rashis* in the northern (*adridh karma*) direction and influencing Mars by half strength signify a body that serves as a conscious vessel for spiritual realization through free will. Venus refines desire into devotion, Jupiter imparts divine wisdom, and Ketu dissolves attachment — their combined trinal influence subdues Mars' raw physicality into disciplined spiritual action. This *adridh karmic* alignment suggests spiritual mastery achieved through mindful engagement rather than ascetic denial. In the native's life, this reflects a body energized by compassion and purpose — strength harmonized by love and awareness. His dynamic service embodied the union of physical vitality and divine consciousness, where action even became an instrument of liberation. The dispositor of the 11th from house from the spiritual significator Ketu is placed in a *moksha rashi* and trine with Jupiter and Ketu. Hence, the body is indeed projecting a significant degree of spirituality through free-willed *karma*.

If we arrange the planets in the **southern direction**, in ascending order of degree, we have **Moon, Rahu** and Rahu here does not significantly influence the body/ego (only 25%) – except for the dispositor of

Rahu being Saturn that has some influence on Mars as the dispositor of Mars is Saturn, and he is conjunct with the dispositor of the 12th house from Ketu – the significator of spirituality.

So, **in summary**: is the body projecting a spiritual essence? The answer is a resounding 'yes'. Does Rahu play a role in driving the mind towards spirituality? The answer is a considerably non-significant 'yes'.

Overall Inference from Parts 1 to 3: Rahu considerably influences spiritual essence through the soul and body, though it does not significantly influence the mind in projecting spirituality. It is simply the aftereffects of the mind attaining spiritual ethos. The results sync with the *Parashari* angle of analysis that Rahu does not generate spiritual realization in the native but plays the role of a major catalyst in helping the native realize spirituality.

Case Study 5
A Renowned Corporate Executive

Section 5.1:
A Narrative of Spiritual Philosophy

The native's spiritual arc reads like a *Vedic* parable about rise, rupture, and re-anchoring in *dharma*. Trained in the hard realism of management, he later met the soft absolutes of *karma*. After a celebrated tenure at McKinsey, his 2012 conviction for insider trading forced a reckoning; even the sentencing judge, Jed Rakoff, called the breach *"a terrible breach of trust,"* yet noted the native's *"extraordinary devotion...to people in need,"* a duality that frames his moral journey. In his memoir he reaches for equanimity: *"The great sages of my Indian heritage had cultivated equanimity and detachment... I strove to emulate them,"* signalling a pivot from success metrics to spiritual measures.

Philosophically, the arc maps onto the *Upanishadic* surgery of the self: *bhidyate hṛdaya-granthih* — *"the knot of the heart is cut; doubts are destroyed; karma is exhausted—when the Highest is seen"* (Mundaka 3.2.9). Encounter with shame and loss can function as such a cutting, if one chooses *sreyas* (the good) over *preyas* (the merely pleasant). The *Gita* prescribes the operative therapy: *"Act without attachment"* (3.19) and *"Evenness of mind is yoga"* (2.48). The native's

Case Study 5: A Renowned Corporate Executive

own reflections explicitly invoke *karma-yoga*—selfless action without clinging to outcomes—suggesting a turn from possession to service.

The world did not reduce him to a single failure. Kofi Annan urged that the court *"recognise him for the good he has done...to improve the lives of millions,"* a reminder that human character contains both light and shadow, and that redemption is a public, not just private, labour. McKinsey's Dominic Barton later said the episode forced the firm to *"keep its focus firmly on values,"* indicating a communal purification in the wake of a leader's fall.

What is the spiritual essence of this trajectory? First, *karma* is pedagogical: failure, properly read, becomes instruction. Second, leadership unmoored from inner truth is brittle—a point echoed by leadership scholar Bill George's warning that high achievers can *"lose their way"* when success outruns self-awareness. Third, authenticity after rupture requires *tapas*: disciplined action aligned with *dharma* rather than image.

A just synthesis, then, is not hagiography but *Vedanta* in motion: the self learns through consequence, steadies through equanimity, and serves through detachment. If early life optimized for achievement, the later movement appears to optimize for meaning. In *Vedic* terms, the corrective is clear: *"Uttisthata, jagrata"*—Arise, awake—not to reclaim status, but to refine the self until action itself becomes a form of worship. And should one ask whether grace attends such striving, the *Gita* answers simply: *"To the devoted, I carry what they lack and preserve what they have."* (9.22).

Rahu and Spirituality

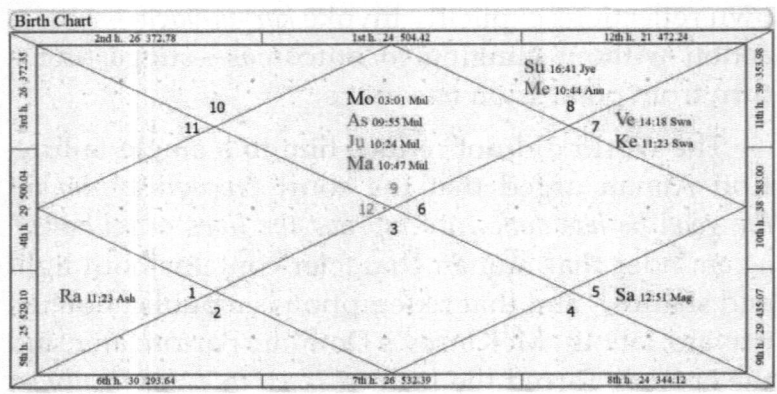

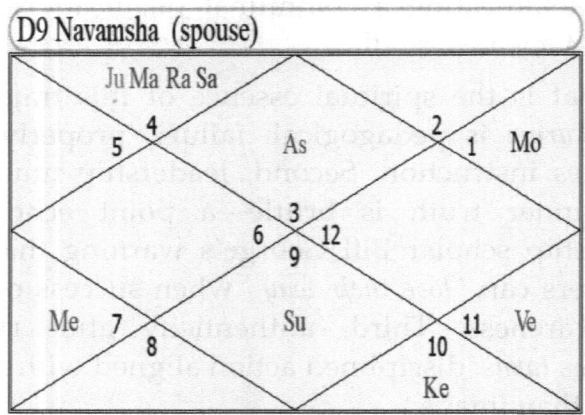

Birth Chart					
As	09:55:20		Moola	Bha	3,Ke/Sa/Me
Su	16:41:03		Jyeshtha	Noh	1,Me/Me/Me
Mo	03:01:24		Moola	Yay	1,Ke/Su/Su
Ma	10:47:54		Moola	Bhe	4,Ke/Sa/Ma
Me	10:44:04	c	Anuradha	Noo	3,Sa/Su/Sa
Ju	10:24:58		Moola	Bhe	4,Ke/Sa/Ve
Ve	14:18:33		Swati	Roh	3,Ra/Me/Sa
Sa	12:51:33		Magha	May	4,Ke/Me/Ju
Ra	11:23:33		Ashwini	Lah	4,Ke/Sa/Ju
Ke	11:23:33		Swati	Ray	2,Ra/Sa/Ve

DOB - 2nd December, 1948, Time - 7:48 AM, Kolkata, India

Case Study 5: A Renowned Corporate Executive

उद्धरेदात्मनात्मानं नात्मानमवसादयेत्।
आत्मैव ह्यात्मनो बन्धुरात्मैव रिपुरात्मनः॥

Let a man lift himself by his own Self; let him not degrade himself. The Self alone is the friend of the Self, and the Self alone is the enemy of the Self. Bhagavad Gita (6.5)

Section 5.2:
A *Parashari* — *Nakshatra* Analysis

We first study the basic potential of the native to inculcate spiritual ethos through a body, mind, soul study of how the trio provides the basic strength needed to develop a spiritual ethos.

5.2.1 Examining the Mind-Body-Soul Synchrony

We first study the basic potential of the native to inculcate spiritual ethos through a body, mind, soul study of how the trio provides the basic strength needed to develop a spiritual ethos.

The lord of the Lagna (significator of body) Jupiter is placed in the Lagna itself in a *dharma rashi* forming *Hamsa yoga*. The Lagna and Lagna Lord are in *Mula nakshatra* which is the *nakshatra* of rootedness and spiritual transformation and ruled by Ketu (a significator of spirituality). The Lagna lord is conjunct with the 8th Lord, Moon (significator of mind) and 5th and 12th Lord, Mars. So, the Lagan is heavily packed with Lagna Lord, 8th Lord, 5th and 12th Lord, all placed in *Mula nakshatra* in *dharma rashi* at very close conjunct degrees. Further Sun (the 9th lord, significator of soul) is placed in the 12th house of spirituality in a *moksha rashi* in Mercury ruled *Jyeshtha nakshatra*. Mars is the Sun's dispositor and conjunct with the Lagna lord and Moon.

In addition, the *Manasa nakshatra* (24th *nakshatra* from *Janam nakshatra* in the 27 *nakshatra* scheme) that signifies the nature of thoughts in the mind, is *Swati nakshatra (nakshatra of independence and freedom)* and lorded by Rahu. Rahu is placed in the 5th house, amplifying a creative mindset and 5th house related attributes. Rahu's (*Manasa nakshatra lord*) dispositor is Mars and Mars is placed in Lagna along with the Moon, the Lagna Lord and Sun's dispositor is the apotheosis for gaining an extremely spiritual mindset due to the mind, body and soul being at the pinnacle of synchronization in *dharma rashi*. Based on D1, it can be inferred that there is a high level static potential promise to experience spiritual transformation. Also, note that both the *Janma* and the *Manasa nakshatras* are *Sulochana nakshatras* in addition to the fact that Ketu is with Venus in the 11th house of gains and Rahu is in the 5th house. The native reacts highly to social stimuli. Hence, the native's spiritual journey will be disrupted by the lack of high Guru-level intelligence.

In D9, the Lagna Lord of D1 is exalted in *moksha rashi* and is conjunct with the 9th Lord, Saturn. Further, Sun is placed in *dharma rashi* aspecting the Lagna of D9 and is in 5/9 axis with Moon (Moon is also in *dharma rashi*). Jupiter is Sun's dispositor and Moon is Jupiter's dispositor which again establishes a strong soul-body-mind connection in D9 for spiritual matters. Moreover, the 5th lord of D9 goes to the 8th house. Hence, D9 further confirms prominent spiritual potential.

5.2.2 Influence of Rahu on Spiritual Potential

Rahu is placed in the 5th house (trine house and *dharma trikon*) in *dharma rashi*, hence it acts as 5th lord and exhibits the properties of Mars, as its dispositor is Mars (5th lord, 12th lord). Please note that Rahu's dispositor, Mars, is the Lagna lord and the 8th lord of the *Kaalpurush* horoscope signifying beginning of life (*rashi* 1) and *rashi* 8 signifying deep spirituality, detachment/end of life. Mars in D1, makes a connection with the 12th house (house of spirituality). This placement of Mars (Rahu's dispositor) further signifies the role of Mars in providing events during its AD/PD for spirituality, as we will see later. Rahu's dispositor, Mars (acting as the 5th lord, and the 12th lord) is conjunct with Jupiter (a *karaaka* of spirituality and the 12th lord in the *kaalpurush kundali*) and the 8th lord - Moon, in Lagna, so Rahu makes a connection with Jupiter and Moon. Further, Rahu makes a trine connection with Saturn (acting as the 3rd lord and the 2nd lord) in the *dharma trikon*. Additionally, Jupiter aspects Rahu providing Rahu with piousness. Rahu is in *Ashwini nakshatra* ruled by Ketu, a significator of spirituality. Ashwini is a *manda nakshatra* (a type of *nakshatra* in the *andhadi* group of *nakshatras*) and will make the native work hard (by generating challenging situations) to be on the spiritual path. Rahu is aspected by Venus (Venus is placed in a *kaam rashi* and in *Swati nakshatra* which is lorded by Rahu itself). In the D9 chart, Rahu is in a *moksha rashi* and is conjunct with Saturn, who is the 8th lord and the 9th lord, and its dispositor Moon is placed in a *dharma rashi* and aspected by Lagan lord Mercury. Mercury as Lagna lord is further aspected by Mars who is conjunct Rahu. In addition, Sun is lorded by exalted Jupiter who is with Saturn acting as 8th lord and 9th lord and aspecting Moon, that in turn aspects Lagna lord Mercury. There is the *Gajakesari Yoga* and a *sannyas yoga* being formed in the D9. Hence, there exists a soul-body-mind synchronization in the D9 chart in supporting the native on the path of spirituality. *It can be reckoned overall that Rahu as a planet can cultivate spiritual ethos in the native but will generate challenges.*

5.2.3 *Dasha* Analysis

Take note that the dispositors of the birth ascendant (Jupiter), Sun (Mars) and Moon (Jupiter) are mutual friends. Hence, while analyzing *dasha* periods, and in accordance with *Sudarshan Paddhati* (SP) principles from the *Parashari* code of *dasha* analysis, we need not perform a logical analysis from all the three reference points (Lagna, Sun, Moon) to arrive at conclusions/inferences.

Sun is the 5th Lord and placed in the 12th house in *Jyestha nakshatra*. It is conjunct with Mercury (10th lord and 7th lord). The native travelled overseas for work during the Sun MD and made remarkable achievements in workspace. Moon's MD brought relocation to different continents along with new heights in career. Mars is the 5th and 12th Lord and placed in ascendant and is conjunct with Jupiter (Lagna lord and 4th lord) and the Moon (8th lord), (Moon & Jupiter form *Gajakesari yoga*). During Mars MD the native reached a pinnacle in his career and set unprecedented milestones, thereby acclaiming global fame and prestige.

Case Study 5: A Renowned Corporate Executive   161

Rahu is placed in the 5th house in *Ashwini nakshatra*. Rahu's placement in the *Ashwini nakshatra* gave a swift and steady growth in native's endeavors at the beginning of Rahu MD and showed its effect during its MD, (Rahu behaving like dispositor Mars and being aspected by Venus from 11th house and Jupiter from Lagna) and the native became a global leader, getting involved in philanthropic projects, became chairman of a world-renowned Institutes in the USA, Co-Chair at UN, served as Board member of several private and public organizations including World Economic Forum. The period of Rahu MD made the native embark on a little too ambitious project which proved to be a turning point in his life. During Rahu-Ketu/ Rahu-Venus *antardashas*, Venus being the 6th and 11th lord and an enemy of Lagna lord, the native was accused of business malpractice. The event got global attention and brought much misery to the native. (Pl Note: The very essence of Venus and Ketu conjunction is to not to be overpowered by hunger for success and money. Ketu was bound to ensure that native learned life lessons based on this conjunction if native watered the roots of gains and desires limitlessly). Mercury is *badhak* here and makes a relation with *khar graha*, Moon, as Moon is the lord of 64th *navamsa* and 22nd *drekkana*. Mercury's dispositor, Mars, is conjunct with the Moon in the Lagna. So, we see that *badhak's* role became active in Rahu-Moon/Rahu-Mars period. He fought a long hauling battle against mighty corporate giants and defended himself in court of law (During Rahu-Sun period; Please note Sun is placed in 12th house and conjunct with *badhak*, Mercury) bravely but still ended up being sentenced to two years imprisonment. The Rahu-Moon period brought a transformation in native's life; He was imprisoned; (Moon being the 8th lord and lowest in degree and winner in planetary battle between Moon, Jupiter and Mars due to their conjunction in the Lagna). The Rahu-Mars AD saw the native spend time in isolation in prison (Mars being the 12th lord is in extremely close conjunction with the Lagna lord). The native's *purva punya* saved him from long term imprisonment as Mars, besides being the 12th lord is also the 5th lord and acted as a savior for the native. We can further say that as Rahu is making a connection with the Lagna lord, the 8th lord, the 5th lord, and the 12th lord, it played a significant role in providing events during its MD that led to self-realization in the native. These events brought about a transformation in native's life and left him a changed man. His philanthropic bent of mind showed in his actions in prison and he is known to have helped several inmates in prison, be it helping them write applications/ letters or helping them set up business and even financing some. In the D1 chart, Rahu is aspected by Venus who is the 11th lord in a *kaam rashi*, and by Jupiter from a *dharma rashi*. Making Rahu as the Lagna being the MD lord, we see Rahu is aspected by both, Venus (7th lord) and Jupiter (9th and 12th lord). In D9, Rahu is conjunct with Jupiter (7th lord and 10th lord), Mars (6th lord and 11th lord), and Saturn (8th lord and the 9th lord). If we make Rahu as the Lagna in D9 being the MD lord, Jupiter is the 9th lord, Mars is the 5th lord, and Saturn is the 8th lord. Hence, Rahu MD gave transformation to the native to move towards developing a spiritual ethos through trials/challenges experience in the material plane.

The Jupiter MD (Jupiter MD started while he was in prison) contributed to his interest in spirituality and he took refuge in the teachings of the Bhagavad Gita. During Jupiter MD, the native wrote a book featuring events from his life and this book imbibed the teaching of Gita. The book has experts from The Gita and confirms the transformation that the native underwent. There was a complete change in native's lifestyle, thought process and aspirations. In the D1 chart Jupiter is conjunct the 8th lord and the 12th lord, both of which are in the *Mula nakshatra* ruled by Ketu (significator of spirituality). Jupiter is exalted in the D9 chart and conjunct Rahu and the 8th lord Saturn. If we make Jupiter as the Lagna in D9, it being the MD lord, Mars is the 5th lord, and Saturn is the 8th lord. Hence, the combined placement of Jupiter in D1 and D9 gave the native the actual spiritual self-realization (inculcated the spiritual ethos) that was seeded by event-driven transformations in the previous Rahu MD through trials/challenges experienced in the material plane. Alternatively, Rahu acted as a catalyst for spiritual realization in the native.

5.2.4 Summarizing Inference

The native's chart prominently depicts potential from birth for spiritual growth and transformation. We also see that there are several *raja yogas* in natives' chart — *Hamsa, Ubhayachara, Chandra mangala, Gaja-Kesari, Kalpadruma/Parijata, Tapasvi yoga*, to name a few. (These strong *yogas* attributed to native being righteous in disposition and purity of mind, polite, generous, long-lasting reputation, sterling character and immense moral fiber, global well-known stature, and *Tapasvi Yoga* led to final spirituality and transformation). He worked on several pristine humanitarian and philanthropic projects while being a trailblazer and leaving an exceptional legacy in terms of work he did in the corporate world & for his country and abroad. Rahu sowed the seed of spirituality by generating materialistic-fall events in the life of native that led to spiritual self-realization, transformation, lifestyle change and interest in teachings of Bhagavad Gita, in the Jupiter MD.

Section 5.3:
A *Nadi* Commentary

We provide THREE alternative, concise, and precise methods of analysis — based on *Bhrigu-Nandi Nadi* (BNN) astrology complementing the *Parashari* analysis of Case Study 5. **The goal is to establish the *Parashari* inference from Case Study 5 independently for each of the alternative methods of analysis.**

The essence of a good astrological analysis is the necessity for it to be validated from multiple schools of Vedic astrological thought. We choose the BNN approach as the alternative school of thought in this book — however, we smoothly integrate and blend an in-depth *nakshatra jyotish* analysis with the BNN framework, as we did with the *Parashari* analysis. While a strong *Parashari* education and a unique predictive *nakshatra jyotish* course are the pillars of the *Dev Jyotish* school of astrology, the BNN analysis was self-learned by Ranjan Pal under the personal guidance of Richa Shukla, and then the learning imparted to Ekta Jain by Ranjan Pal and Richa Shukla.

Case Study 5: A Renowned Corporate Executive

5.3.1 Method 1 (*Bhrigu Nandi Nadi*)

The significator of spirituality is Ketu. Based on BNN and as established in previous cases, Ketu is the planet that can grant spiritual realization to a native. So, we will see (a) whether the placement of Ketu is of sufficient strength to provide a spiritual outlook to the native and (b) whether and to what extent Rahu influences Ketu to support the native realizing spiritual ethos. Unlike in *Parashari jyotish*, there is no need to do a dynamic analysis in BNN astrology (e.g., via progressions and transits) of Rahu to establish its quantum of influence on native spiritual ethos. This is because the static *Nadi* analysis is sufficiently causal to judge the quantum of Rahu's effects.

Decision Making Factor #1

For the native in Case Study 5, we have Ketu placed with Venus, **Ketu + Venus,** conjunct in 11 *rashi* with Ketu at a lower degree than Venus. As part of the 7th house from Ketu analysis, we have **Moon + Jupiter + Mars + Rahu + Saturn** (trines with each other from the 7th house from Ketu in ascending order of degree in *dharma rashi*). The Ketu + Venus combination (in *kaam rashi* in 11th house) makes the native attain flagship status in amassing wealth and luxuries. In a *Kaam rashi*, this combination becomes the journey from desire to detachment — the true alchemy of Venus under the light of *moksha*-giver Ketu. Seventh from Ketu combination of Moon + Jupiter + Mars + Rahu + Saturn in *dharma rashi* indicates action-oriented individual with ethics, and boundless growth in career in foreign lands. Rahu, when joining these planets in *dharma trikon*, magnifies desires and adds a restless, unconventional, or socially reformative dimension. Rahu with Mars and Jupiter produces mission-oriented intensity — a reformer, revolutionary, or explorer of new domains of thought or action. Moon and Rahu, together distorts perception, causing *illusion or idealistic obsession*. Saturn's influence on this combination adds structure and discipline. The native oscillates between higher inspiration (Jupiter) and psychological overdrive (Rahu–Moon), learning eventually to transform passion into wisdom. There is a direct potent influence of these 5 planets on Ketu. **All planets are in *dharma rashis*, and together with Rahu play a significant role in providing high spiritual impetus to the native. As Ketu and Venus are in *kaam rashis*, realization will not be ultimate but profound and will culminate in the ineffable bliss of moksha. The influence of Rahu and other planets from *dharma rashi* will lead to the culmination of the final bliss.**

The elements in the same trine from the 7th house from Ketu have a strong modifying/influencing effect to the significance impact of Ketu of making a native realizing (or not) spiritual ethos. Rahu is always part of this trine to no surprise, the interesting thing to see is how the other planets together with Rahu shape the quantum of impact, as we have done above. It might be tempting to also check for the trine from the 2nd to the placement of Ketu – however, since we are interested in the role of Rahu, we skip this step for now and will return to the analysis of such trines when we integrate *nakshatra* astrology with BNN astrology.

Case Study 5: A Renowned Corporate Executive

Decision Making Factor #2

For the native in Case Study 5, we have Mercury as the lord of the 12th house from **Ketu**. Since Ketu is the significator of spirituality in BNN astrology one must check for the 12th from Ketu (12th house is the house of *moksha/dissolution* from any signification). There is no planet in the trine 12th to Ketu which has an *artha rashi*. So, we see that no planet is placed in the *Artha trikon* for the native. The dispositor of 12th to Ketu is Mercury who is placed 2nd to Ketu in a transformative *moksha rashi* along with Sun (the significator of soul). Hence, it can be said that 12th to Ketu contributes to the influence on Ketu from the *moksha rashi* of Scorpio via dispositor of 12th to Ketu, Mercury.

This is also the trine from the 7th from 12th to Ketu. We have the combination of **Mercury + Sun** (in ascending order of degree) in **transformative *moksha rashi*** in 12th house denoting native's knowledge; business decisions being influenced by status and authority. **Rahu and its trine combination have no direct influence or role to play here on Ketu significance based on sign placement** (we do not include a *nakshatra* analysis here that is left for subsequent Methods 2 and 3).

Decision Making Factor #3

For the native in Case Study 5, we have Sun as the lord of the 11th house from **Ketu**. We have Saturn placed in the 11th from Ketu. Since Ketu is the significator of spirituality in BNN astrology one must check for the 11th from Ketu (11th house analysis checks for catalytic factors contributing to a significator – in our case Ketu of spirituality). We have Saturn placed 11th to Ketu and **Moon + Jupiter + Mars + Rahu + Saturn** (in ascending order of degree) in the trine combination. **Relate this combination to Decision Making Factor #1 earlier, and it is evident why Rahu is a big catalytic factor in the spiritual journey of the native.** If we take the trine from the 7th from the 11th house from Ketu, we get Ketu and Venus that being in *Kaam rashis*, spoils the non-materialistic essence towards ultimate spiritual realization.

If we now consider Sun as the lord of the 11th house from Ketu, we have the combination **Mercury + Sun** (in ascending order of degree) in a transformative *moksha rashi*. There is no planet in 7th from this combination. When we summarize the 11th from Ketu influence, in essence **Rahu gives considerable spiritual impetus to the native on his journey. However, Ketu and Venus placement in *Kaam rashi*, does not give ultimate realization (i.e., the blissful *moksha*).**

Decision Making Factor #4

For the native in Case Study 5, we have Venus as the dispositor of Ketu placed in a *kaam rashi* and is conjunct with Ketu. We have **Moon + Jupiter + Mars + Rahu + Saturn** (trine with each other from the 7th house from Ketu in ascending order of degree) in *dharma rashis*. The 7th from Venus has strong **Rahu** connection. **Hence, in view of DMF#4, Rahu's influence on Ketu gives a significant impetus to the native on his journey to realize spiritual ethos.**

Summary: Does the placement of Ketu give a strong spiritual outlook to the native? The answer is a

Case Study 5: A Renowned Corporate Executive

Planet	R/C	Sign	Degree	Speed	Nakshatra	Pada	RL	NL	SL	SS	Status	SB
Lagna		Sag	09:55:20		Moola	3	Ju	Ke	Sa	Me		
Sun		Sco	16:41:03	01:00:53	Jyeshtha	1	Ma	Me	Me	Me	Grt.Fr.	1.00
Moon		Sag	03:01:24	13:14:58	Moola	1	Ju	Ke	Su	Su	Enemy	0.80
Mars		Sag	10:47:54	00:45:46	Moola	4	Ju	Ke	Sa	Ma	Neutr.	1.53
Mercury	C	Sco	10:44:04	01:34:17	Anuradha	3	Ma	Sa	Su	Sa	Frnd.	1.21
Jupiter		Sag	10:24:58	00:13:15	Moola	4	Ju	Ke	Sa	Ve	Own	1.15
Venus		Lib	14:18:33	01:13:56	Swati	3	Ve	Ra	Me	Sa	Moolt.	0.95
Saturn		Leo	12:51:33	00:01:39	Magha	4	Su	Ke	Me	Ju	Neutr.	1.20
Rahu		Ari	11:23:33	-00:06:01	Ashwini	4	Ma	Ke	Sa	Ju	Neutr.	
Ketu		Lib	11:23:33	-00:06:01	Swati	2	Ve	Ra	Sa	Ve	Neutr.	

'yes' from most of the four Decision Making Factors. Does Rahu play a major role in the native experiencing spiritual ethos? The answer is a 'yes' from multiple DMFs. The results sync with the *Parashari* analysis.

5.3.2 Method 2 (BNN with *Nakshatra*)

Since, our analysis base is BNN astrology, like in Method 1 we will work with the same Decision Making Factors (DMFs). It is sufficient to see **(a) whether the placement of Ketu is of sufficient strength to provide a spiritual outlook to the native and (b) whether and to what extent Rahu influences Ketu to support the native realizing spiritual ethos.** Most importantly we will consider the strength of the *nakshatra* sub-lords of the planets related to these factors. The following parameters are relevant for study for each decision making factor: (i) a planet's ***nakshatra* sub-lord**, (ii) the **sub-lord's *nakshatra* lord:** the planet ruling the *nakshatra* in which the sub-lord is situated, and the (iii) the **sub-lord's sign lord:** the planet ruling the sign in which the sub-lord is situated. We could go more granular in our analysis at the nakshatra level, i.e., analyse sub-sub-lords, however, this would imply a very accurate birth time within seconds of the native. This is something that is hardly ever guaranteed.

Decision Making Factor #1

For the native in Case Study 5, we have **Ketu + Venus** (trine with each other in ascending order of degree). As part of the 7th house from Ketu analysis, we have **Moon + Jupiter + Mars + Rahu + Saturn** (trine with each other from the 7th house from Ketu in ascending order of degree) and placed in *dharma rashis*.

Case Study 5: A Renowned Corporate Executive 171

Ketu is placed in the *nakshatra* of Rahu in the *pada* ruled by separative planet Saturn. Rahu and Saturn are placed in a *Dharma rashi* and are in same trine, in 5th and 9th house respectively. If we now look at Venus that is conjunct with Ketu, Venus is also placed *nakshatra* of Rahu in the *pada* ruled by Mercury. Rahu is placed in *dharma rashi* and Mercury is placed with Sun in the transformative *moksha rashi* in 12th house. Ketu's sub-lord is Saturn (Saturn is trine with Rahu). Saturn's *nakshatra* lord is Ketu. Ketu's *nakshatra* lord is Rahu. **Hence the spiritual significator, Ketu is influenced by Rahu and provides strength to the native to realize spiritual ethos.** Ketu is conjunct with Venus. Venus's sub-lord is Mercury. Mercury's *nakshatra* lord is Saturn (which is in trine with Rahu) and Saturn's sign lord is Sun (Sun is conjunct with Mercury in transformative *rashi* lorded by Mars and Mars is in trine with Rahu). **Rahu influences Ketu and the trine in catalysing spiritual impetus.**

As part of the 7th house from Ketu analysis, we have **Moon + Jupiter + Mars + Rahu + Saturn** (trines with each other from the 7th house from Ketu in ascending order of degree). Moon's *nakshatra* sub-lord is Sun. Sun's *nakshatra* lord is Mercury, and Sun's sign lord is Mars (Mars is Rahu dispositor and in trine with Rahu). Jupiter's *nakshatra* sub-lord is Saturn (Saturn is in trine with Rahu). Saturn's *nakshatra* lord is Ketu (Ketu's *nakshatra* lord is Rahu). Saturn's *rashi* lord is Sun (Sun's dispositor, Mars makes a connection with Rahu). Mars's *nakshatra* sub-lord is Saturn (Saturn is in trine with Rahu). Saturn's *nakshatra* lord is Ketu (Ketu's *nakshatra* lord is Rahu). Saturn's sign lord is Sun (Sun's dispositor, Mars makes a trine connection with Rahu). Rahu's *nakshatra* sub-lord is Saturn (Saturn is in trine with Rahu). Further analysis for Saturn will be similar as explained above. Saturn's *nakshatra* sub-lord is Mercury (Mercury is lorded by Mars that is in trine to Rahu). Mercury's *nakshatra* lord is Saturn (Saturn is in trine to Rahu). Saturn's sign lord is Sun (dispositor of Sun makes a trine connection with Rahu). We see an extremely strong connect of Rahu with all planets. **In summary, Rahu significantly influences the DMF #1 to enable the native experience spiritual ethos.**

Now we look at 7th from Ketu. Moon, Jupiter, Mars, Rahu and Saturn, are in *nakshatra* of Ketu (5 planets in same trine 7th to Ketu in *nakshatra* lorded by Ketu). Moon is in *pada* ruled by Sun; Jupiter, Mars and Rahu are in *pada* ruled by Saturn and Saturn is in *pada* ruled by Mercury. **Hence the spiritual significator has enormous strength for the native to realize spiritual ethos and is also influenced by Rahu — however, Ketu being in a *kaam rashi* affects the purity of the realization.**

Decision Making Factor #2

For the native in Case Study 5, we have Mercury as the lord of the 12th house from **Ketu**. There is no planet placed here or in this trine. Since Ketu is the significator of spirituality in BNN astrology one must check for the 12th from Ketu (12th house is the house of *moksha/dissolution* from any signification). Mercury is placed in 12th house in a transformative *moksha rashi* in the *nakshatra* of Saturn in the *pada* lorded by Sun. Sun is conjunct with Mercury. Sun is placed in

Case Study 5: A Renowned Corporate Executive

nakshatra of Mercury in *pada* of Mercury. So, Sun and Mercury have *pada* lord exchange and influence each other strongly. The lord of this house is Mars who is placed in *nakshatra* of Ketu in *pada* lorded by Saturn. **The 12th house from Ketu has decent strength to make the native realize spiritual ethos.** The trine from the 7th from 12th of Ketu has **Mercury + Sun (in ascending order of degree). Hence the 12th house from Ketu is NOT influenced by Rahu in imparting spiritual ethos.**

Mercury is placed in the *nakshatra* of Saturn and the *nakshatra* sub-lord is Sun. Mercury's *nakshatra* lord, Saturn makes a relation with Rahu being in same trine in *dharma rashi*. Mercury is conjunct with Sun whose *nakshatra* lord is Mercury. Further, Mercury and Sun have Mars as the sign lord and Mars makes a trine relation with Rahu. There are no planets in this trine. The trine from the 7th from 12th from Ketu has **Mercury + Sun** (in ascending order of degree). Mercury's *nakshatra* sub-lord is Sun. Sun's *nakshatra* lord is Mercury. Sun's sign lord is Mars (Mars makes a trine connection with Rahu). Sun's *nakshatra* sub-lord is Mercury and Mercury's nakshatra lord is Saturn. Mercury's sign lord is Mars (Mars has a trine relation with Rahu). **In summary, Rahu considerably influences the DMF #2.**

Decision Making Factor #3

Since Ketu is the significator of spirituality in BNN astrology one must check for the 11th from Ketu (11th house analysis checks for catalytic factors contributing to a significator – in our case Ketu of spirituality). For the native in Case Study 5, we have Sun as the *dharma rashi* lord of the 11th house from Ketu. We have Saturn placed 11th from Ketu. **Saturn is placed along with Moon + Jupiter + Mars + Rahu in this trine providing impetus to Ketu to realize spiritual essence.** Relate this combination to DMF #1 earlier, and it is evident why Rahu is a big catalytic factor in the spiritual journey of the native. If we now consider Sun as the lord of the 11th house from Ketu, we have the combination **Mercury + Sun** (in ascending order of degree). Relate DMF#2 analysis here. Hence, **overall Rahu influences the 11th house from Ketu and promotes Ketu to impart spiritual ethos to the native.**

Sun's nakshatra sub-lord is Mercury. Mercury's *nakshatra* lord is Saturn and Saturn is in trine with Rahu. Mercury's sign lord is Mars and Mars is also in trine with Rahu. So, the lord of 11th from Ketu, Sun, makes a connection with Rahu. Saturn is placed 11th from Ketu and we have Moon + Jupiter + Mars + Rahu + Saturn combination (in ascending degree order) in trine with Saturn. We have Ketu + Venus in trine to the 7th house from the 11th from Ketu. The analysis from DMF#1 repeats here and we can decipher that Rahu makes a strong connect. **In summary, Rahu significantly influences the DMF #3 in the native realizing a spiritual ethos.**

Decision Making Factor #4

For the native in Case Study 5, we have Venus as the dispositor of Ketu and is located in a *kaam rashi*. We have **Ketu + Venus** (ascending order of degree) conjunct in *moksha rashi* in 11th house. Relate this

Case Study 5: A Renowned Corporate Executive

combination to **DMF #1** earlier, and it is evident why Rahu is a big catalytic factor in the spiritual journey of the native. **Overall, Rahu gives a significant impetus to the native on his journey to realize spiritual ethos.**

Venus's *nakshatra* sub-lord is Mercury. Mercury's sign lord is Mars and Mars is in trine with Rahu. We have the *artha rashi* trine 7th from Venus which is empty. Both Ketu and Venus are in the *nakshatra* of Rahu and the sub-lord analysis also establishes Rahu connect. **In summary, Rahu influences the DMF #4.**

Summary: Does the placement of Ketu give a strong spiritual outlook to the native? The answer is a 'yes' based on majority of the four DMFs. Does Rahu play a role in the native experiencing spiritual ethos? The answer is a 'yes' from majority of Decision-Making Factors 1-4. The results sync with the *Parashari* analysis.

5.3.3 Method 3 (BNN with *Karmic* Angles)

We wish to analyze in **three parts** using the *karmic Nadi jyotish* principles the strength of Rahu in influencing each of the mind, body, and soul to realize a spiritual ethos. After all, these are the basic pillars that eventually decide whether a native will be able to realize spiritual ethos in their lifetime. **If the connection is strong in at least two out of the three cases, we can say that Rahu has been significantly instrumental in promoting spirituality within the native.** Unlike in *Parashari jyotish*, there is no need to do a dynamic analysis (e.g., via progressions and transits) of Rahu to establish its quantum of influence on native spiritual ethos. This is because the static *Nadi* analysis is sufficiently causal to judge the quantum of Rahu's effects.

Dridh-Adridh Karma Axes: In *Nadi jyotish*, directions embody the metaphysics of *karma* itself. **East and West** anchor *dridh karma* — duties to father, guru, and ancestors that bind the soul to its inescapable obligations. **East**, aligned with Sun and Jupiter, signifies *dharma*, authority, and righteous beginnings; **West** blends closure and entanglement, largely fixed through Saturn's weight, though softened by Venus's negotiable pleasures. **North and South** anchor *adridh karma* - mutable desires and worldly pursuits shaped by free will. **North**, guided by Mercury and Rahu, points to growth, commerce, and ambition; while **South**, linked with Mars, Ketu, and Moon, carries ancestral debts, *tapas*, and *karmic* reckonings. In summary, East pulls a native towards *dharmic* duty, West toward worldly entanglement, North toward ambition, and South toward purification.

Thus, the four directions mark not mere space but the soul's *karmic* geography: some pathways immovable, others pliable. The horoscope becomes a compass of necessity and possibility, mapping destiny's fixity against the field of conscious striving. One may ask: why not diagonal directions? In *Nadi jyotish*, only the **four cardinal directions** - East, West, North, and South—are used, not the intermediates like Northeast or Northwest. This is because Vedic cosmology is fundamentally **fourfold**, based on sunrise and sunset, solstices and equinoxes, day and night. Each direction is tied to specific *grahas* and *karmic* qualities: East (Sun, Jupiter), West (Saturn, Venus),

Case Study 5: A Renowned Corporate Executive

North (Mercury, Rahu), South (Moon, Mars, Ketu). This framework mirrors the *dik-palas* (directional guardians) of Vedic ritual, which are cardinal. By limiting to four, *Nadi* emphasizes clarity: destiny is seen through primal axes of *dharma*, desire, past, and closure, without diluting meaning in diagonals.

We provide the planetary directional compass diagram for Case Study 5.

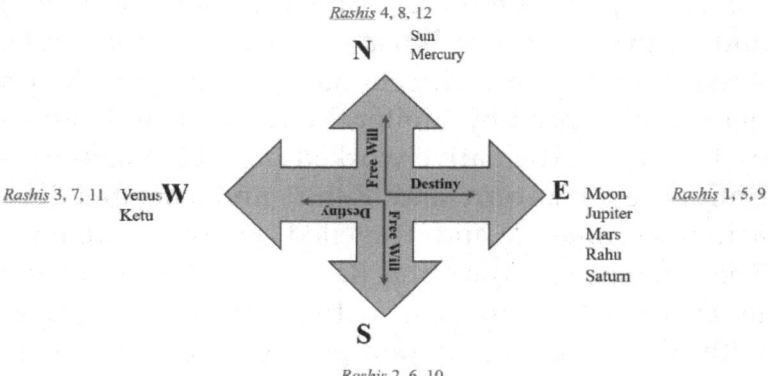

Part 1

We first analyse the planet **Moon – the significator of the mind**, to judge whether (a) the mind is inherently spiritual and (b) and how Rahu plays a role in driving the mind towards spirituality.

We observe that Moon occupies a *dharma rashi* along with Jupiter and Mars. Saturn and Rahu are in trine, and they all occupy the eastern direction (in fire sign) because they are in 1, 5, 9 positions from each other. If we arrange the planets in the **eastern direction** in ascending order of degree, we have the sequence **Moon, Jupiter, Mars, Rahu and Saturn** –

an extremely potent combination of planets in *dharma rashi*. Moon is also modified and influenced by planets placed in opposite direction i.e., **western** direction. Here we have **Ketu and Venus** (in ascending order) who are placed in trine opposite to Moon.

If we arrange the planets in the eastern direction in ascending order of degree, we have **Moon + Jupiter + Mars + Rahu + Saturn**. Moon (*karaka* of mind), Jupiter (*karaka* of *jeev*/ life force), Mars (*karaka* of *deha*/ ego) and Saturn (*karaka* of *karma*), all are in *dharma rashi*. According to *Nadi* directionality principles Moon here is influenced by Jupiter, Mars, Rahu and Saturn by full 100%. The native worked in foreign countries (influence of Saturn and Rahu) and changed jobs across continents and travelled across continents. The influence of Mars and Rahu triggered obsession to make it big, and the native was a trail blazer with his pioneering accomplishments in a career in foreign land. Influence of Jupiter (attributes related to wisdom, philosophy, nobility and wealth) and Saturn (career/ profession/ activity) made him establish legacy in higher learning in the form of inception of globally renowned prestigious institute. The native was affiliated with top global institutes of higher learning and worked in capacity of advisor/ chairman with global organizations like UN, World Economic Forum and several esteemed private organizations. It was the 75% influence of Ketu and Venus (in ascending order) from the opposite western direction that spearheaded the native to establish his flagship in career and philanthropic efforts. This influence of Ketu and Venus (from *Kaam rashi*) led him to amass wealth and luxuries in life and upheld flagship status

Case Study 5: A Renowned Corporate Executive

in not just Venus related *karaktatvas* but also Saturn, Mars and Jupiter related *karaktavas* as Ketu + Venus combination influenced not just Moon (the mind) but also Jupiter + Mars + Rahu + Saturn. So, we see that Moon (*Karaka* of mind) is influenced by Jupiter (*karaka* of life force and attributes related to wealth, wisdom, nobility, philosophy), Mars (*Karaka* of *deha*/ego attributing to power, enemies), Rahu (*karaka* of *karmic* compulsion attributing to illusion/ *maya*) and Saturn (*significator of Karma*) by 100% as they are in trine with one another and by Ketu (significator of *moksha*/ flagship) and Venus (significator of *bhog*/ luxuries) by 75% from the opposite direction.

The eastern and western direction is that of destiny (*dridh karma*), and the native is driven by destiny to do *karma* on significations in these directions. Hence Jupiter, Mars, Rahu, Saturn, Ketu and Venus, all influence the mindset of the native by destiny as part of the *dridh karma*. Ketu is influenced 100% by Venus being conjunct in a *kaam rashi* and Ketu influences the mind (Moon) by 75%. Rahu influences the mind by 100% being in the same *dharma* trine as Moon. So, the mind will not realize spirituality till it has experienced the epitome of *bhog* (due to the significant 75% influence of Ketu + Venus from *kaam trine*). Rahu plays a key role in influencing the mind here and since the native underwent Rahu *mahadasha* in his lifetime, Rahu played a critical role in creating events that played as a catalyst and led to spiritual realization during its *dasha*.

If we now look at 12th from Moon, it's the *moksha trine* (northern direction) and Mercury (*karaka* of *buddhi*) is positioned in *moksha* trine along with Sun (*karaka of atma*/ soul). When we arrange the planets in northern direction in ascending order, we have Mercury + Sun. So, Sun (authority, fame) influences the speech, intellect, business acumen of the native. This combination has 25% influence on the mindset of the native as these planets are 12th from the Moon. 7th from 12th of Moon is southern direction and this trine has no planets. The northern and southern directions are of the *adridh karma* or the free will. So, the native uses his intellect for free will *karmas* which is 100% influenced by Sun from a transformative *moksha rashi*.

So, **in summary**: Is the mind spiritual? The answer is 'yes'. Does Rahu play a role in driving the mind towards spirituality? The answer is a resounding 'yes'. However, Rahu is not the only main contributor, even though it is the precipitating factor driving the native to doing *dridh karma*. Mars, Jupiter, Saturn, Ketu and Venus also contribute to spiritual mindset of the native.

Part 2

We now analyse the planet **Sun — the significator of the soul**, to judge whether (a) the soul is projecting spirituality and (b) and how Rahu plays a role in driving the soul towards projecting spirituality.

We observe that Sun (the *atma* karaka) is placed in transformative Scorpio *moksha rashi* in the 12th house in the northern direction. Mercury is conjunct with Sun here.

Sun is the significator of the soul and Mercury is the significator of *buddhi* and both are in the *moksha*

Case Study 5: A Renowned Corporate Executive 181

rashi of transformation. We now arrange the planets in the **northern direction** in ascending order of degree. We have the sequence **Mercury + Sun**. It is evident that the intellect of the native is primarily influenced by the soul of the native. According to *Nadi* directionality principles Sun influences Mercury in full (100%) because Sun is conjunct and in trine with Mercury.

We now look at planets in the **southern direction** (7th to Sun) in ascending order of degree. We have no planets here. Venus (*karaka* of *bhog*) is the lord of the house 7th to Sun and is placed 12th to Sun conjunct with Ketu (*karaka* of *moksha*/ flagship) in the **western direction**. According to *Nadi* directionality principles Sun (significator of the soul) here is influenced by Venus (*karaka* of *bhog*/ luxuries) and Ketu (*karaka* of *moksha*/ flagship) by 25% because Ketu and Venus are 12th to Sun. Ketu + Venus influence Sun from the western direction (direction responsible for *dridh karma*).

If we look at planets second to Sun, we see the potent combination of Moon + Jupiter + Mars in *dharma rashi* with Saturn and Rahu in trine to them. So, we have Moon (significator of mind) + Jupiter (significator of philosophy/wisdom/life force) + Mars (significator of ego) + Rahu (Significator of illusion/ maya) + Saturn (significator of *karma*) combination is 2nd from Sun in Eastern direction in *dharma rashi* which exerts 50% influence on the *atma karaka*, Sun. This is a powerful and overpowering influence considering that its coming from the axis of *dridh karma* from a *dharma rashi*. The native's soul evolves through disciplined struggle, guided emotion, and reformative action. Hence, we see that Sun has dominant influence from **eastern direction** of *dridh karma* from *dharma trikon* giving spiritual impetus to the soul. Rahu is placed *in dharma trikon* and its dispositor is also placed in the same trine in the direction of *dridh karma* confirming that Rahu plays a very critical role as a catalyst for spiritual ethos for the native.

So, **in summary**: does the soul project spirituality? The answer is a resounding 'yes'. Does Rahu play a role in driving the mind towards spirituality? The answer is a resounding 'yes'. Rahu is not the main contributor. Moon, Jupiter, Mars, Saturn and Mercury play a big contributing role in influencing the soul towards spirituality.

Part 3

We want to analyse the planet **Mars — the significator of the body and ego**, to judge whether (a) the body is inherently spiritual and (b) and how Rahu plays a role in driving the body and ego towards spirituality. However, since Moon and Mars are in the same direction, the analysis and inference for Part 3 is exactly same as that in Part 1. In other words, is the body projecting spiritual essence? The answer is positively 'yes'. Does Rahu play a role in driving the soul towards spirituality? The answer is a resounding 'yes'.

Overall Inference from Parts 1 to 3: Rahu considerably influences spiritual essence through the mind, soul and body, though it does not significantly influence the mind in projecting spirituality. It acts more as a catalyst for the mind attaining spiritual ethos. The results sync with the *Parashari* angle of analysis that Rahu does not generate spiritual realization in the native but plays the role of a major catalyst in helping the native realize spirituality.

Case Study 6
A Renowned Yogi

Section 6.1:
A Narrative of Spiritual Philosophy

The native stands as a radiant symbol of India's eternal spirituality adapted for the modern age. His rational, questioning mind initially doubted religion until his encounter with Sri Ramakrishna Paramahamsa, who offered him not doctrine but direct mystical experience. This shifted Vivekananda from intellectual scepticism to experiential conviction, echoing the *Upanishad* principle: *"Neti, neti"* — truth must be realized, not merely described.

His proclamation that *"all religions are true"* was not a syncretic compromise but a Vedantic insight drawn from the *Rig Veda (1.164.46): Ekam sat vipra bahudha vadanti* — *"Truth is One, the wise speak of it in many ways."* This universality became his philosophical anchor and the hallmark of his mission.

While rooted in *Advaita Vedanta*, the native insisted that realization must flow into action. He declared: "They alone live who live for others; the rest are more dead than alive." His doctrine of *"Practical Vedanta"* extended the *Upanishad* realization of unity into social service. He transformed *jnana* into *karma*, teaching that "service to man is service to God." This radical vision redefined *moksha* as not an escape from the

Case Study 6: A Renowned Yogi

world but liberation expressed through compassion and *loka-sangraha* (the welfare of all). The *Bhagavad Gita* (3.19) captures this ethic: "*tasmad asaktaḥ satatam karyam karma samacara*" — "*Act without attachment, and one attains the Supreme.*" Vivekananda embodied this ideal, balancing detachment with ceaseless action.

Contemporaries recognized his unique power. Romain Rolland hailed him as "*the living voice of India's soul.*" Sri Aurobindo observed: "*He was the soul-force of the Mother's future, carrying the word of the eternal.*" Mahatma Gandhi admitted, "*I learned from him what patriotism truly means.*" His famous exhortation — "*Arise, awake, and stop not till the goal is reached*" — became both spiritual mantra and political rallying cry.

The native's *moksha* was not mere personal transcendence but *jivanmukti* — liberation while living. Under Ramakrishna's guidance, he experienced *samadhi* where the ego dissolved in *Brahman*. Yet, he refused to remain absorbed; instead, he turned this realization outward. "*I am a voice without form,*" he declared, echoing the *Taittiriya Upanishad's* dictum: "*Brahmavid apnoti param*" (2.1) — "*The knower of Brahman attains the Supreme.*"

Thus, the natives' liberation sanctified worldly action. His life testified that *moksha* is not flight but transformation — the discovery of the Self as universal, lived through fearless service and boundless compassion.

Rahu and Spirituality

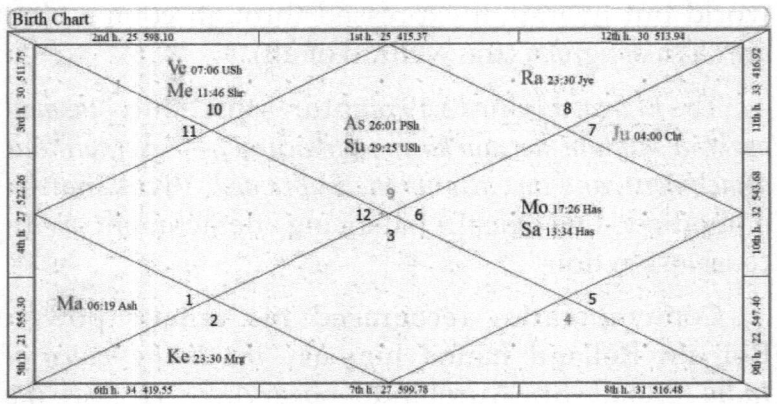

D9 Navamsha (spouse)

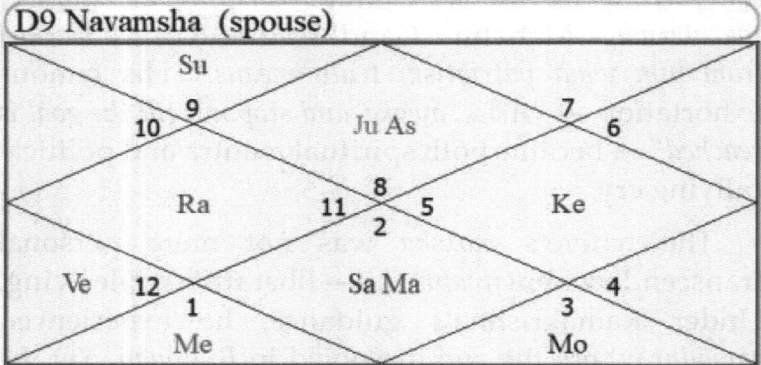

Birth Chart

As	26:01:47		P.Shad.	Dah	4,Ve/Ke/Ve
Su	29:25:23		U.Shad.	Bay	1,Su/Ra/Ra
Mo	17:26:47		Hasta	Nuh	3,Mo/Sa/Ra
Ma	06:19:25		Ashwini	Chay	2,Ke/Ra/Sa
Me	11:46:22	c	Shravana	Khi	1,Mo/Ma/Ve
Ju	04:00:50		Chitra	Ree	4,Ma/Ve/Ju
Ve	07:06:10	c	U.Shad.	Jee	4,Su/Ke/Ve
Sa	13:34:25		Hasta	Shah	2,Mo/Ra/Su
Ra	23:30:30		Jyeshtha	Yee	3,Me/Ma/Ju
Ke	23:30:30		Mrigashi	Vay	1,Ma/Ma/Ju

DOB - 12th January 1863, Time - 6:33 AM, Kolkata, India

भिद्यते हृदयग्रन्थिश्छिद्यन्ते सर्वसंशयाः ।
क्षीयन्ते चास्य कर्माणि तस्मिन् दृष्टे परावरे ॥

When He who is both the high and the low is realized, the knot of the heart is cut, all doubts are resolved, and all karma is exhausted. **[Mundaka Upanishad (3.2.9)]**

Section 6.2:
A *Parashari* – *Nakshatra* Analysis

We first study the basic potential of the native to inculcate spiritual ethos through a body, mind, soul study of how the trio provides the basic strength needed to develop a spiritual ethos.

6.2.1 Examining the Mind-Body-Soul Synchrony

We first study the basic potential of the native to ascertain spiritual ethos through a body, mind, soul study of how the triad provides the basic strength needed to develop a spiritual ethos.

The Lagna has Sun who is the 9th lord. Sun is placed in its own *nakshatra* in the *dharma pada*. The Lagna is placed in the *nakshatra* of Venus in the *moksha pada*. The lord of the Lagna (significator of body), Jupiter, is placed in the 11th house in a *kaam rashi* in *Chitra nakshatra* (lorded by Mars *and nakshatra of celestial artist of creation & transformation)* and is aspected by Mars (5th lord & 12th lord) from a *dharma rashi*. Lagna Lord (and 4th lord) Jupiter is aspected by 5th lord and 12th lord Mars from a *dharma rashi*. Jupiter's dispositor is Venus and is placed in the 2nd house in *Uttarashada nakshatra* (Lorded by Sun) thus establishing a relationship between body and soul.

The Moon (significator of mind) is the 8th lord (house of transformation) and placed in 10th house in an *arth rashi* in *Hasta Nakshatra* (Lorded by Moon itself) and is conjunct with Saturn forming a *sannyas yoga*. Moon's dispositor is Mercury, which is conjunct with Lagna Lord's dispositor, Venus who is placed in the *nakshatra* of Sun. So, we see an elevated level of synchronization between Lagna, mind and soul. Further Sun (the 9th lord, significator of soul) is placed in the Lagna in a *dharma rashi* in *Uttarashada nakshatra* (Lorded by Sun itself and a *nakshatra* of determination and higher knowledge). It must be noted that the Sun is the planet with the highest degree and the closest to the degree of Lagna (Lagna is in *Purvashada nakshatra*, a *nakshatra* of invincibility and creative fire, which is lorded by Venus). This amplifies the fact that the soul has an innate desire for creation, higher learning, and transformation.

In addition, the *Manasa nakshatra* (24th *nakshatra* from *Janma nakshatra*) that signifies the nature of thoughts in the mind, is *Ashlesha nakshatra (nakshatra of kundalini energy, transformation and hidden wisdom)* and lorded by Mercury. Mercury is placed in the 2nd house and is conjunct with Lagna Lord's dispositor, Venus. Mercury is in *Shravana nakshatra* (Lorded by Moon and *nakshatra* of listening, learning and spiritual awakening). Hence, we see that the *Manasa nakshatra lord*, Lagan Lord, Sun and Moon are in union for gaining an extremely spiritual mindset due to the mind, body and soul being at the apex of synchronization. It can be inferred from D1 that the native has an extortionate static potential to experience spiritual transformation.

Case Study 6: A Renowned Yogi

In D9, the Lagna is with 5th lord Jupiter in a *moksha rashi*. The Lagna is aspected by the Lagna lord Mars. The Lagna lord of D1, Jupiter, is placed in Lagna in *moksha rashi* 8 (a *rashi* of transformation). Jupiter is placed in Lagna aspecting an exalted Venus (Jupiter's dispositor in D1) who is the 12th lord in the 5th house in a *moksha rashi*. Sun is placed in the 2nd house in a *dharma rashi* and is aspected by Mars. Sun and the 9th lord Moon mutually aspect each other. Moon is placed in the 8th house of transformation in *kaam rashi*. The dispositor of the Moon in D9 is in the house of the Lagna lord that aspects the Sun. So, we see that Lagna Lord of D1, Sun and Moon establish a connection in D9 amicably. Hence, D9 further confirms the high static promise for the native to inculcate high spiritual ethos.

6.2.2 Influence of Rahu on Spiritual Potential

Rahu is placed in the 12th house of spirituality in the *moksha rashi* 8 in D1 in *Jyestha nakshatra* (Lorded by Mercury and *nakshatra* known for inner transformation). Hence, Rahu acts as 12th lord and its dispositor Mars, who is the 5th lord and 12th lord (placed in *Ashwini nakshatra* which is lorded by Ketu, a significator of spirituality) and is placed in the 5th house in a *dharma rashi*. Mars aspects this Rahu influencing Rahu strongly with Martian qualities from a *dharma rashi* and 5th house of *purva punya*. It can be inferred that Mars and Rahu dasha (MD/ADs) could play a significant role in enabling spiritual transformation in native. In D9, Rahu is placed in 4th house in Rahu's co-owned *rashi* of *kumbh and* is aspected by *rashi* lord Saturn. It should be noted that

Jupiter acting as 5th lord aspects Rahu's dispositor, and Lagna lord Mars in D9, thereby granting this Rahu inherent piousness to experience spiritual ethos.

6.2.3 *Dasha* Analysis

Take note that dispositors of the birth ascendant (Jupiter), Sun (Jupiter) and Moon (Mercury) are mutual friends. Hence, while analyzing *dasha* periods, and in accordance with *Sudarshan Paddhati* (SP) principles from the *Parashari* code of *dasha* analysis, we need not perform a logical analysis from all the three reference points (Lagna, Sun, Moon) to arrive at conclusions/inferences.

Rahu acts as the 12th lord and Mars, as its dispositor is Mars. The native met his Guru during Rahu-Saturn period which proved to be a turning point of native's life. With the blessings and guidance of his Guru, the native imbibed the spirit of renunciation and heard the inner calling for the greater purpose in life. Rahu's placement in the 12th house of spirituality in *Jyestha nakshatra* emphasizes the soul's purpose and desire for inner transformation. This inner transformation started in the Rahu period when the native's father and the native's spiritual Guru passed away. Note here that Rahu is 12th from the Sun (*pitrukaraka* and the 9th lord), indicating a loss of father and Guru in this *dasha*. Rahu MD played a key role in natives' life by introducing the native to his Guru and bringing in realization of purpose of his life.

Making Rahu (MD lord) as the ascendant, the Lagna lord, Jupiter is placed 12th from Rahu. 12th house being house of losses, the native lost his birth

Case Study 6: A Renowned Yogi

identity and received a new name during this period and is popularly recognized by his new name till this day. In addition, Jupiter is the *karaka* of a Guru, and being in 12th from MD lord and being in the 8th from his own house also justifies the loss of the native's Guru during this period. Venus is the lord of the 6th and 11th house in D1, and Ketu is placed in 6th house. Rahu-Ketu & Rahu-Venus periods were difficult and turning points for the native as the native lost his father during the Rahu-Ketu period (Sun as *pitrukaaraka* is placed in 8th house from Ketu) and had to take up complete responsibility for his family. The native also lost his Guru during Rahu/Venus *dasha*. Note that Sun as 9th lord signifying a Guru is placed in the 12th from Venus. Also, from the Moon Lagna, Mars and Moon are in 6/8 axis of each other, and Jupiter is not in a good position with respect to the Moon Lagna. Hence, Rahu-Mars and Rahu Jupiter periods brought him challenges in the mind. However, in these difficult times, Rahu MD gave the native complete self-realization and spiritual transformation. Hence, Rahu is indeed the seed of spiritual ethos in the native. However, this native was not a common man whose spiritual climax was yet to arrive. In other words, the native was a spiritual giant whose spiritual 'best' was yet to come. This came in the Jupiter MD, where Jupiter is the Lagna lord and the 4th lord in the chart, and aspected by 5th and 12th lord Mars.

Jupiter is Lagna lord and is placed in the 11th house of fulfillment of desires in *Chitra nakshatra* ruled by 12th lord Mars. It was at the beginning of

Jupiter MD and end of the Jupiter AD that the native meditated uninterrupted for three continuous days in South India and attained *moksha* (according to historical sources); traveled to the USA, and in the Saturn AD that the native gave a historic captivating speech on religious tolerance in Chicago. Saturn aspects the 4th house and 7th house of fame. Jupiter MD also spearheaded the inception of Vedanta Society of New York, followed by centers in Boston and San Francisco. Jupiter, mutually aspects Mars (12th lord and 5th lord) and this aspect of 12th lord on Jupiter, who is the Lagna lord does promise spiritual upliftment during its AD. If we make Jupiter - the MD lord, as the ascendant, it is aspected by 2nd lord and 7th lord Mars that is placed in the transformative *Ashlesha nakshatra* ruled by Mercury - the 9th lord and the 12th lord. Hence, the native attaining *moksha* in the Jupiter/Jupiter period is justified. Saturn is 4th lord and 5th lord from the Jupiter ascendant and placed in the 12th house in the *nakshatra* of the 11th lord - hence the fame and name during this period. In D9, Jupiter has moved to 12th relative to the D1. Hence the long-distance travel during Jupiter MD confirmed from the D9 chart.

Special Point: It should be noted that the *Indu Lagna* falls in the 3rd house in *rashi* 11, in D1 and is aspected by Jupiter. Sun (in *Uttarashada nakshatra*, a nakshatra of higher knowledge) is placed 11th from the *Indu Lagna* so it can be conjectured that natives' gains were in the form of wisdom. Placement of Rahu/Ketu in *kendra* from the *Indu Lagna* further confirms that native's purpose was to gain spiritual wealth and not material wealth.

6.2.4 Summarizing Inference

The native was a highly evolved soul who took human form to accomplish missions that were revolutionary and historic. We see that native's chart promised an epitome of self-realization and spirituality and the native left right after completing those tasks. There were several *raja yogas* in natives' chart - *Vesi, Sunphaa, Guru-Mangal, Kalpadruma. Tapasvi, Sanyaas,* to name a few. These strong yogas conferred on him with a stellar personality and will to work on humanitarian and spiritual missions, selflessly. This case is a classic example where even though the native was born an evolved soul, and also faced expansive spiritual progress in the Rahu MD (including renouncing the world and taking *sannyas*), absolute *moksha* (i.e., merging with the Divine) was only attained by the native in the Jupiter MD. Hence, Rahu cannot be taken as the contributor to the native attaining absolute *moksha*, but indeed gave enough spiritual progress in the Rahu MD (including renunciation) that is equivalent of a *moksha* for the commoner. The native attained *moksha* or the highest spiritual ethos in the period of Jupiter.

Section 6.3:
A *Nadi* Commentary

We provide THREE alternative, concise, and precise methods of analysis – based on *Bhrigu-Nandi Nadi* (BNN) astrology complementing the *Parashari* analysis of Case Study 6. **The goal is to establish the *Parashari* inference from Case Study 6 independently for each of the alternative methods of analysis.**

The essence of a good astrological analysis is the necessity for it to be validated from multiple schools of Vedic astrological thought. We choose the BNN approach as the alternative school of thought in this book – however, we smoothly integrate and blend an in-depth *nakshatra jyotish* analysis with the BNN framework, as we did with the *Parashari* analysis. While a strong *Parashari* education and a unique predictive *nakshatra jyotish* course are the pillars of the *Dev Jyotish* school of astrology, the BNN analysis was self-learned by Ranjan Pal under the personal guidance of Richa Shukla, and then the learning imparted to Ekta Jain by Ranjan Pal and Richa Shukla.

6.3.1 Method 1 (*Bhrigu-Nandi Nadi*)

The significator of spirituality is Ketu. In BNN astrology, only this planet can grant spiritual realization to a native. Hence, unlike in the *Parashari* analysis we need not check whether Rahu provides a spiritual ethos. It cannot. Simply put, BNN saves us effort to test this that takes a significant effort to test via *Parashari jyotish*. It is sufficient to see **(a) whether the placement of Ketu is of sufficient strength to provide a spiritual outlook to the native and (b) whether and to what extent Rahu influences Ketu to support the native realizing spiritual ethos.** Unlike in *Parashari jyotish*, there is no need to do a dynamic analysis in BNN astrology (e.g., via progressions and transits) of Rahu to establish its quantum of influence on native spiritual ethos. This is because the static *Nadi* analysis is sufficiently causal to judge the quantum of Rahu's effects.

Decision Making Factor #1

For the native in Case Study 6, we have Ketu placed with combination - **Venus + Mercury + Saturn + Moon + Ketu** (trine with each other in ascending order of degree) in *artha rashis*. As part of the 7th house from Ketu analysis, we have **Rahu** (trine with each other from the 7th house from Ketu in ascending order of degree) in *moksha rashis*. The Venus + Mercury + Saturn + Moon + Ketu combination in an *artha* sign makes the native enjoy luxury of earning mammoth flagship status in wealth of spirituality, earned via *karma* associated with attributes of Ketu. The native has 5 planets in *artha* trine. Ketu's significations influence Venus + Mercury + Saturn + Moon. The planet representing *karma*, Saturn, is present here and the native's *karma* was influenced by Ketu, Moon, Mercury and Venus. The native used his stellar oratory skills (Mercury) and travelled (Moon) nationally and internationally to spread the message of Hindu spiritual thought and advocated for both religious tolerance and universal acceptance. The native founded Ramakrishna Math to impart spiritual training and education and for social service and humanitarian work. He played a crucial role in the Hindu revivalist movement and contributed significantly to the rise and development of Indian nationalism in colonial India.

Rahu in *moksha rashi* opposite this trine influenced native's *karma* in foreign land. His historic speech in Chicago gave him a landmark flagship for disseminating Hindu philosophy and later establishing branches of Vedanta Society in the Unites

States. He also travelled in Europe to propagate the message of Vedanta philosophy.

The elements in the same trine from the 7th house from Ketu have a strong modifying/influencing effect on the significance impact of Ketu of making a native realizing (or not) spiritual ethos. Rahu is always part of this trine to no surprise, the interesting thing to see is how the other planets together with Rahu shape the quantum of impact, as we have done above.

Decision Making Factor #2

For the native in Case Study 6, we have Mars as the lord of 12th house from Ketu and placed in 12th from **Ketu**. Since Ketu is the significator of spirituality in BNN astrology one must check for the 12th from Ketu (12th house is the house of *moksha/dissolution* from any signification). We have Mars placed 12th from Ketu, and Mars + Sun in trine from the 12th house from Ketu in a *fire rashi*. So, native's action and ego are influenced by nationalism and mentors/father figure (in the native's case in form of Guru). The trine 7th from this has Jupiter in *kaam rashi* and *kaam trikon*. Nationalistic action was influenced by knowledge and philosophy (Jupiter). This combination helped the native play a pivotal role in shaping Indian nationalism by igniting national consciousness through spiritual and moral rejuvenation. He emphasized a unified national identity rooted in India's spiritual heritage and the concept of inner divinity, while championing social reform and service to the masses as vital means to uplift the nation from the yoke of colonial subjugation. **Rahu has no role to play here based on sign placement (if we do not include a *nakshatra***

Case Study 6: A Renowned Yogi 197

analysis here that is left for subsequent Methods 2 and 3).

Decision Making Factor #3

Since Ketu is the significator of spirituality in BNN astrology, one must check for the 11th from Ketu (11th house analysis checks for catalytic factors contributing to a significator – in our case Ketu of spirituality). For the native in Case Study 6, we have Jupiter as the lord of the 11th house from **Ketu**. There is no planet placed here, but **Rahu** is placed in this trine. **So, Rahu plays a pivotal catalytic role here.** If we consider 7th to the 11th to Ketu, we have Venus + Mercury + Saturn + Moon + Ketu (in ascending order of degree). We have discussed the results of this combination in DMF#1. **Rahu's placement in trine 11th from Ketu amplifies this substantially giving an impetus to spiritual ethos.**

Decision Making Factor #4

For the native in Case Study 6, we have Venus as the dispositor of Ketu and is in an *artha rashi*. We have **Venus + Mercury + Saturn + Moon + Ketu** (trine with each other in ascending order of degree) in *artha rashi*. This combination forms a powerful trine and makes the native do *karma* related to learning, duty and service toward mother/land. Saturn and Ketu cut emotional ties, while Mercury and Venus gift refined intellect and creativity influenced by mysticism. The Moon, influenced by Ketu and Saturn, turned the mind inward, creating a seeker whose *karma* becomes the doorway to wisdom, philosophy, and spiritual contribution. The trine houses from the 7th house of Venus have **Rahu** alone. The Rahu trine signifies foreign influence on this powerful combination leading the native to establish his flagship in foreign lands by propagating Vedanta philosophy and setting up Vedanta societies abroad. Relate this combination to **DMF #1** earlier, and it is evident why **Rahu does play pivotal catalytic factor in the spiritual journey of the native.**

Summary: Does the placement of Ketu give a strong spiritual outlook to the native? The answer is an absolute 'yes' from each of the four DMFs. Does Rahu play a positive role in the native experiencing spiritual ethos? The answer is a 'yes' from DMF #s 1-4. The results sync with the *Parashari* analysis.

6.3.2 Method 2 (BNN with *Nakshatra*)

Since our analysis base is BNN astrology, like in Method 1 we will work with the same DMFs, and be light on the BNN part of the analysis (detailed in Method 1). It is sufficient to see using *nakshatras* **whether and to what extent Rahu influences Ketu to support the native realizing spiritual ethos.** When it comes to doing an analysis using *nakshatra* principles using KP astrology, three KP parameters are relevant for study for each decision making factor: (i) a planet's ***nakshatra* sub-lord**, (ii) the **sub-lord's *nakshatra* lord:** the planet ruling the *nakshatra* in which the sub-lord is situated, and the (iii) the **sub-lord's sign lord:** the planet ruling the sign in which the sub-lord is situated. Each *nakshatra* span of 13d20' is unequally divided into degree space owned by 9 sub-lords proportional to *Vimshottari dasha* duration.

Case Study 6: A Renowned Yogi

Decision Making Factor #1

For the native in Case Study 6, we have **Venus + Mercury + Saturn + Moon + Ketu** (trine with each other in ascending order of degree) in *artha rashis*. Venus is in the *nakshatra* of Sun in the *pada* of Ketu. Mercury is in the *nakshatra* of Moon in the *pada* of Mars. Saturn is in the *nakshatra* of Moon in the *pada* of Rahu. Moon is in the *nakshatra* of Moon in the *pada* of Saturn. Ketu is in *nakshatra* of Mars in the *pada* of Rahu. As per KP principles, Venus is in the *nakshatra* of Sun and has Ketu as its sub-lord. Ketu's *nakshatra* lord is Mars and Ketu's sign-lord is Venus. Mercury is in the *nakshatra* of Moon and its sub-lord is Mars. Mars's *nakshatra* lord is Ketu and sign-lord is Mars itself. Saturn is in the *nakshatra* of Moon and its sub-lord is Rahu. Rahu's *nakshatra* lord is Mercury and sign-lord is Mars. Moon is in *nakshatra* of Moon itself, and its sub-lord is Saturn. Saturn's *nakshatra* lord is Moon and sign-lord Mercury. Ketu is in *nakshatra* of Mars and its sub-lord is Mars. Mars is in *nakshatra* of Ketu and its sign-lord is Mars. When we see influence at *nakshatra* and sub-lord level, we see that the native's enjoyment and gains come from spiritual pursuits and his *karma* is influenced by Rahu which led the native to propagate Vedanta philosophy in foreign lands in a big way.

As part of the 7th house from Ketu analysis, we have **Rahu** (trine from the 7th house from Ketu) and placed in *moksha rashis*. Rahu is placed in *nakshatra* of Mercury in *pada* of Mars. As per KP principles, Rahu is placed in *nakshatra* of Mercury and has Mars as its sub-lord. Mars's *nakshatra* lord is Ketu and sign-lord is Mars itself. Mars being the sub-lord and sign lord of Rahu makes Rahu's influence on Ketu as highly action oriented. The results of this are seen in form of native travelling extensively overseas and his iconic historic speech in Chicago and several others later and extensive role in spreading spiritual teachings, dedication to social services, education, and humanitarian work.

If we now look at the trine houses from the 2nd house from Ketu, we get **Jupiter** in the trine of *kaam rashi*. Jupiter is in the *nakshatra* of Mars and in the *pada* of Venus (that is in trine with Ketu). As per KP principles, Venus's *nakshatra* lord is Sun and its sign-lord is Saturn. The native desires knowledge and philosophical pursuits are the aim of the native at soul level.

Rahu influences Ketu significance and plays a significant role in spiritual impetus in native.

Decision Making Factor #2

For the native in Case Study 6, we have Mars as the lord of the fiery 12th house from **Ketu**. Since Ketu is the significator of spirituality in BNN astrology one must check for the 12th from Ketu (12th house is the house of *moksha/dissolution* from any signification). We have a **Mars + Sun** standing on the trine from the 12th house from Ketu in a *fire rashi* (*Dharm rashi trikon*) – hence, we see that the *Guru*, Mentor, have significant influence on action/ ego of the native. The *Guru* gave him direct God-experience, faith in his mission, and the vision that serving humanity is the highest worship. Without the *Guru*, the disciple

Case Study 6: A Renowned Yogi

would have remained a brilliant but restless mind; with the *Guru*, he became the voice of India's spiritual nationalism."

The trine houses from the 7th from Mars + Sun (and the 12th house from Ketu) is comprised only of **Jupiter**. Jupiter is in the *nakshatra* of Mars and in the *pada* of Venus that forms a trine with Ketu. This combination makes the native become a *karmic* agent of dharma — blending leadership, energy, and righteous counsel.

Decision Making Factor #3

For the native in Case Study 6, we have **Rahu** in *moksha* trine of the 11th house from **Ketu**. Since Ketu is the significator of spirituality in BNN astrology one must check for the 11th from Ketu (11th house analysis checks for catalytic factors contributing to a significator – in our case Ketu of spirituality). Rahu is in the *nakshatra* of Mercury and in the *pada* of Mars. As per KP principles, Rahu is placed in *nakshatra* of Mercury and has Mars as its sub-lord. Mars's nakshatra lord is Ketu and sign-lord is Mars itself.

If we now consider the trine houses from the 7th to the 11th house from Ketu, we have the combination **Venus + Mercury + Saturn + Moon + Ketu** (trines with each other in ascending order of degree) in *artha rashis*. A detailed analysis of this combination is written in DMF#1.

Rahu's placement in *moksha* trine in *nakshatra* of Mercury in pada of Mars manifested as brilliant, restless intellect, a fearless tongue, and daring actions. His sharpness in debate and command over logic made him an undefeatable arguer, while his courage allowed him to challenge both orthodox tradition and Western materialism. Guided firmly by *dharma* under his Guru Sri Ramakrishna, this fiery combination transformed into a force of truth. It made the native a fearless thinker, bold innovator, and spiritual warrior who carried India's message to the world and secured success on foreign soil.

Decision Making Factor #4

For the native in Case Study 6, we have Venus as the dispositor of Ketu and is located in an *artha rashi*. We have **Venus + Mercury + Saturn + Moon + Ketu** (trines with each other in ascending order of degree) in *artha rashis*. The analysis is same as DMF#1.

Summary: Does the placement of Ketu give a strong spiritual outlook to the native? The answer is a 'absolute yes' from each of the four DMFs. Does Rahu play a positive role in the native experiencing spiritual ethos? The answer is a 'yes' from DMF #s 1-4. The results sync with the *Parashari* analysis.

6.3.3 Method 3 (BNN with *Karmic* Angles)

We wish to analyze in **three parts** using the *karmic Nadi jyotish* principles the strength of Rahu in influencing each of the mind, body, and soul to realize a spiritual ethos. After all, these are the basic pillars that eventually decide whether a native will be able to realize spiritual ethos in their lifetime. **If the connection is strong in at least two out of the three cases, we can say that Rahu has been significantly instrumental in promoting spirituality within the native.** Unlike in *Parashari jyotish*, there is no need

Case Study 6: A Renowned Yogi

Planet	R/C	Sign	Degree	Speed	Nakshatra	Pada	RL	NL	SL	SS	Status	SB
Lagna		Sag	26:01:47		Poorvashadha	4	Ju	Ve	Ke	Ve		
Sun		Sag	29:25:23	01:01:07	Uttarashadha	1	Ju	Su	Ra	Ra	Grt.Fr.	1.18
Moon		Vir	17:26:47	13:06:59	Hasta	3	Me	Mo	Sa	Ra	Neutr.	1.12
Mars		Ari	06:19:25	00:30:33	Ashwini	2	Ma	Ke	Ra	Sa	Moolt.	1.74
Mercury	C	Cap	11:46:22	01:39:05	Shravana	1	Sa	Mo	Ma	Ve	Enemy	1.33
Jupiter		Lib	04:00:50	00:05:24	Chitra	4	Ve	Ma	Ve	Ju	Neutr.	1.07
Venus	C	Cap	07:06:10	01:15:23	Uttarashadha	4	Sa	Su	Ke	Ve	Neutr.	1.00
Saturn		Vir	13:34:25	00:00:19	Hasta	2	Me	Mo	Ra	Su	Neutr.	1.46
Rahu		Sco	23:30:30	-00:01:34	Jyeshtha	3	Ma	Me	Ma	Ju	Debil.	
Ketu		Tau	23:30:30	-00:01:34	Mrigasira	1	Ve	Ma	Ma	Ju	Debil.	

to do a dynamic analysis (e.g., via progressions and transits) of Rahu to establish its quantum of influence on native spiritual ethos. This is because the static *Nadi* analysis is sufficiently causal to judge the quantum of Rahu's effects.

***Dridh-Adridh Karma* Axes:** In *Nadi jyotish*, directions embody the metaphysics of *karma* itself. **East and West** anchor *dridh karma* — duties to father, guru, and ancestors that bind the soul to its inescapable obligations. **East**, aligned with Sun and Jupiter, signifies *dharma*, authority, and righteous beginnings; **West** blends closure and entanglement, largely fixed through Saturn's weight, though softened by Venus's negotiable pleasures. **North and South** anchor *adridh karma* - mutable desires and worldly pursuits shaped by free will. **North**, guided by Mercury and Rahu, points to growth, commerce, and ambition; while **South**, linked with Mars, Ketu, and Moon, carries ancestral debts, *tapas*, and *karmic* reckonings. In summary, East pulls a native towards *dharmic* duty, West toward worldly entanglement, North toward ambition, and South toward purification.

Thus, the four directions mark not mere space but the soul's *karmic* geography: some pathways immovable, others pliable. The horoscope becomes a compass of necessity and possibility, mapping destiny's fixity against the field of conscious striving. One may ask: why not diagonal directions? In *Nadi jyotish*, only the **four cardinal directions** - East, West, North, and South—are used, not the intermediates like Northeast or Northwest. This is because Vedic cosmology is fundamentally **fourfold**, based on

Case Study 6: A Renowned Yogi

sunrise and sunset, solstices and equinoxes, day and night. Each direction is tied to specific *grahas* and *karmic* qualities: East (Sun, Jupiter), West (Saturn, Venus), North (Mercury, Rahu), South (Moon, Mars, Ketu). This framework mirrors the *dik-palas* (directional guardians) of Vedic ritual, which are cardinal. By limiting to four, *Nadi* emphasizes clarity: destiny is seen through primal axes of *dharma*, desire, past, and closure, without diluting meaning in diagonals.

We provide the planetary directional compass diagram for Case Study 6.

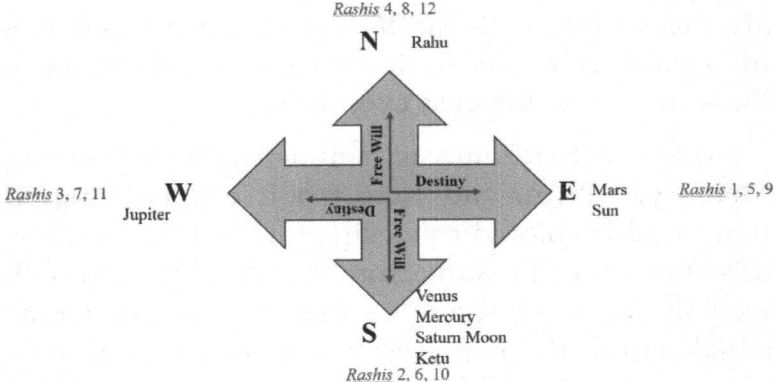

Part 1

We first analyze the planet **Moon — the significator of the mind**, to judge whether (a) the mind is inherently spiritual and (b) and how Rahu plays a role in driving the mind towards spirituality.

We observe that Moon occupies the southern direction (the *Earth sign*) of the *Kaalpurusha* chart. If we arrange the planets in the southern direction in ascending order of degree, we have the sequence

Venus, Mercury, Saturn, Moon and Ketu in *artha rashi trikon*. According to *Nadi* directionality principles Moon here is influenced by these planets in full (100%) because these planets are in trine with one another. So, Moon, the karaka of mind is 100% influenced by Venus (the significator of *bhog*), Mercury (the significator of *buddhi*), Saturn (the significator of *karma*) and Ketu (significator of spirituality and flagship). So, we see here that Ketu influences the mind of the native by 100%. We have Rahu opposite to this in the northern direction and it influences Moon (significator of mind) by 75%. The northern and southern directions are that of free will (*adridh karma*) and the native is in 'certain sense' free to do *karma* on significations in these directions towards evolution.

Moon in the South is hemmed between Venus, Mercury, Saturn, and Ketu, so it can be inferred that mind is colored by desire, intellect, karma, and detachment, while Rahu from the North pulls it with worldly allure or *maya*. As these directions denote *adridh karma*, the native is free to shape destiny — either rising through *karmic* discipline and spirituality or falling into worldly restlessness and illusion. In this case the native chose the higher path — transmuting *bhog*/enjoyment into devotion, intellect into wisdom, struggle into service for motherland (Saturn + Moon – influence of motherland on *karma*), detachment into renunciation, and Rahu's expansion into the voice of Indian nationalism. The mind consciously chose to harmonize all influences → *bhog* transformed into devotion (Venus), Vedantic sharp intellect and stellar oratory skills (Mercury), discipline and service (Saturn), renunciation and flagship (Ketu).

Case Study 6: A Renowned Yogi

Rahu in *moksha rashi* became his power to cross the seas, mesmerize Western audiences, and globalize Vedanta. The native stands as a shining example of how free will (*adṛiḍh karma*) can transform destiny. Born into poverty and burdened by family struggles, his restless mind was torn between worldly allure, intellectual brilliance, and the pull of renunciation. Yet, guided by the teachings of his Guru Sri Ramakrishna, he chose consciously to channel his inner conflicts into strength. Instead of being consumed by illusion or withdrawal, he used his free will to harmonize intellect with spirituality and service. In doing so, he carried India's timeless wisdom to the world, awakened national pride, and left an indelible mark as a spiritual nationalist who shaped modern India's identity.

If we arrange planets in the **western direction** (the direction of *dridh karma* or destiny) in ascending order of degree we have Jupiter (significator of wisdom, higher philosophy) there alone in this trine. According to *Nadi* directionality principles, Moon here is influenced by half power (50%) because they are in trine with one another from the 2nd house from Moon. This placement of Jupiter on the Western axis of *dṛiḍh karma*, endows the native with knowledge and wisdom flow as *karmic* inheritance, making the soul a natural teacher, counselor, or protector of truth. The mind is influenced by this strong pursuit of higher self.

If we arrange planets in the **eastern direction** (the direction of *dridh karma* or destiny) in ascending order of degree, we have the sequence **Mars and Sun** –

friendly combination for spiritual essence. According to *Nadi* directionality principles Moon is influenced by these planets with minimum power (25%) because they are in trine with one another from the 12th house of Moon. Mars (significator of ego/*deha*/action) and Sun (significator of soul/ *atma*/ authority/ Guru) in the Eastern direction, signify that the native is bound by destiny to act with fiery courage and authority. This combination influences the mind by 25%.

Thus, while the East axis of *dridh karma* propelled the mind into divine action, the West refined his mind through spiritual wisdom. Together they reveal a soul whose destiny was to unite *karma* and wisdom, embodying service rooted in realization— *the mind of a yogi guided by the light of a guru and the fire of divine purpose.*

So, **in summary**: is the mind spiritual? The answer is not a resounding 'yes' (partly). Does Rahu play a positive role in driving the mind towards spirituality? The answer is a 'yes'.

Part 2

We now analyse the planet **Sun — the significator of the soul**, to judge whether (a) the soul is projecting spirituality and (b) and how Rahu plays a role in driving the soul towards projecting spirituality.

Sun is placed in Eastern direction, the direction of *dridh karma* in *dharma rashi*. If we arrange all planets here in this *dharma* trine, we have the combination of Mars + Sun. Sun, the significator of soul, authority, *Guru*, leadership placed in *dridh karma* axis carries forward *karmas* destined from past related to

Case Study 6: A Renowned Yogi

Guru/ fatherly role, government/service, dharmic authority. Mars's placement in the East (destiny-driven), shows fated *karmas* of action and struggle. This combination indicates a soul bound to perform bravery, protection, leadership, conflict, or *karmic* battles in this lifetime. With Mars and Sun together in eastern direction, the native was Karmically bound to act as a warrior-saint: fiery courage (Mars) fused with radiant authority (Sun). This destined energy made him a protector of *dharma* and a fearless voice for India. Sun gave him royal authority in speech, while Mars gave a passionate fire. His words at the 1893 Chicago Parliament of Religions shook the West — this was not mere choice, but the unfolding of *karmic* necessity. Wherever he went, he inspired reform, nationalism, and awakening— Mars compelled action, Sun compelled visibility. His "Arise! Awake!" call is the pure voice of Mars–Sun *dridh karma* axis. With Mars and Sun in the Eastern *dridh karma*, the native was destined to embody fiery courage and radiant leadership. Bound by *karmic* necessity, he became a fearless orator, reformer, and protector of India's spiritual heritage — carrying the flame of *dharma* to the world and igniting the fire of nationalism at home.

As discussed in Part 1, the **western** direction (the direction of *dridh karma*) and has Jupiter in *kaam rashi* trine which influences Mars + Sun by 100%. So overall the Eastern destiny of fiery courage (Mars + Sun) met the Western destiny of *dharmic* wisdom (Jupiter). Compelled by past-life *karma*, he became both a fearless warrior for Indian nationalism and a Guru for the world — a spiritual flame that illumined East and West alike. Bound by *karmic* inheritance, he carried forward his Guru's grace, spread Vedanta globally, and awakened India's soul — fulfilling a destiny that was written beyond free will.

If we arrange the planets in South (the direction of *adridh karma*), we have Venus + Mercury + Saturn + Moon + Ketu in *artha rashi* trine. These influence Sun by 50% because they are in trine with one another from the 2nd house from Sun. We have seen the effect of this combination in Part 1 and can safely infer that Sun gets momentum and influence from this combination to perform *dridh karma* related to *dharma* and spirituality. This powerful combination supports the native on path of spiritual impetus and achieving the destined goals.

If we arrange the planets in North (the direction of *adridh karma*), we have Rahu in *moksha rashi* trine. This Rahu influences Sun + Mars combination by 25% because it's in trine houses 12th to Sun. Rahu influence motivates the soul to perform *karma* in foreign lands (as discussed in detail in Part 1).

In **summary** is the soul projecting spiritual essence? The answer is a resounding 'yes'. Does Rahu play a positive role in driving the soul towards spirituality? The answer is a 'partly yes'.

Part 3

We now analyze the planet **Mars — the significator of the body (*deha*) and ego**, to judge whether (a) the body is aligned to be projecting spirituality and (b) and how Rahu plays a role in driving the body towards projecting spirituality.

Case Study 6: A Renowned Yogi

We observe that **Mars** is placed in Eastern direction of *dridh karma* in a fire rashi along with Sun. Please refer to Part 2 for detailed analysis.

So, **in summary**: is the body projecting spirituality? The answer is somewhat 'yes'. Does Rahu play a positive role in driving the body towards spirituality? The answer is 'partly'.

Overall Inference from Parts 1 to 3: Rahu does strongly influence spiritual essence through the mind, and partly via body and soul. The results sync with the *Parashari* angle of analysis and even get more fine-grained with the *Nadi* analysis that says the body, mind, and soul are each aligned with a spiritual essence that is good and exert strong impetus towards realizing spirituality. **In truth, Rahu holds but a marginal influence over the native's spiritual ethos. The soul had already attained realization, and its embodiment in human form was only to discharge the ordained duties entrusted by destiny.**

Case Study 7
A Spiritual Communication Businesswoman

Section 7.1:
A Narrative of Spiritual Philosophy

The native's trajectory reflects the paradox of modern religiosity: devotion infused with spectacle. Rooted in the Vedic current of *bhakti*, her devotional *kathas* and *bhajans* embody *sraddha* (faith) and *bhakti-marga* (the path of devotion). Yet, as Jain philosophy reminds us, true liberation (*moksha*) requires *aparigraha* (non-possession), for attachment obscures the soul. This dual inheritance sets the stage for her controversy.

A Dior tote episode ignited debate. Critics asked: *Is spirituality here a vocation of service, or an enterprise cloaked in sanctity?* One voice argued: "She preaches simplicity but lives in luxury — devotion has become monetized." Such critiques resonate with Jain suspicion of any blending of wealth with renunciation, as *Mahavira* taught that even subtle desire corrupts purity. Her defence — "I've never asked anyone to renounce... I'm a normal girl" — places her closer to the *Bhagavad Gita's karma yoga*: acting in the world without compulsory asceticism. The *Bhagavad Gita* (3.19) says: "*Act without attachment, and in this way attain the Supreme.*" Yet, the question remains: is her

Case Study 7: A Spiritual Communication Businesswoman

luxury aligned with non-attachment, or does it signal indulgence rationalized as spirituality?

Philosophically, this touches the ancient problem of *vidya* and *avidya*. If her teachings inspire devotion but her lifestyle suggests material aspiration, is she reconciling these or commodifying the sacred? Scholars like Heinrich Zimmer warned that modern *gurus* often *"confuse the mythic with the personal,"* projecting charisma as sanctity. Critics may argue she embodies precisely this — religion as a brand, devotion as commerce.

The Jain *Uttaradhyayana Sutra* cautions: *"Wealth, however great, cannot cleanse the soul of karma; only renunciation burns the bonds."* This adds sharper weight to her dilemma: devotion shines, but luxury risks *karmic* residue.

Yet one must also concede: the Vedic tradition allows multiple *yogas*. Perhaps her path is not of saintly renunciation but of *loka-sangraha* — engaging the world while channelling devotion. The controversy, then, is less about hypocrisy than about authenticity: whether her *bhakti* uplifts beyond wealth, or whether materialism dilutes its flame.

ईशावास्यमिदं सर्वं यत्किञ्च जगत्यां जगत् ।
तेन त्यक्तेन भुञ्जीथा मा गृधः कस्यस्विद्धनम् ॥

— *All this — whatever moves in this world — is enveloped by the Lord. Protect it through renunciation; do not covet the wealth of another.*
—*Isa Upanishad, Verse 1*

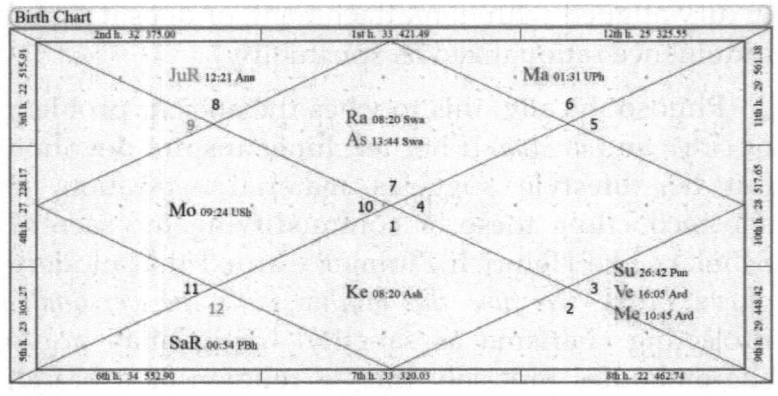

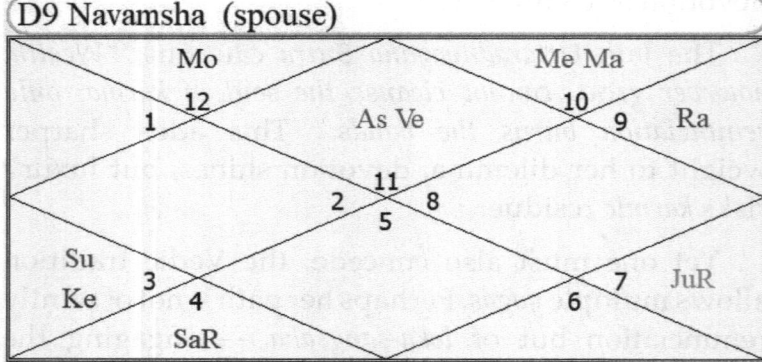

Birth Chart				
As	13:44:41	Swati	Roh	3,Ra/Me/Ra
Su	26:42:09	Punarvasu	Hah	3,Ju/Ve/Ve
Mo	09:24:43	U.Shad.	Jee	4,Su/Ve/Sa
Ma	01:31:36	U.Phalg.	Toh	2,Su/Ju/Sa
Me	10:45:58	Ardra	Gha	2,Ra/Sa/Sa
Ju	12:21:40 R	Anuradha	Noo	3,Sa/Ma/Ju
Ve	16:05:22	Ardra	Nga	3,Ra/Ve/Ra
Sa	00:54:50 R	P.Bhadra.	Dee	4,Ju/Ma/Sa
Ra	08:20:13	Swati	Roo	1,Ra/Ra/Su
Ke	08:20:13	Ashwini	Cho	3,Ke/Ju/Ke

DOB - 13th July, 1995, Time - 2:00 PM, Sujangarh, India

Nanassa saraha bhikkhu, appagaho bahussuto |
Lobhamulu sava pava, lobho savvaparam pi dukkham ||

—Knowledge is honored, restraint is praised, and learning is esteemed. All sin has its root in greed; indeed, greed is the source of all sorrow.

—*Uttaradhyayana Sutra (9.24)*

Section 7.2:
A *Parashari – Nakshatra* Analysis

We first study the basic potential of the native to inculcate spiritual ethos through a body, mind, soul study of how the trio provides the basic strength needed to develop a spiritual ethos.

7.2.1 Examining the Mind-Body-Soul Synchrony

We first study the basic potential of the native to inculcate spiritual ethos through a body, mind, soul study of how the triad provides the basic strength needed to develop a spiritual ethos.

The Lagna or birth ascendant is placed in a *kaam rashi* and in the *Swati nakshatra* who is ruled by Rahu placed in its own *nakshatra*. The lord of the Lagna (significator of body) Venus acting as the 8th lord, is placed in the 9th house in a *kaam rashi* in *Ardra nakshatra* (lorded by Rahu and a *nakshatra* of transformation and inner awakening). The Lagna lord, Venus (also the lord of 8th house of transformation), is conjunct with Sun (11th lord) and Mercury (9th lord and 12th lord) in the 9th house. The dispositor of Lagna lord, Venus, and Sun is Mercury which is conjunct with both and placed in the 9th house.

The Sun (significator of soul) is the 11th lord, has the highest degree amongst all planets and is placed in the 9th house, in a *kaam rashi*, and in the *Punarvasu nakshatra* (lorded by Jupiter, a *nakshatra* of reward, hope and growth). This explains native's epitome of desire for reward, hope and growth.

The Moon (significator of mind and 10th lord and forming the *Kemadruma Yoga*) is placed in the 4th house and in an *artha rashi* and in the *Uttarashada nakshatra* (lorded by Sun who is placed in the 9th house) aspects the 10th house of career. The Moon is further in a 5/9 trine with 2nd lord and 7th lord Mars. Moon's dispositor is retrograde Saturn (10th lord of *kaal purush kundli*) and its placed in 6th house of service in *Purva Bhadrapada nakshatra* (lorded by Jupiter and a *nakshatra* of mystical energies, transformation and higher learning). In addition, the *Manasa nakshatra* (the 24th *nakshatra* from the *Janma nakshatra*) that signifies the nature of thoughts in the mind, is *Anuradha nakshatra (nakshatra of devotion and friendship)* and lorded by Saturn (Saturn is Moon's dispositor). It can be inferred that the Lagna lord, Venus, Sun, Moon and *Manasa nakshatra lord* are in extreme synchronization and deeply intertwined to the 9th house, the 8th house *of* transformation, the 11th house of wish fulfilment, for spiritual and religious transformation potential. *However, the native is very business and gain minded in her pursuits, as evident by the placement of key planets in kaam and artha rashis.* In addition, both the *Janma nakshatra* and the *Manasa nakshatra* of the native are *manda nakshatras* (a type/group of *andhadi nakshatras*) implying the native

Case Study 7: A Spiritual Communication Businesswoman 217

will get to attaining high spiritual ethos (promised by above mentioned factors) only after a lot of hard work in life and is not gifted spiritually.

In D9, Venus (9th lord of D9) - the Lagna lord of D1 is placed in the Lagna in *kumbha rashi* (a *kaam rashi* of community and humanitarian focus) and aspected by Jupiter (11th lord and 2nd lord of D9). In addition, Venus moves 9 places relative to D1, i.e., it's in the *bhagyamsa* in the *Rasi Tulya Navamsa*. Sun is placed in 5th house in a *kaam rashi* and is conjunct with Ketu (significator of spirituality) and is in the 5/9 trine with Venus (lagna lord of D1) and Jupiter. The Moon is placed in the 2nd house in a *moksha rashi* and its dispositor, Jupiter, is placed in the 9th house. Saturn is the Lagna lord of D9 (its dispositor is the Moon) and is aspected by an exalted Mars and Mercury (5th lord and 8th lord of D9) from the 12th house of spirituality. We see that Venus (Saturn is the dispositor), Sun and Jupiter make a trine connection in a *kaam trikon*. Moreover, the Moon (Jupiter is the dispositor) and Saturn (Moon is the dispositor) form a 5/9 *moksha* trine. Hence, the D1 and the D9, both confirm significant promise potential for (business) gains by the native via spiritual activities.

The *Indu Lagna* falls in 9th house where Lagna lord, Venus, Mercury, and Sun are placed in *rashi* 3 (*rashi of communication*) and 11th from *Indu lagna* has Ketu in a *dharma rashi* indicating possibility of wealth accumulation via spiritual preachings and speech (*e.g.,* by being a *kathavachak,* like the native). The native has a religious and philosophical bent of mind but will strive to achieve material opulence.

7.2.2 Influence of Rahu on Spiritual Potential

Rahu is placed in the Lagna in a *kaam rashi* in D1, and in the *Swati nakshatra* (lorded by Rahu). Rahu acts as the Lagna lord and Venus — its dispositor. Venu is placed in the 9th house in a *kaam rashi* and conjunct with Sun and Mercury. Rahu is placed in the *kaam trikon* but is in a *dharma rashi* and in trine with Sun, Mercury and Venus. This placement could promote financial gains through religious/ *dharmic* pursuits. In D9, Rahu is placed in the 11th house in a *dharma rashi* and aspected by Sun (7th lord of D9) from 5th house. Rahu's dispositor, Jupiter, is placed in the 9th house (and 11th from its own house) further confirming the material pursuits via religion in D9 as well.

7.2.3 *Dasha* Analysis

Take note that the dispositors of the birth ascendant (Venus), Sun (Mercury) and Moon (Saturn) are mutual friends. Hence, while analysing *dasha* periods, and in accordance with *Sudarshan Paddhati* (SP) principles from the *Parashari* code of *dasha* analysis, we need not perform a logical analysis from all the three reference points (Lagna, Sun, Moon) to arrive at conclusions/inferences.

The Moon is the 10th lord, placed in the 4th house (forming the *Kemadruma Yoga*) and aspects the 10th house of career. The dispositor of the Moon is a retrograde Saturn in a *dharma rashi* but in a *kaam trikon*, and aspecting the 12th house, and being aspected by Mars. The native had to work hard during this phase of life in matters of spirituality. During Moon MD, the native started singing *bhajans* and *Bhagavad Gita* verses and performing at community *satsangs*. In the D9 chart, the Moon is in the 2nd house (of earnings), in a *moksha rashi* and in a 5/9 trine with Saturn. In addition, it is in the 6th *amsa* in the *Rasi Tulya Navamsa*, indicating hard work in this MD using speech talent to chant the name of God. Moreover, making Moon as the ascendant being the MD lord, the 7th house of fame is activated. This is realized via the 2nd lord going into the 3rd house and being aspected by the 11th lord from the 9th house, and by the 12th lord from the 11th house.

Mars is the 7th lord and 2nd lord and placed in the 12th house of spirituality in *Uttar Phalguni nakshatra* (lorded by Sun, a *nakshatra* of radiant flame of creativity and passion; Sun being 11th lord from birth ascendant and 12th lord from the Mars ascendant). The Mars MD spearheaded the native towards religious learning of *Puranas*. This primarily because Mars mutually aspects Saturn the 5th lord from Mars ascendant. It was during the Mars MD, Mars AD that she received *deeksha* from her Guru and commenced her journey formally as a *Katha Vachak*. Note that this was a sort of a transformation and Mars is the 8th lord from both the birth ascendant and the Mars ascendant. In D9, Mars is in the 12th house with speech *karaka* Mercury and mutually aspected by 12th lord Saturn.

Rahu is placed in Lagna in *Swati nakshatra*. The Ascendant is also placed in *Swati nakshatra* and the Lagna Lord, Venus is also placed in *Ardra nakshatra, also* lorded by Rahu. Rahu has a huge influence on native and confers her an enigmatic, charming personality (Venus being dispositor and in friendly sign) that connects with masses instantaneously and has enabled her to create an enormous fan following nationally & internationally. The Lagna lord is conjunct with Mercury (9th lord and 12th lord) in 9th house along with the Sun (significator of fame) in *rashi* 3 (*rashi* of communication). Sun plays a key role in fulfilment of desires for the native as its the 11th lord and placed 11th from 11th house giving fame through speech. Sun is also in the *Punarvasu nakshatra, a nakshatra* known for reward, growth and hope. Rahu-Jupiter gave exceptional oratory skills to the native. Jupiter is placed in the 2nd house (so she uses her speech to earn money through Jupiter significances such as spiritual communication) in *Anuradha nakshatra* lorded by the 4th and 5th house. Jupiter's dispositor is Mars and is placed in the 12th house of spirituality, and mutually aspected by 4th and 5th lord. The deity of *Swati nakshatra* is *Saraswati devi* and presence of Rahu in *Swati nakshatra* blessed the native with stellar oratory skills and Venus's (dispositor of Rahu) conjunction with Mercury in *rashi* 3 (a *rashi* of communication) further amplified this. Rahu MD has played a pivotal role in the native fulfilling her desires for material success and fame through spiritual communication. The highlight of Rahu MD so far was during the Rahu-Venus period (Rahu and Venus being in trines and conjunct fame *karaka* Sun, apart from Venus being the Lagna lord) when the native received a national award from the Prime Minister of the country. In the D9, Rahu is aspected by Sun who is the 7th lord (of fame and *pada praapti*). Making Rahu as the ascendant makes it aspected by 9th lord Sun; its dispositor Jupiter being in 5/9 trine with Sun, and a 5/9 trine with 11th lord Venus. The trines are of the *kaam* type (i.e., planets placed in *kaam rashis*) and hence material growth through spiritual communication will be the flavour of the Rahu MD. Note that the 2nd house of speech from Rahu (with Rahu being ascendant) is occupied by 5th lord and 12th lord Mars, aspected by 2nd and 3rd lord Saturn, and conjunct 7th and 10th lord Mercury. The material growth via a speech career on spiritual sayings is guaranteed in the Rahu MD.

The native is still running her Rahu MD and has yet to witness Jupiter and Saturn MDs. But Jupiter and Saturn MD should play a significant role in granting spiritual ethos to the native as she would have fulfilled much (if not all) of her material desires by the end of Rahu MD. Jupiter is placed in a *rashi* of transformation in Saturn lorded *nakshatra*. There is a *nakshatra* exchange between Saturn and Jupiter and both aspect the 8th house of transformation. Jupiter is Saturn's dispositor (6th lord) and also aspects Saturn. The native will likely spend on philanthropic projects targeted for elderly people in society. Saturn (placed in *moksha rashi* in 6th house and aspected by an exalted 10th lord, Mars, in D9) being at a very low degree in D1 in 6th house, its *dasha* could trigger a very high level of spiritual ethos.

7.2.4 Summarizing Inference

The native is blessed with a chart having immense static potential promise for religious and spiritual transformation - but a potential that has not yet materialized into spiritual transformation. The public 'falsely' perceives the native to be spiritually realized which she is not, as of yet (but will probably later in life). There are several *yogas* in the native's chart like the *Kemadruma, Adhi, Chaamara, Saraswati, Lakshmi, Vipreet Raj Yoga* blessing the native with an exceptionally charismatic personality and oratory skills. While Rahu has not yet sown the seed of spirituality, Rahu's dasha has imparted tremendous awakening in the religious sphere and transformed the native to a sensational *Kathavachak* with exceptional oratory skills of national fame. Rahu cannot be taken as significant bestower to the engendering of spirituality or spiritual transformation in the native but has bestowed the native with desire for material gains and fame via religion and dharmic endeavors. The natives chart assures tremendous scope of spiritual transformation during the Jupiter and Saturn MD periods.

Section 7.3:
A *Nadi* Commentary

We provide THREE alternative, concise, and precise methods of analysis — based on *Bhrigu-Nandi Nadi* (BNN) astrology complementing the *Parashari* analysis of Case Study 7. **The goal is to establish the *Parashari* inference from Case Study 7 independently for each of the alternative methods of analysis.**

The essence of a good astrological analysis is the necessity for it to be validated from multiple schools of Vedic astrological thought. We choose the BNN approach as the alternative school of thought in this book – however, we smoothly integrate and blend an in-depth *nakshatra jyotish* analysis with the BNN framework, as we did with the *Parashari* analysis. While a strong *Parashari* education and a unique predictive *nakshatra jyotish* course are the pillars of the *Dev Jyotish* school of astrology, the BNN analysis was self-learned by Ranjan Pal under the personal guidance of Richa Shukla, and then the learning imparted to Ekta Jain by Ranjan Pal and Richa Shukla.

7.3.1 Method 1 (*Bhrigu Nandi Nadi*)

The significator of spirituality is Ketu. In BNN astrology, only this planet can grant spiritual realization to a native. Hence, unlike in the *Parashari* analysis we need not check whether Rahu provides a spiritual ethos. It cannot. Simply put, BNN saves us effort to test this that takes a significant effort to test via *Parashari jyotish*. It is sufficient to see (a) whether the placement of Ketu is of sufficient strength to provide a spiritual outlook to the native and (b) whether and to what extent Rahu influences Ketu to support the native realizing spiritual ethos. Unlike in *Parashari jyotish*, there is no need to do a dynamic analysis in BNN astrology (e.g., via progressions and transits) of Rahu to establish its quantum of influence on native spiritual ethos. This is because the static *Nadi* analysis is sufficiently causal to judge the quantum of Rahu's effects.

Decision Making Factor #1

For the native in Case Study 7, we have Ketu placed in *dharma rashi*. Ketu is placed alone here in *dharma rashi* so Ketu on its own does have a positive placement to promote spiritual impetus. As part of the 7th house from Ketu analysis, we have Rahu in *kaam rashi*. If we look at trine from Rahu we have the combination of Rahu + Mercury + Venus + Sun. If we consider the retrograde motion of Jupiter and Saturn, then they also join this combination, and we have an array of six planets influencing Ketu from 7th to Ketu, Saturn + Rahu + Mercury + Jupiter + Venus + Sun from *kaam rashi* trine. So, we see that the *karma* of native is influenced by fame, authority (Sun) in creative philosophical spiritual discourses (Jupiter + Venus) via singing, storytelling (mercury) leading to mass following in not just country of origin but internationally (Rahu). The influence of Jupiter and Venus on Mercury and Rahu makes her a mesmerising *katha vachak* with phenomenal following. The native leverages higher religious learning for fame, professional advancement and wealth creation. We see that Rahu's trine has a magnanimous influence on Ketu, but **cannot say that Rahu provides or influences true essence of spirituality here.**

Decision Making Factor #2

As Ketu is the significator of spirituality in BNN astrology one must check for the 12th from Ketu (12th house is the house of *moksha/dissolution* from any signification). For the native in Case Study 7, we have Jupiter as the lord of the 12th house from Ketu. We have Saturn + Jupiter placed in the trine from the 12th house from Ketu in a *moksha rashi*. It is evident that the native does *karma* related to significator of Jupiterian attributes motivated by higher knowledge and religion. This aligns well with the role of the

Case Study 7: A Spiritual Communication Businesswoman

spiritual significator Ketu. The trine from the 7th from the 12th house of Ketu has Mars + Moon in *artha rashi* suggesting instability in action or indecisiveness in *deha*. So, Jupiter and Saturn could exert spiritual impetus to the native. **Rahu has no role to play here based on sign placement.**

Decision Making Factor #3

As Ketu is the significator of spirituality in BNN astrology one must check for the 11th from Ketu (11th house analysis checks for catalytic factors contributing to a significator – in our case Ketu of spirituality). For the native in Case Study 7, we have Saturn (*karaka of karma*) as the lord of the 11th house from Ketu. If we consider the retrograde motion of Saturn, then Saturn can be said to be placed 11th from Ketu. We have Saturn + Rahu + Mercury + Jupiter + Venus + Sun (in ascending order of degree). Relate this combination to DMF #1 earlier, and it is evident that Rahu does not influence the spirituality significator in a positive way towards the significations of spirituality. On the contrary, Rahu pushes the native towards projection of pseudo spirituality and using religious discourses for wealth creation. The powerful and unique Rahu trine combination makes the native a globally acclaimed religious bhakti *katha vachak* with tremendous fan following worldwide. If we now consider the trine houses from the 7th to the 11th house from Ketu, we have the combination of Ketu sitting alone in *dharma rashi*. The dispositor Mars, forms the trine combination of Mars + Moon in *artha rashi*. So, the dispositor is influenced by Moon making the *deha* indecisive. Hence, spirituality is being used for professional and monetary gains. **Rahu does not play a role in giving actual spiritual impetus here based on its sign placement** (unless we deal with a *nakshatra* analysis).

Decision Making Factor #4

For the native in Case Study 7, we have Mars as the dispositor of Ketu and is in an *artha rashi* as part of the combination Mars + Moon (in ascending order, Moon being in trine to Mars in *artha trikon*). We reemphasize that the native's ego/ *deha* is influenced by Moon and can lead to wavering actions, indecisiveness. Action done by native in areas of spirituality could be wavering, not consistent and natives' ideas about spirituality could change from time to time and could be motivated towards accumulation of wealth. The trine houses from the 7th house of Mars are influenced by a retrograde Saturn and retrograde Jupiter in *moksha rashi*. The native's mind and ego is influenced by a *karma karak* Saturn and higher religious knowledge *karaka* Jupiter (placed in *moksha rashi*). So, Jupiter and Saturn exert spiritual impetus on native's mind. **Rahu does not play a role here based on its sign placement** (unless we deal with a *nakshatra* analysis).

Summary: Does the placement of Ketu give a strong spiritual outlook to the native? The answer is a partial yes, provided from each of the four DMFs. Does Rahu play a positive role in the native experiencing spiritual ethos? The answer is a 'No' from collated Decision Making Factors 1-4. The results sync with the *Parashari* analysis. Note, that we did not delve into the positivity or negativity with which Rahu influences spiritual ethos. That is not the focus of the research.

Case Study 7: A Spiritual Communication Businesswoman

Planet	R/C	Sign	Degree	Speed	Nakshatra	Pada	RL	NL	SL	SS	Status	SB
Lagna		Lib	13:44:41		Swati	3	Ve	Ra	Me	Ra		
Sun		Gem	26:42:09	00:57:12	Punarvasu	3	Me	Ju	Ve	Ve	Enemy	1.32
Moon		Cap	09:24:43	14:54:48	Uttarashadha	4	Sa	Su	Ve	Sa	Frnd.	1.25
Mars		Vir	01:31:36	00:34:29	Uttara Phalg.	2	Me	Su	Ju	Sa	Neutr.	1.06
Mercury		Gem	10:45:58	01:47:48	Ardra	2	Me	Ra	Sa	Sa	Own	0.91
Jupiter	R	Sco	12:21:40	-00:03:38	Anuradha	3	Ma	Sa	Ma	Ju	Grt.Fr.	1.41
Venus		Gem	16:05:22	01:13:31	Ardra	3	Me	Ra	Ve	Ra	Neutr.	1.18
Saturn	R	Pis	00:54:50	-00:00:42	Poorvabhadra	4	Ju	Ju	Ma	Sa	Enemy	0.87
Rahu		Lib	08:20:13	-00:10:37	Swati	1	Ve	Ra	Ra	Su	Neutr.	
Ketu		Ari	08:20:13	-00:10:37	Ashwini	3	Ma	Ke	Ju	Ke	Neutr.	

7.3.2 Method 2 (BNN with *Nakshatra*)

Since, our analysis base is BNN astrology, like in Method 1 we will work with the same Decision Making Factors (DMFs). It is sufficient to see (a) whether the placement of Ketu is of sufficient strength to provide a spiritual outlook to the native and (b) whether and to what extent Rahu influences Ketu to support the native realizing spiritual ethos. We consider the strength of the *nakshatra* sub-lords of the planets related to these factors. The following parameters are relevant for study for each decision making factor: (i) a planet's *nakshatra* sub-lord, (ii) the sub-lord's *nakshatra* lord: the planet ruling the *nakshatra* in which the sub-lord is situated, and the (iii) the sub-lord's sign lord: the planet ruling the sign in which the sub-lord is situated. We could go more granular in our analysis at the *nakshatra* level, i.e., analyse sub-sub-lords, however, this would imply a very accurate birth time within seconds of the native. This is something that is hardly ever guaranteed.

Decision Making Factor #1

For the native in Case Study 7, we have Ketu alone in its trine in a *dharma rashi*. Ketu is in the *nakshatra* of Ketu in the *pada* of Jupiter. If we consider the retro motion of Jupiter, then Jupiter is conjunct with Rahu and clearly influences Rahu. Hence, Ketu's significance are significantly influenced by Rahu. Ketu is in the *nakshatra* of Ketu and has Jupiter (placed in *moksha rashi*) as its sub-lord. Ketu (*nakshatra* lord) is alone in the trine of *dharma rashi*. The dispositor of Ketu is Mars (placed in *Artha rashi*) and is in the

Case Study 7: A Spiritual Communication Businesswoman 229

trine with Moon. Jupiter has Saturn as its *nakshatra* lord and is placed in the *rashi* of Mars that is in trine with Moon. Hence, Ketu significance of spirituality is boosted, but is not influenced by Rahu.

As part of the 7th house from Ketu analysis, we have Rahu + Mercury + Venus + Sun (trine with each other from the 7th house from Ketu in ascending order of degree) and placed in *Kaam rashis*. If we consider the retro motion of Jupiter and Saturn, then they also join the Rahu trine and we have Saturn + Rahu + Mercury + Jupiter + Venus + Sun. Jupiter is conjunct to Rahu (due to Retro motion) and dispositor of Mars is in trine to Rahu. Saturn is placed in *nakshatra* of Jupiter and has sub-lord Mars. Mars's *nakshatra* lord is Sun and it's placed in *rashi* of Mercury. Rahu is placed in *nakshatra* of Rahu and has sub-lord Rahu. Rahu's *nakshatra* lord is Rahu and its *rashi* lord is Venus. Mercury is placed in *nakshatra* of Rahu and has sub-lord Saturn (Retro Saturn in trine to Rahu). Saturn is in *nakshatra* of Jupiter and its *rashi* lord is Jupiter. Jupiter is placed in *nakshatra* of Saturn and has sub-lord Mars. Mars is placed in *nakshatra* of Sun and its *rashi* lord is Mercury. Venus is placed in nakshatra of Rahu and its sub-lord is Venus. Venus's nakshatra lord is Rahu and its *rashi* lord is Mercury. Sun is placed in *nakshatra* of Jupiter and has sub-lord Venus. Venus is placed in *nakshatra* of Rahu and its sign lord is Mercury. The dispositor of Mars, Venus, Sun and Mercury is Mercury and its in trine with Rahu. Rahu's influence is significant at nakshatra and sub-lord level. **It is evident Rahu significantly influences the spiritual Ketu significance of the** native but it will be incorrect to say that its in a complete positive way.

If we now look at the trine houses from the 2nd house from Ketu, we get Mars + Moon in the *artha* trine. Mars is in *nakshatra* of Sun (Sun is in trine to Rahu) and has Jupiter as its sub-lord. Jupiter has Saturn as *nakshatra* lord and Mars as its sign lord. Moon is in *nakshatra* of Sun and has Venus as its sub-lord. Sun and Venus, both are in trine to Rahu. Venus has Rahu as the *nakshatra* lord and Mercury (Mercury is in trine to Rahu) as the sign lord. So, we see a strong connect of Moon (*karaka* of mind) with Rahu. **So, we see influence of Rahu in trine 2nd from Ketu.**

Decision Making Factor #2

Since Ketu is the significator of spirituality in BNN astrology one must check for the 12th from Ketu (12th house is the house of *moksha/dissolution* from any signification). For the native in Case Study 7, we have Jupiter as the lord of *moksha rashi*, 12th house from Ketu. Jupiter is retro and if we consider the retro motion of Jupiter its conjunct with Rahu. We have Saturn + Jupiter in this *moksha rashi* trine, 12th from Ketu. Saturn is in *nakshatra* of Jupiter and its sub-lord is Mars. Mars's *nakshatra* lord is Sun (Sun is in trine to Rahu) and *rashi*/sign lord is Mercury (Mercury is in trine to Rahu). Jupiter is in *nakshatra* of Saturn and its sub-lord is also Mars. Retro Jupiter is conjunct with Rahu and dispositor of Mars is in trine with Rahu. Retro Saturn is in trine with Rahu and dispositor of Mars is in trine with Rahu. So, we see that Rahu influences both, Saturn and Jupiter and exerts influence 12th from Ketu.

Case Study 7: A Spiritual Communication Businesswoman

The trine from the 7th from the 12th house of Ketu has Mars + Moon. (the analysis is same as in DMF #1) **We again see remarkable influence of Rahu on this trine. Hence Rahu influences 12th from Ketu.**

Decision Making Factor #3

Since Ketu is the significator of spirituality in BNN astrology one must check for the 11th from Ketu (11th house analysis checks for catalytic factors contributing to a significator – in our case Ketu of spirituality). For the native in Case Study 7, we have Saturn as the lord of the 11th house, (a *kaam trikon* house) from Ketu. We also have a retrograde Saturn (if we consider the retro motion of Saturn) placed in the 11th from Ketu. We have Rahu + Mercury + Venus + Sun (trine with each other in 11th house from Ketu in ascending order of degree) and placed in *Kaam rashis*. If we consider the retro motion of Jupiter and Saturn, then they also join the Rahu trine and we have Saturn + Rahu + Mercury + Jupiter + Venus + Sun. Further *nakshatra* analysis is same as in DMF #1.

If we now consider the trine houses from the 7th to the 11th house from Ketu, we have the combination of Ketu sitting alone. Ketu is in the *nakshatra* of Ketu and has Jupiter (If we consider retro motion of Jupiter, its conjunct with Rahu) as its sub-lord. Jupiter is placed in transformative *moksha rashi* and is retro. Jupiter's *nakshatra* lord is Saturn (if we consider retro motion of Jupiter, its in trine with Rahu) and *rashi*/sign lord if Mars. **Hence, Ketu's significance is notably influenced by Rahu.**

Decision Making Factor #4

For the native in Case Study 7, we have Mars as the dispositor of Ketu and is located in a *artha rashi* as part of the combination Mars + Moon. The dispositor of Mars (Mercury) is in trine with Rahu. Mars is in *nakshatra* of Sun (Sun is in trine to Rahu) and has Jupiter as its sub-lord. Jupiter has Saturn as *nakshatra* lord and Mars as its sign lord. If we consider retro motion of Saturn and Jupiter, they both are trine to Rahu. Moon is in *nakshatra* of Sun and has Venus as its sub-lord. Both Sun and Venus are in trine with Rahu. Rahu has a significant role to play in influencing Ketu significance when we go deeper into a *nakshatra* analysis.

We reemphasize that the native's action are motivated by higher knowledge, religion, authority and fame. Rahu has a significant role to play in influencing Ketu significance when we go deeper into a *nakshatra* analysis.

Summary: Does the placement of Ketu give a strong spiritual outlook to the native? The answer is a partial 'yes' from each of the four DMFs. Does Rahu play a positive role in the native experiencing spiritual ethos? Rahu has a significant influence, but the native will first experience the epitome of *bhog* (in terms of amassing wealth via *karma* involving religious pursuits), before experiencing real spiritual ethos later in life. The consensus from Decision Making Factors 1-4 is seen that Rahu's influence does not support pure spiritual bliss but pseudo spirituality. The native uses religion for professional gains and is yet to experience the true essence of spiritual bliss.

Case Study 7: A Spiritual Communication Businesswoman

Jupiter and Saturn have the inert potential to realize the spiritual ethos in the native. The native is very young so there is a huge possibility that the native will experience the epitome of spiritual bliss in future. The results sync with the *Parashari* analysis. Note, that we did not delve into the positivity or negativity with which Rahu influences spiritual ethos. That is not the focus of the research.

7.3.3 Method 3 (BNN with *Karmic* Angles)

We wish to analyze in **three parts** using the *karmic Nadi jyotish* principles the strength of Rahu in influencing each of the mind, body, and soul to realize a spiritual ethos. After all, these are the basic pillars that eventually decide whether a native will be able to realize spiritual ethos in the lifetime. **If the connection is strong in at least two out of the three cases, we can say that Rahu has been significantly instrumental in promoting spirituality within the native.** Unlike in *Parashari jyotish*, there is no need to do a dynamic analysis (e.g., via progressions and transits) of Rahu to establish its quantum of influence on native spiritual ethos. This is because the static *Nadi* analysis is sufficiently causal to judge the quantum of Rahu's effects.

Dridh-Adridh Karma Axes: In *Nadi jyotish*, directions embody the metaphysics of *karma* itself. **East and West** anchor *dridh karma* — duties to father, guru, and ancestors that bind the soul to its inescapable obligations. **East**, aligned with Sun and Jupiter, signifies *dharma*, authority, and righteous beginnings; **West** blends closure and entanglement, largely fixed through Saturn's weight, though softened by Venus's negotiable pleasures. **North and South** anchor *adridh karma* - mutable desires and worldly pursuits shaped by free will. **North**, guided by Mercury and Rahu, points to growth, commerce, and ambition; while **South**, linked with Mars, Ketu, and Moon, carries ancestral debts, *tapas*, and *karmic* reckonings. In summary, East pulls a native towards *dharmic* duty, West toward worldly entanglement, North toward ambition, and South toward purification.

Thus, the four directions mark not mere space but the soul's *karmic* geography: some pathways immovable, others pliable. The horoscope becomes a compass of necessity and possibility, mapping destiny's fixity against the field of conscious striving.

One may ask: why not diagonal directions? In *Nadi jyotisha*, only the four cardinal directions—East, West, North, and South—are used, not the intermediates like Northeast or Northwest. This is because Vedic cosmology is fundamentally fourfold, based on sunrise and sunset, solstices and equinoxes, day and night. Each direction is tied to specific *grahas* and *karmic* qualities: East (Sun, Jupiter), West (Saturn, Venus), North (Mercury, Rahu), South (Moon, Mars, Ketu). This framework mirrors the *dikpalas* (directional guardians) of Vedic ritual, which are cardinal. By limiting to four, *Nadi* emphasizes clarity: destiny is seen through primal axes of *dharma*, desire, past, and closure, without diluting meaning in diagonals.

Case Study 7: A Spiritual Communication Businesswoman

We provide the planetary directional compass diagram for Case Study 7.

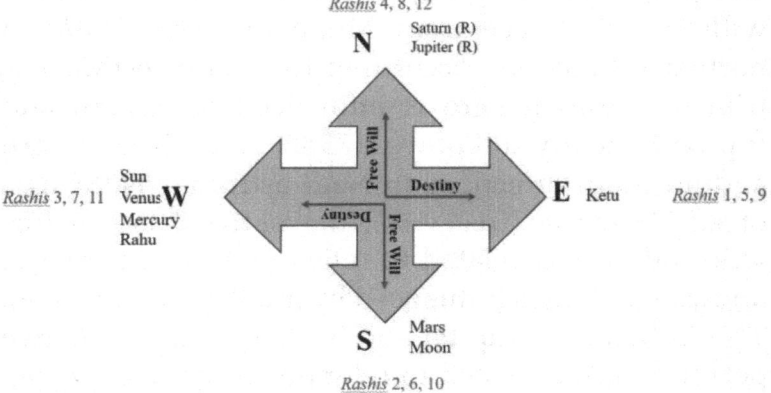

Part 1

We first analyze the planet **Moon — the significator of the mind**, to judge whether (a) the mind is inherently spiritual and (b) and how Rahu plays a role in driving the mind towards spirituality.

We observe that Moon occupies the southern direction (an *artha* sign) of the *Kaalpurusha* chart. If we arrange the planets in the southern direction in ascending order of degree, we have the sequence Mars, Moon in an *artha rashi*. It is evident that the native's ego/ action/ *deha* is influenced by mind. According to *Nadi* directionality principles Moon here is influences Mars in full (100%) because these planets are in trine with one another. So, the karaka of mind is 100% influenced by Mars the karaka of action, aggression, ego and *deha*. It can be concluded that the mind is action oriented.

Note that retrograde Saturn (*karaka* of *Karma*) and retrograde Jupiter (significator of religious learning and philosophy and higher learning) and is in trine with the 7th house from Moon in *moksha rashi* in northern direction. According to *Nadi* directionality principles Moon here is influenced by Saturn and Jupiter in nearly full power (75%). Since the southern and northern directions in Nadi astrology is the axis of a*dridh karma* (free will), the native has the free will to do *karma* related to religious learning, higher knowledge that is influenced by intelligence, and ego. This influence of Jupiter and Saturn makes the native perform karma related to religious discourses. When retrograde Jupiter and Saturn occupy the northern direction, the native becomes an awakened worker of *dharma* — a soul that consciously uses wisdom and discipline to elevate collective consciousness. The retrograde Jupiter and Saturn in the northern direction make the mind evolve through self-effort, reflection, and responsibility. In native's case, it reflects a soul that consciously reclaims its Guruhood — teaching and serving as an act of free will, not destiny. The native/s mind is action oriented and she has established her position as a charismatic *Katha-Vachak* with tremendous following.

If we arrange the planets 12th to Moon, we have Ketu, significator of spirituality in eastern direction in *dharma rashi*. Ketu is the only planet that is the *dharma* trine. Ketu in eastern direction of *dridh karma* signifies a destiny rooted in renunciation and self-realization, a native born to act under divine compulsion. Ketu in the East shows that her very birth purpose (*dridh*

Case Study 7: A Spiritual Communication Businesswoman

karma) is spiritual emancipation through action — *karma yoga* spiritualized *by bhakti*. According to *Nadi* directionality principles, Moon here is influenced by planets in this trine with minimum power (25%) because they are in trine with one another from the 12th house from Moon. This is the axis of *dridh karma* so this implies that natives mind is influenced by the spirituality *karaka* by 25%.

Now we see the planets in trine 2nd to Moon. We have an array of planets — Rahu, Mercury, Venus and Sun (in ascending order) in this trine in western direction in *Kaam trikon*. If we consider the retro motion of Saturn and Jupiter, then they also join this trine of *dridh karma*. So, we see that Saturn (*Karaka of Karma*), Rahu (significator of illusion or *Maya*), Mercury (significator of *buddhi*), Jupiter (significator of wisdom, higher knowledge, religious learning), Venus (significator of luxury, *bhoga*), Sun (significator of soul), all are placed in western direction and influence the *karaka* of mind, Moon by 50%. This is the axis of *dridh karma* that the native is destined to perform. This combination reflects a soul whose destiny (west direction of *dridh karma*) radiates through intellect, devotion, and humility in the mind (Moon placed in south), creating a life of inspired action. The retro *Guru* and retro *Shani* internalize wisdom and discipline; Mercury and Venus refine it into speech and devotion; Rahu and Sun project it to the world. The Moon receives all this as luminous awareness — a mind acting freely, yet in perfect harmony with divine will. It is evident that the native harnesses her sharp intellect and higher religious learning to carve a flourishing profession as a *katha-*

vachaka. In doing so, she not only amasses wealth but also establishes her flagship authority in the domain. Her charming and magnetic communication style serves as the vehicle through which she commands influence, consolidates her position, and radiates spiritual as well as professional distinction.

So, in summary: is the mind spiritual? The answer is partial 'yes'. Does Rahu play a role in driving the mind towards spirituality? The answer is a 'no' (non-significant).

Part 2

We now analyse the planet **Sun — the significator of the soul**, to judge whether (a) the soul is projecting spirituality and (b) and how Rahu plays a role in driving the soul towards projecting spirituality.

We observe that Rahu, Mercury, Venus and Sun are placed in the western direction in *kaam rashi* and are placed in trine so influence each other by 100%. According to *Nadi* directionality principles Sun here is influenced by these planets with maximum power (100%). This combination shows the native has fame, authority in creative arts using speech, intellect in home country and abroad. This is the direction of *dridh karma* so it can be inferred that the native is destined to perform *karmas* related to this axis and planets. If we consider the retrograde motion of Jupiter and Saturn, they join this combination and we can infer that they also exert 100% influence on Sun. So, we can say that the soul's desire is to the attain fame/position of authority in profession related to religion as a *katha-vachak*.

Case Study 7: A Spiritual Communication Businesswoman

Ketu is the significator of spirituality, and Sun is the significator of the soul. Ketu is placed opposite to Sun in eastern direction in *dharma trikon* and exerts 75% influence on trine of Sun. It is then evident that Ketu (from the eastern direction of *dridh karma* or destiny) provides spiritual essence to the soul of the native because it is in trine with the 7th house from Sun. According to *Nadi* directionality principles Sun is influenced by Ketu with nearly full power (75%) because Sun is in trine with Ketu. As Ketu influences Rahu that is in trine with Sun, Rahu does have an influence on the soul projecting spirituality.

If we arrange planets in the northern direction (the direction of *adridh karma* or free will) in ascending order of degree we have the sequence Saturn, Jupiter. These planets are lying in the *moksha rashis*. According to *Nadi* directionality principles Sun here is influenced by these planets with nearly half power (50%) because they are in trine with one another from the 2nd house from Sun. Saturn is a separative planet and Jupiter signifies philosophy and higher learning. Being placed in *moksha trikon*, this combination has the power to exert spiritual ethos influence. Thus, it can be said there is sufficient influence power of Saturn and Jupiter on Rahu to be able to infer that Rahu does not have non-significant role to play on the soul projecting spirituality.

The southern direction consists of Mars and Moon combination in *artha trikon* with a 25% power influence on Sun.

So, in summary: is the soul projecting spirituality? The answer is a resounding 'yes'. Does Rahu play a role in driving the mind towards spirituality? The answer is a 'yes'.

Part 3

We want to analyze the planet **Mars — the significator of the body and ego,** to judge whether (a) the body is inherently spiritual and (b) and how Rahu plays a role in driving the body and ego towards spirituality. However, since Moon and Mars are in the same direction, the analysis and inference for Part 3 is exactly same as that in Part 1. In other words, is the body projecting spiritual essence? The answer is *not* a resounding 'yes'. Does Rahu play a role in driving the soul towards spirituality? The answer is a 'no' (non-significant).

Overall Inference from Parts 1 to 3: Rahu does not strongly influence spiritual essence through the mind and body, though it significantly influences the soul projecting spirituality. The results sync with the *Parashari* angle of analysis that Rahu does not generate spiritual realization in the native. However, the results get even more fine-grained with the *Nadi* analysis that says the body, mind, are not aligned with Rahu in projecting spirituality but the soul is aligned with Rahu in this regard. Since two out of the three (Sun, Moon, and Mars) are not being influenced by Rahu on the lines of spiritual realization, we can say that Rahu does not generate spiritual ethos in the native.

Conclusion

Through a systematic, multi-layered analysis grounded in *Parashari*, *Nakshatra*, and *Nadi Jyotisha* techniques, this essay addressed the all-important question — *can Rahu give high spiritual ethos to a native?* The inquiry was approached not as a matter of belief or tradition, but as a **rigorous, evidence-based investigation,** combining **scriptural annotations** with a **statistical analysis of 50 horoscopic case studies (with 7 shared here).**

The convergence of results across all three methodological frameworks provides a **high degree of statistical confidence** in the conclusions derived. Two major discoveries emerged from the study:

1. **Scriptural Evidence:** In the classical *Jyotisha* texts and *shlokas* describing the prerequisites for *moksha* or elevated spiritual realization, **Rahu is conspicuously absent.** None of the canonical verses attribute direct spiritual deliverance or liberation to Rahu.

2. **Empirical Evidence:** From the comprehensive analysis of the case studies, it was **statistically established** that while Rahu can **initiate, support,** or **sustain** a spiritual lifestyle or high spiritual ethos within the native, it **cannot act as the direct giver of *moksha*.** Rahu's influence may seed detachment, intensify the desire for transcendence, or amplify spiritual conduct inherited from other planetary periods, but

it does not generate the state of spiritual realization itself.

In essence, Rahu functions as a **catalyst and sustainer**, not as the **source or granter** of spiritual attainment. It can stimulate the soul's movement toward divine realization by providing worldly experiences that force inner evolution, yet the ultimate state of liberation remains governed by the grace and agency of *sattvic grahas* in their higher manifestations.

Thus, this argumentative and statistically validated analysis firmly concludes that **Rahu may seed and sustain spirituality but cannot be its ultimate giver**. This conclusion stands consistent across *Parashari*, *Nakshatra*, **and** *Nadi* **frameworks**, providing a rare triangulated validation of a single spiritual principle — that **the path of illusion can serve the path of realization, but cannot itself confer it.**

In the grand architecture of the cosmos, Rahu symbolizes the *veil of illusion* through which truth is revealed. It is the paradoxical teacher — the one who leads by negation. By plunging the soul into shadows of desire, confusion, and restlessness, it silently serves the divine order by forcing the seeker to turn inward toward the real light of awareness. In this way, **Rahu does not give** *moksha* **— it provokes it.** The shadow itself becomes the means through which light is known.

Bibliography

1. Sharma, Girish Chand (2006) *Brihat Parashara Hora Shastra.* Sagar Publications
2. Charak, K. S (2020) *Laghu ParashariAn Exquisite Exposition of Vimshottari Dasha.* Uma Publications
3. Vasudev, P. K. *Manasagri.* Sagar Publications
4. Ojha, Gopesh Kumar (2014) *Phaldeepika.* Motilal Banarsidass Publishers
5. Bhasin, J. N(2020) *The Sarvartha Chintamani of Vyankatesh Sharma.* Sagar Publications
6. Bhasin, J. N.(1972) *Astro Sutras.* Sagar Publications
7. Sastri, P. S(2020) *Kalidasa Uttar Kalamrita.* Ranjan Publications
8. Iyer, N. Chidambaram (2013)*Brhat-Samhita of Varaha-Mihira.* Parimal Publications
9. Sastri, P. S (2013) *Brihat Jatak.* Ranjan Publications
10. Vasudev. Gayatri Devi. (2020) *The Art of Interpreting Horoscopes.* Motilal Banarsidass International
11. Sharma, Shiv Raj. (1995)*The Mystery of Rahu in a Horoscope.* Sagar Publications
12. Raman. B.V. (2025) *How to Judge a Horoscope Volume 1.* Motilal Banarsidass International
13. Raman. B.V (2025) *How to Judge a Horoscope Volume 2.* Motilal Banarsidass International

14. Jain, Manik Chand (2009) *Rahu & Ketu (Moon's Nodes) in Predictive Astrology.* Sagar Publishers
15. Jain, Manik Chand (2014) *Karmic Control Planets.* Ranjan Publications
16. Rao, K. N. (2011). *Kaal Sarp Dosha - Why such fright?* Vani Publications
17. Mishra, Suresh Chandra. (2019) *Vedic Jyotisha for Beginners.* Vedic Astro India
18. Mishra, Suresh Chandra. (2019) *Light on Bhavas.* Vedic Astro India
19. Mishra, Suresh Chandra. (2021) *A Textbook of Nakshatra Jyotisha.* Vedic Astro India
20. Bagal, Narendra Nath. (1965) *Formulas for Astrology and Horoscopes in India*, Sanskrit Pustak Bhandar
21. Gaur, A. K. (2015) *Professions: Inclination, Fructification, and Career Profile.* Alpha Publications
22. Shukla, A. B.(2019) *Nadi Praveshika- A Handbook for Teachers & Students.* Indian Council of AstrologicalSciences (ICAS)
23. Rao, R G. (2007)*Fundamentals of Rao's System of Nadi Astrology.* Ranjan Publications
24. Rao, R. G. (2008) *Bhrigu Nandi Nadi: A Classical Work Based on Nadi Technique of Prediction.* Ranjan Publications
25. Naik, Satyanarayana. (2009) *Orbital Providence Scholarly Exposition on Nadi Astrology.* Sagar Publishers

26. Krishnamurthi. K. S. (2016) *Predictive Stellar Astrology*. Krishman & Co.
27. Pal Ranjan. (2025) *Does Rahu Give Spiritual Ethos? An Argumentative Analysis in Jyotish*. Motilal Banarsidass International
28. Pal Ranjan. (2025) *Navamsa – A Practical Treatise on Prediction*. Motilal Banarsidass International
29. Parmanand Swami. (2020) *The Upanishads*. Prakash Books
30. Jagadiswarananda Swami. (1953) *Devi Mahatmayam (Glory of the Divine Mother)*. Vedanta Press & Bookshop
31. Debroy Dipavali. (2006) *The Holy Vedas – Rig Veda, Yajur Veda, Sama Veda, Atharva Veda* B. R. Publishing Corporation
32. Easwaran Eknath. (2007) *The Upanishads (Easwaran's classics of Indian Spirituality)* Nilgiri Press
33. Jacobi Herman. (2015) *Uttaradhyayana Sutra*. Createspace Independent Publishers

Biographies

Richa Shukla, MA, PhD; *Jyotish Alankara, Jyotish Acharya* is a renowned professional astrologer based in Gurgaon (Gurugram), India with over 25 years of practice experience. She has an M.A. and Ph.D. in Indian history. Her illustrious clientele ranges across the world spanning Asia, Australia, Europe, and the USA, and include (among many others) engineers, doctors, politicians, eminent secretaries, corporates, and administrative officers.

Richa has received numerous awards in Vedic astrology; has appeared on multiple national news channels (*Speaking Tree/ Times Now/ Zindagi with Richa*); and has written astrology columns in leading Indian newspapers. She has a hysterical social media fan following with over 4,00,000 people subscribing to her YouTube Channel *Astrology by Richa*. She is the Founder of the Dev Jyotish school of astrology and has learnt Vedic astrology under her father J. P. Agnihotri, esteemed astrologers in UP, under Shri K. N. Rao, and faculty at the *Bharatiya Vidya Bhavan Institute of Astrology*, New Delhi, India.

Ranjan Pal, MS, PhD, has been into *jyotish* and Vedic philosophy since 2000. He is a *jyotish* scholar, and an author having authored the two popular titles: *Does Rahu Give Spiritual Ethos: An Argumentative Analysis in Jyotish*, and *Navamsa: A Practical Treatise on Prediction* — both published by Motilal Banarsidass

International. In his professional work sphere, Ranjan is a computer scientist, decision scientist, and applied mathematician at the Massachusetts Institute of Technology, USA and serves on the faculty of the MIT Sloan School of Management. He conducts and leads research at the MIT Sloan School of Management in the field of cybersecurity; consults for Fortune 100 Global MNCs; and is an invited member of a World Economic Forum working group. Ranjan has an MS and a PhD in computer science.

Prior to joining MIT, Ranjan held cybersecurity research positions at Princeton University, USA and the University of Cambridge, UK. He was a faculty member of the University of Michigan, USA, and a visiting faculty of King's College London, Tsinghua University, Indian Institute of Management Ahmedabad, Indian Institute of Management Calcutta, Indian Institute of Technology Delhi, the Indian School of Business, and the All India Institute of Medical Science, and the Dhirubai Ambani Institute of Information and Communications Technology. He has given more than 50 invited talks around the globe on his academic research.

Ranjan is an astrology research student of Dr. Richa Shukla. He has been associated with *jyotisha* since a mid-teenager (for more than 20 years) and has been schooled in Vedic astrology by his late father (as part of a 150-year family tradition) who was a faculty member and Acting Director of the Indian Institute of Management (IIM) Calcutta. Ranjan's primary astrological interests are in the logical, philosophical, mathematical, and scientific foundations of Vedic astrology. His goal is to make the exposition of Vedic astrology a simple, structured, and logical task for the student mass studying the subject. Besides Vedic astrology, he is an ardent follower of the reasoning behind the Vedic *Advaita* philosophy.

Ekta Jain, BTech, MBA is a seasoned Human resource professional with over 25 years of experience; She specializes in advising ERP / SAP/ Data Analytics / Cyber Security professionals in the field of Information Technology and is currently the CEO of Alliance Consultants Inc, in USA. She has a B.Tech (with a Gold Medal) from Nagpur University and an MBA in Human Resource Management from Delhi University. She has diverse experience in activities ranging from Talent Acquisition, Immigration, HRIS, Compensation and Benefits, Training and Development, Diversity & Organization Restructuring.

She is a student of Vedic astrology with Dr. Richa Shukla and a practicing *Vaastu* professional. She is an active volunteer at the Jain Center of Greater Atlanta and Child Rights and You - America (Non-profit organization that works for Child rights). She is deeply interested in the philosophical aspects of Jainism and Indian culture. Ekta is also a trained *Kathak* dancer.